BLUE FUNNEL

Voyage East

by

Richard Woodman

An Publication

'This is life at sea, warts and all, and a better book because of it.'

Sea Breezes

Published by:-

Avid Publications,
Garth Boulevard,
Bebington,
Wirral,
Merseyside. UK.
CH63 5LS
Telephone / Fax: (44) 0151 645 2047

e-mail info: @ AvidPublications.co.uk

website: http//www.AvidPublications.co.uk

BLUE FUNNEL - VOYAGE EAST
by Richard Woodman

ISBN 1 902964 04 7 © Richard Woodman 1988

This edition 2002, 2005

The author and the publisher are particularly grateful to the Trustees of the National Museums and Galleries on Merseyside for allowing reproduction from their collections of the photographs within this work as well as the images of Blue Funnel vessels on the front and rear covers.

A CIP record for this book is available from the British Library.

Front Cover : *Perseus* passing the rock of Gibraltar, circa 1960s.
From an original painting by Walter Thomas (1894-1971].
Rear Cover : *Patroclus* circa 1967.

The right of Richard Woodman to be identified as the author of this work has been asserted by him in accordance with the Copyright, Designs and Patent Act, 1993.

Edited, typeset and cover © William David Roberts MA, Avid Publications 2002.

Cover Design: Janice Rickards

No part of this publication may be reproduced, stored in a retrieval system or transmitted in any form or by any other means, electronic, mechanical, photocopying, recording or otherwise without the prior permission of the publisher.

Other books, DVDs, and videos are available direct from Avid Publications

Details of these are at the rear of this book.

Contents

	Page
Foreword	v
Thoughts from Merseyside	vi
Introduction	vii
Departure	1
Outward Bound	24
A Dismal but Profitable Ditch	48
The Gate of Tears	56
Flying Fish Sailors	67
The Smell of Many Mornings	85
The City of Angels	101
The Isle of Fragrant Waters	117
Lotus Eating	135
Red Barbarians	146
A Change of Orders	167
The Land below the WInd	177
Homeward Bound	196
Visitations of Fate	211
The Channels	223

The two photographic sections in the book contain some of Alfred Holt's 'China Boats' through the years. They are not in any order at all and are shown to give a flavour both of the beauty and utility of a typical 'Blue Flue' vessel.

Pages viii, ix and x. Maps showing the outward bound and homeward bound route of a typical 'voyage east'.

Page 230 -231: A cross section through a typical Blue Funnel ship.

BLUE FUNNEL

What was life like aboard a British vessel in the last great days of the Merchant Navy? *Blue Funnel - Voyage East* takes us in one of the Holt Line's 'China Boats' on a typical trip out of the Mersey, to the Far East and back again by way of Suez. The time is the 1960s and it is a style of seafaring now totally lost among today's container ships and roll on - roll off ferries.

On board the cargo vessel *Antigone* we keep the long watches of the night, observe officers and men, sea and weather, in every mood. We learn about the transvestites of Singapore and the almond- eyed whores of Hong Kong, as well as the intricacies of derricks and cargo stowage; human hair and hog bristle from China, liquid latex and palm oil from Malaya. We can puzzle over the mysteries of navigation, what motivates the First Mate and why any sane man should go to sea, far from home and the love of good women.

The author draws on his many years service in cargo liners similar to *Antigone* to capture the sights, smells, enormous satisfactions and aching sadness that attended the 'carriage of general cargo in open stows'.

Richard Woodman is an award-winning author who has been involved in sailing since boyhood. From serving as an indentured midshipman with 'Blueys', he achieved his First Mates certificate with the company before going on to obtain his Masters certificate later in his seagoing career.

The author has since crossed the Atlantic under sail and he is an adviser to the World Ship Trust. He currently chairs the Technical Committee of the National Historic Ships Committee, under the aegis of the National Maritime Museum.

Richard began writing at sea and has some two dozen novels to his credit including the fourteen titles in the Nathaniel Drinkwater series.

Voyage East

FOREWORD
by Mike Stammers, FRHS
Keeper - Merseyside Maritime Museum

I first came across Richard Woodman's *Voyage East* by chance. Late in 1988 I was in London with a bit of time to spare between meetings. I went into a large bookshop in Piccadilly. I was not looking for anything in particular. But nautical titles always attract my attention and I happened on *Voyage East*. The Blue Funnel ship on the cover commended it to me and a few moments examination of Richard's novel convinced me that I had to have it. Such was the grip of his story I had practically finished the book by the time I had arrived back at Liverpool Lime Street station that night.

As the curator of the Merseyside Maritime Museum I knew something of the history of the Line and its remarkable managers and indeed at that time we still had George Holt, the last of the Holts to hold a senior position in the company serving on our board of Trustees. We also had a number of superb scale models of Blue Funnel cargo liners including the *Peleus* of 1949 which was one of the larger passenger carrying vessels of the Line. She is currently on show in the *Lifelines: A Story of Merchant Ships and Seamen* gallery in the Museum and she gives some idea of the robust and distinctive appearance of a typical Blue Funnel ship.

But models do not provide any idea of what it was like to serve on such a ship or all the manifold complications of sailing between many ports with a multiplicity of cargoes. Nor do they provide any insight into the life on board and the many conditions and characters who found themselves working together on a long round voyage. Richard's work has the feel of authenticity about it besides it being a good story. It is a superb account of what it was like aboard a British cargo liner before the container ships hurried all the old ships to the breaker's yard.

Voyage East has already gone through a second edition as *Antigone* and deserves this new edition. The author and publisher have agreed to return to the original title and to make it that bit special there are photographs of some of the ships mentioned in the story. The Blue Funnel ships will long be remembered especially on Merseyside. Besides being an excellent sea story, *Voyage East* will contribute to perpetuating that memory.

BLUE FUNNEL

THOUGHTS FROM MERSEYSIDE

Though I never sailed on a Blue Funnel cargo liner I did work on one, the *Priam*, in the late 1960's. Though my employer Cammell Laird, didn't realise it, I was under age to be working outside of the Birkenhead shipyard. However my supervising Fitter, Kenny Mortimer and I, thought we'd ' say nowt' for the chance to work away from the yard for a change. The result of this little adventure was the company's legal inability to pay me overtime, so they gave me a couple of days off with pay instead.... (I was getting around £8.00 a week at the time!) Oh! and a severe bollocking from my foreman too! In fact the *Priam* was at the time berthed in the 'home dock' of the Blue Funnel line, Vittoria Dock in Birkenhead, and it is from this self same dock that *Voyage East* begins.

I do remember though the beauty of the '*Bluey*' liner and wanting to sail away in her, as just about everyone in my hometown had sailed with '*Blue Flues*', and this is why Richard Woodman's account of a typical '*Voyage East*' is so important for this island's history and our own history on Merseyside.

This is what it was like, warts and all, to sail on a typical cargo liner during the heyday of Britain's maritime trading in the middle of the 20th century. The Scouse Dockers are here, the deckhands from Tranmere and Bootle, and the young trainee officers from Bebington and Aigburth, as well as the strong influence of the Welsh Officers and men who sailed with '*Blue Flues*' .... not for nothing was Blue Funnel also well known as '*The Welsh Navy*'......... the author sailed with them all.

Here too is the legendary Egyptian '*Gully-gully*' man and the 'surprising' distractions of Singapore... all part of a sea voyage to the Orient.
Blue Funnel - *Voyage East* will not disappoint. *Bon voyage!*

David Roberts MA, Maritime Historian. Merseyside 2002

Voyage East

INTRODUCTION

The cargo liner *Antigone* never existed. Yet more than thirty years ago ships like her left the ports of the United Kingdom daily, bound to the four corners of the world. Now they are gone, replaced by a mere handful of British registered container ships and the merchant fleets of flags of convenience, third world nations and the former Comecon countries. In a bewilderingly short period the once pre-eminent British Merchant Navy has ceased to exist, taking into obscurity the men who served at sea as well as the vast infrastructure that supported them, and leaving only a legacy of public indifference and personal bitterness.

But although *Antigone*, her Master and crew are creative reminiscences, this is not entirely a work of fiction. Rather, I have attempted an evocation, a synthesis from several sources of a typical voyage to the Far East in the last days of British mercantile sea power. Whilst the ship is imaginary her owners are not. Alfred Holt's Blue Funnel Line was a sterling example of the best of that multitude of ships which once flew the British ensign. If I have taken liberties with chronology I have been less free with mood or language. I make no apology for this; such ships were microcosms of human existence and so had their full share of lusty behaviour and rather senseless profanity.

Though highly subjective, this is not a work of autobiography, and the first person of the narrator should be viewed accordingly. However, most of the events here described occurred at one time or another and all of the characters will, I hope, be recognised by those who sailed on these ships as something other than stereotypes. In short, and to use Joseph Conrad's words from his introduction to *The Mirror of the Sea*, this book is '*an imaginative rendering ... a record of a phase ... an attempt to set down graphically the feelings and emotions born from the experience of a ... useful calling*'; for this is how it seemed to me as a young man.

I have retained the foreign names common at the time of *Antigone's* voyage, particularly in the case of China, where the new Pinyin transliteration remains confusing to British readers. Similarly tonnages remain at their contemporary values and it is hoped that the majority of technical terms can be deduced from the profile of *Antigone* on pages 230-231.

Richard Woodman

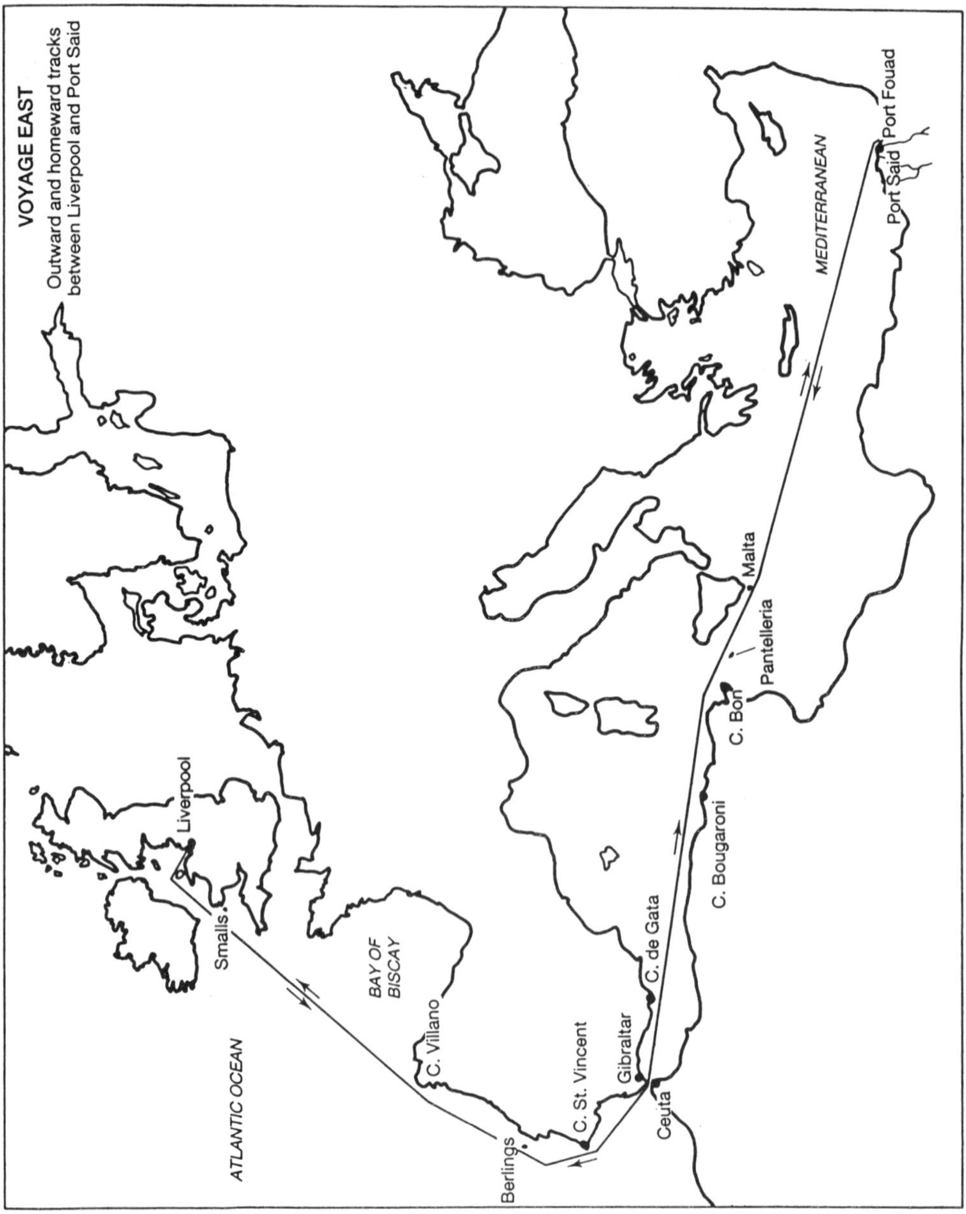
VOYAGE EAST
Outward and homeward tracks between Liverpool and Port Said
Liverpool
Smalls
ATLANTIC OCEAN
BAY OF BISCAY
C. Villano
Berlings
C. St. Vincent
Gibraltar
Ceuta
C. de Gata
C. Bougaroni
C. Bon
Pantelleria
Malta
MEDITERRANEAN
Port Said
Port Fouad

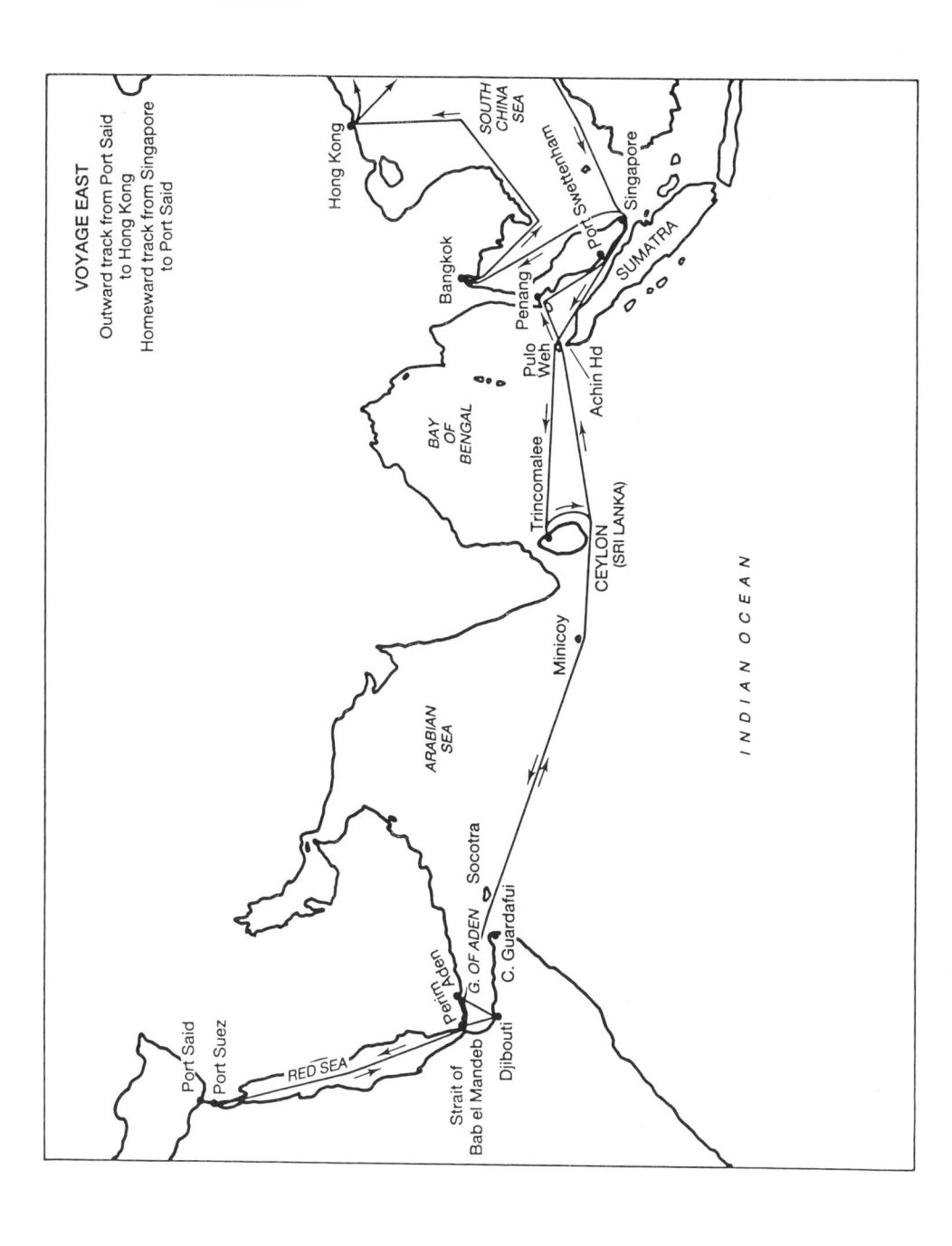

Voyage East

VOYAGE EAST
Outward track from Port Said to Hong Kong
Homeward track from Singapore to Port Said

VOYAGE EAST
"The Coast"
Penang outward
to
Singapore homeward
Hsinkiang
KOREA
JAPAN
HONSHU
Nagoya
Kobe
Yokohama
Shimizu
Shimonoseki
YELLOW
SEA
Shanghai
EAST
CHINA
SEA
CHINA
TAIWAN
STRAIT
TAIWAN
Hong Kong
LUZON
Manila
PHILIPPINE ISLANDS
NORTH PACIFIC
OCEAN
Bangkok
GULF
OF
THAILAND
SOUTH CHINA SEA
PALAWAN
SULU
SEA
Penang
MALAYSIA
Port Swettenham
Jessleton
Labuan
Sandakan
Bohihan
Tawau
Sabah
SARAWAK
Singapore
BORNEO
(KALIMANTAM)
SUMATRA
INDONESIA
JAVA

BLUE FUNNEL

Voyage East

by

Richard Woodman

BLUE FUNNEL

A typical dockside scene at a Blue Funnel berth.

departure

We came together first in the Shipping Office in Birkenhead, the cream and green paintwork of its walls marking it as Board of Trade territory. In a grubby hall furnished with a counter, grilles and desks, populated by thin-lipped clerks and filling with tobacco smoke, we formed an untidy queue. Signing on the Blue Funnel cargo liner *Antigone,* we had been variously told, would take place at ten o'clock that morning.

We were unremarkable in our appearance. The ubiquitous jeans of the ratings were topped by Beatle crops, or the already dated slicks of air-blown bow-waves riding out above foreheads and hungover eyes. Cavalry twill and hacking jacket was the shoreside uniform of the second and third mates; a crumpled suit that had clearly been slept in on a night train from Scotland adorned a preoccupied and apparently elderly man. A noisy group of north-country voices identified the junior engineers, while a venturesome fellow in slacks and pullover, cocksure and handsome in a sallow way, lit another cigarette and tried to look as if he had done this sort of thing before; the experienced put him down as Sparks, the radio officer.

'First tripper,' remarked the Bosun jerking his head. An old Blue Funnel hand, the Bosun was a Welshman, as broad as he was tall and with a powerful physique. His face had been tanned by the tropic sun except for the paler crow's feet round his eyes. His teeth were white too, startlingly white, when he grinned.

'New teeth, eh?' jibed the carpenter, a tall Liverpudlian with a searing accent, the shoulders of a navvy and a paunch over which strained the buttons of his open-necked shirt.

They shared a match and added to the hard Scouse joking as the queue jostled, its members eyeing each other, figuring out the forthcoming pecking order, a company of seamen undergoing metamorphosis into a ship's company.

'Good leave, Chippy?'

'Fuckin' gear, Bose ... . 'Ow d'you gerron, La?' Chippy punctuated his sentences with fervid drags at his hand-rolled cigarette. He held it cupped, pinched, with its burning end tucked inwards towards his palm.

'The missus screwed me for a new suite....'

'Fuckin' 'ell ...'

We hailed from all over the United Kingdom, although the majority of the ratings were Merseysiders, from Birkenhead or Liverpool itself. The Bosun was one of many who came from beyond the River Dee to man Alfred Holt's Blue Funnel cargo-liners and gave them their nickname of 'The Welsh Navy'. There was also a vagrant Scot or two, with the pinched faces and sharp aggression of Glaswegians.

Conspicuous among us, the four apprentices were in uniform, their plain black reefers distinguished by the button and twist of gold bullion lace upon each lapel. They wore no white patch like their naval cousins, but Alfred Holt's apprentices were called midshipmen and considered themselves, without hyperbole, to be in the same tradition of Drake. Their ages varied from sixteen to twenty and the senior was as capable as any navigating officer, working out his last qualifying months of sea-time to sit his second-mate's examination. The youngest was pale and acned, his new hat vast upon his head as he peered uncertainly about him. Like the Sparks it was his first voyage. Technically the midshipmen did not sign on. They were indentured to the Company, but their names, their next of kin and their documents were examined by the Shipping Master and entered on the articles.

We shuffled forward, producing our certificates of competency, signing against our appropriate rank or rating, obeying the half understood ritual that had grown sacred with usage. It was born out of the long struggle between capital and exploited labour and acted out in the no man's land of the Shipping Office under the impartial eye of Government bureaucracy. The rates of pay and scales of food had minimum levels, set by the National Maritime Board; but Holt's were a good company, their food and pay well above these. Upon us lay the obligation to earn good profits in return by making the forthcoming voyage a success.

It was a requirement of the rite of 'signing-on' that the Master opened

Voyage East

the articles first, but this formality had usually been attended to much earlier than our shambling arrival. Nor did we hear the articles read aloud by the Shipping Master superintending the Mercantile Marine Office; these were things honoured in the breach. But we looked for the Old Man's name. They were famous in their way, these shipmasters, imprinting their personalities and idiosyncrasies on the elusive atmosphere that distinguished one cargo-liner from her class-sisters. We had a reasonable chance of knowing who the Master was to be unless, as on this occasion, the Company had been carrying out one of its periodic reshuffles. As each man picked up the ball-point pen to sign his name with slowly formed characters, illegible flourish or pedantic thoroughness, he scanned the top of the printed form, deciphering the powerful scrawl that opened our mutual 'agreement'.

Was it Typhoon Charlie, or Scarface, or Radar Roberts? Was it Drunken Duncan, or Bucket-Mouth or Coco McBain? If we had not already sailed with these men, hearsay provided an abundance of rumour. Stubbs never wore the Company's uniform beyond the Mersey Bar; Goodyear, a commander in the Royal Naval Reserve, went to the other extreme and sported a brass-buttoned waistcoat beneath his reefers. China Dick Richards had reboarded his torpedoed ship during the last war and brought her water-logged hull and its precious cargo safely into port. Others were known by their Christian names, or their initials, but all possessed some bubble of reputation, be it good, bad or plain awkward.

That day the word went whispering up and down the line: our Old Man was 'China Dick', Captain Richard Richards, an Ap Richards from the Welsh coastal town of Newquay where every house was reputed to have produced at least one master's certificate. His soubriquet caused the laughter which was our first corporate act, our first coming-together as a crew.

'He's a right bastard ...' It was said somewhere behind the preoccupied Scot in the crumpled grey suit who was bent over the articles at that moment, signing his name below that of Captain Richards. The remark met knowing nods.

'A prick . . .'

It would have been unthinkable to suggest he had a single virtue.

'I thought Ding-Dong was Ole Man ... hey, Bose, didn' youse say Ding-Dong Bell was the Old Man?' The complaint whined among the coiling cigarette smoke.

'He used to be. Been transferred to the *Cyclops*, see,' and in a lower voice to the Carpenter, 'Christ, Chippy, right little sod moaning already ...' There was a click of new teeth over the enunciation of those sharp, Merioneth Ts'.

'Dey doan know when dere well off, dese days ...' commiserated the Carpenter.

The Scot in the crumpled suit straightened up and smiled thinly at the man behind the grille. Vague recognition passed between them. Screwing the top on his fountain pen and recovering his own master's certificate from the Shipping Master, the worried-looking man scooped up his grubby Burberry raincoat and passed along the line of men, ignoring the nudges that marked his passage, acknowledging only the brief greetings of his old, if socially distant, shipmates, the Bosun and Carpenter.

'Dat's de Mate.'

There was a subtle but pointed emphasis on the mauled definite article. The Scot had signed on against the rank 'First Mate', but to all on board, including Captain Richards, he was *the* Mate, the most committed of the entire ship's company, for in practice most of the economic burden of the voyage would rest upon his shoulders and its success depend very largely upon his competence. He would undoubtedly be the first of this motley company to repair on board.

I signed against the designation 'Extra Third Mate' as the Shipping Master scrutinised my Second Mate's certificate, but henceforth I was in fact to be known as the *Antigone's* Fourth Mate, or perhaps 'Four-O' to Captain Richards when he was in a benign mood. I had, however, an undeniably better label than my colleague, the Third Mate. His rank entitled him to be called 'Third', which the sailors would render into demotic Scouse as 'Turd'.

After the Master we signed on in no special order. There were four engineers and three 'assistant' engineers, two electricians, the new 'sparks'

Voyage East

and his senior partner, who doubled as purser. Following him came a sleek, rotund man eminently fitting Caesar's criteria for obvious contentment and easily identified in his alpaca suit as the Chief Steward. Where appropriate the particulars of our certificates were entered on the Articles, together with our discharge-book numbers which we surrendered to the Master for the duration of the voyage and which formed a running record of our service, competence and sobriety. We aspired to the rubber-stamped 'V.G.' of 'very good' and feared the 'D.R.' that was the equivalent of professional obloquy, for it meant 'decline to report' and stunk of bad character. The midshipmen presented their linen indentures and married men arranged their allotments of pay to dependent relatives. For most of us a gracious surrender to the bureaucratic process was the speediest way to secure release from the stifling hall. Besides, our last, stolen minutes of freedom must not be wasted.

We stepped out into the sleeting rain of Hamilton Square, already coalescing into groups. We had begun to cut ourselves off from the land, although we still trod it, and in the pub the process of parturition continued. Here the knots were tied and we made ourselves known to those whom cynics called 'Board of Trade acquaintances', formed by circumstance rather than choice. Events would cause dislike, disinterest or occasionally life-long friendship. Later, when the bruising barman hung up the towels, when our liberty could no longer be stretched by the most robust imagination, we went in search of our baggage and the ship.

'Bloody sailors,' the barman said as we slouched out into the dismal afternoon, 'not the same as when I was at sea.'

The ship was loading at Cathcart Street, berthed in Vittoria Dock. She shared the quay with two other Blue Funnel liners at varying stages of loading. Opposite Holt's 'China Boats', three India and Pakistan-bound Clan Line vessels were similarly occupied. The dock policemen nodded our taxi through the gate.

'The bastard'll want a ten-bob note to let us out when we get home again,' the Second Mate remarked without rancour as the taxi rumbled over ancient cobbles, 'or have all your gear out among the pigeon-shit just when you want to get the one o'clock train from Lime Street...'

BLUE FUNNEL

The taxi edged along the quay between the warehouses and the sudden bulk of the ship. *Antigone - Liverpool* we read briefly upon her high cruiser stern, white letters on a black hull; dark ropes with their rat-guards fanned down from the Panama leads to the cast-iron bollards that lined the quay. Around us the dockers lounged and smoked, waiting for the rain to ease.

'Lazy bastards,' my companion said as they stared at us.

On the decks the high peaks of untidily erected hatch tents hung from the derrick runners. The wide maw of the warehouse revealed stacks of cased Guinness stout and rows of waiting cars. A flock of feral pigeons clattered out, across the windscreen of the taxi and over the ship, black against the grey scud coming in low from the Irish Sea. The taxi squealed to a halt on the slimy cobbles and we piled out, the two of us, into the downpour, sliding on the filth and the gleaming reflections of the immobilised cranes. I paid and my companion looked up at the blank windows of the crane cabs.

'All pissed off for a smoke-oh.'

The taxi drew away, leaving us with trunks, cases and sextant boxes in the pouring rain. A second taxi arrived, and the Third Mate and the Purser emerged. The gangway stretched upwards to the dry, inviting comfort of the superstructure.

'God helps those who help 'emselves.'

'This no belong proper for white-men.'

We commenced a friendship with over-laboured clichés and humped our combined possessions aboard.

Since she arrived home from her previous voyage *Antigone* had been coasting, visiting the several British and Continental destinations of her homeward consignments of cargo. From Gladstone Dock on the Liverpool side of the River Mersey where she began her discharge, she had been north to Glasgow, then through the Minch, round Cape Wrath and through the fierce tides of the Pentland Firth before crossing the North Sea to Hamburg, Bremerhaven and Rotterdam. From the Waalhaven on the River Maas where her last tank of liquid latex, her last chests of tea and bales of Malayan rubber were landed, she had begun to load her outward cargo of 'general'. This comprised anything under the sun and included kitchen

Voyage East

sinks.

From the Maas she had returned to the Elbe, loading the produce of industrial Germany at the Oderhafen and then recrossed the North Sea for a brief stop at Grangemouth for steel and chemicals. The previous voyage she had been up the Baltic as far as Riga, but not this trip. She had loaded Scotch Whisky at Shieldhall on the Clyde before crossing the Mersey Bar and locking into Vittoria Dock to complete her outward lading.

For this coastal voyage she had been manned by an *ad hoc* crew. Apart from a few of the last voyage's officers due for transfer, extended leave or examination, and the much put-upon Chinese, it was made up by men between permanent ships or from the 'Pool', a register of unemployed seamen run under the auspices of the Board of Trade from which a shipping company drew manpower if its contracted employees were insufficient. They had had a good coasting, a few days in a floating dry-dock at Howaldtswerke in Hamburg, and not too much fog, despite the fact that it was already late autumn. Vittoria Dock marked the end of the old and the start of the new odyssey, the forty-fourth foreign voyage made by the *Antigone*.

She had been built, like so many of her sisters, at the Caledon Yard at Dundee in 1949, the year the Communists took over China and Holt's lost their great wharf at Pootung on the Whang-Pu River below Shanghai. She was 487 feet long with a beam of 64 feet. Her long black hull with its pink boot-topping had a distinctive curve to the line of its sheer and was topped by three white painted 'islands'. Amidships, the longest, was known as the centre-castle and bore the main accommodation and the huge blue funnel with its black top. The scantlings of her hull were massive, row upon row of rivets strapped her plating and frames, her stringers and her beams to a specification far above the most stringent requirements of Lloyds. Holt's ships were built for anything, typhoon-proof and uninsured, the Company's confidence resting with their ships and men, rather than underwriters. She was owned by the Ocean Steamship Company Limited, for whom Alfred Holt and Company acted as managers. The Ocean Steamship Company had been founded by the innovative engineer Alfred Holt just a hundred years earlier in 1866, and the commercial empire had expanded to absorb the China Mutual Steamship Company, the Knight Line, the Indra Line and, at last, their chief and most successful rivals, the Glen and Shire Lines owned by MacGregor and Gow, who alone retained their own funnel colours. Blue Funnel ships were divided under Ocean or China Mutual ownership. But these were pettifogging notions, not comprehended by simple sailors because, in practice, they were indistinguishable from one another. *Antigone* was a Blue Funnel liner, a 'Blue Flue', a 'China Boat'.

Her Danish-designed Burmeister and Wain diesel engine had been built under licence by Kincaid's of Glasgow; its seven cylinders developed 8,000 horsepower and gave her heavy-loaded hull a speed of sixteen knots. In a ship's day of twenty-four hours she could make good 384 nautical miles. Her gross registered tonnage, a measurement based upon her total cubic capacity calculated at 100 cubic feet per ton, was 7,800 and her net tonnage (the same figure less the spaces necessary for her crew, engines, fuel and navigation) was 4,500. She was capable of lifting total deadweight of 9,300 tons. For most of the forthcoming voyage she would sell her capacity, the vast spaces of her 'tween decks and lower holds, at a unit-rate of 40 cubic feet, the notional 'space-ton' of her trade.

As we scrambled aboard, sweating and swearing in the rain, hauling our gear up a gangway perversely designed, so it seemed, for the passage of a single drunk, our nostrils were assailed by exotic smells. There were scents of copra, the more pungent whiff of rubber and the faint, elusive aroma of tea, all coming from the ventilators that found the upper deck along the centre-castle alleyway. No trace of these commodities remained on board, yet their lingering perfumes had an odd, nostalgic power. We leaned on the rail, pausing to catch our breath, with two decks still to go.

Below us a narrow strip of water ran between ship and quay where the floating wooden fenders held the hull clear of the granite coping stones. The vibration of the generators which provided auxiliary power to the domestic services of the ship set up tiny ripples in the filthy water and these radiated and reverberated in a mathematically precise wave-form between the hull and dock-wall. From the quay dockers stared incuriously back at us from the warehouse doors, having watched our antics scaling the gangway

Voyage East

with our traps.

'Bloody class warfare,' growled the Purser scowling at them. The remark set us in motion again. As we lumbered up to the promenade deck and negotiated the final ladder to the boat deck the squeal of more taxis braking sounded from the quay now far below us. While we gasped on the boat-deck at last, a crane driver ascended to his cab, silhouetted against a solitary patch of blue sky. We watched as the tall jib jerked into motion and the weighted hook plumbed the quay. The midshipmen were pulling their gear out of two taxis, the senior was waving the crane-driver round to where his companions were manoeuvring their trunks into a purloined cargo-net. We watched dumbly as their personal effects were hoisted smoothly onto the deck alongside us, to be dumped right outside the half-deck door. Calling to his men, the Senior Midshipman took the gangway steps two at a time. I noticed the raw recruit was left to pay the taxi. The lounging dockers grinned up at us. One sensed a kind of solidarity, abandoned when one gained one's first 'ticket'.

'That young man', said the Second Mate, 'has more leadership potential than is good for him ... ah, Middy!'

The Senior Midshipman had reached the boat-deck unencumbered and unwinded.

'Sir?' He looked round at us, eyes wary, taking in the pile of trunks.

'Bring our gear along to the officers' accommodation, please.' The Second Mate led us forward, beneath the monolithic blue funnel that reared above us.

'Time you buggers arrived.'

The preoccupied Scot had shed his crumpled suit. He wore instead a threadbare reefer uniform, the three gold bars on his sleeve interlaced with a diamond. He seemed to have grown taller and younger, uncoiled from the stooped self-effacement of his civilian anonymity in the Shipping Office. The small, neat black knot of his tie nestled under a starched detachable collar and bespoke a precise man. The Scots accent was muted, yet carried a weight of authority and one noticed for the first time a pair of powerful shoulders. He produced a filled pipe, tamped it and lit a match, eyeing us over the undulating flame. He was blocking our entry into the officers'

BLUE FUNNEL

alleyway; we were exposed on the boat-deck and the rain continued to bucket down, despite the expanding patch of blue sky that indicated an approaching shift in the wind. He was provoking a response. I had paid the taxi; it was time rank took on its obligations. We looked at the Second Mate expectantly.

'I'm sorry sir ... slight delay getting our gear together...'

We 'sir-ed' the mate in those days, particularly under such circumstances.

'Bullshit.'

The word fell athwart our hawse like a cannon shot, helped by the explosion of smoke from his mouth. But it was said without malice; he knew full well where we had been and was only letting us know he knew.

'Come on, get out of that bloody rain...'

Our arrival displaced the coasting crew. They drifted away, on leave, to courses, or to ship-keep the other 'Bluies' loading along the dock. Most of the final cargo supervision here was undertaken by the Company's own stevedores. One by one the hatches filled, the beams and hatch-boards were shipped, the triple tarpaulins pulled over and Chippy and his mate drove home the hardwood wedges around each coaming. Previously swung untidily outboard clear of the access to the hatches in this port of tall, dockside cranes, the derricks were now brought inboard and lowered into their crutches by the Bosun and his 'Crowd'. We mates occupied ourselves in pre-sailing preparations, familiarising ourselves with the ship. Although an individual, she was one of a numerous class, almost all identical in build and with the richly unpronounceable names of Greek mythology. The Homeric nomenclature was indiscriminate in its choice. Alfred Holt, rating his great adventure into ship-owning akin to the stories from the *Iliad* and the *Odyssey* that had thrilled his youth, had named his first Far East bound ship *Agamemnon*. This heroic strain had been followed ever since and there had always been an *Agamemnon*, an *Achilles* and an *Ajax* in the fleet. Equally valiant were the newer *Menelaus* and *Maron*, or the big steamships on the Australian service, the *Hector*, *Helenus* and the lovely *Nestor*. But there were less glorious names like our own and *Cyclops*, the hideous *Gorgon* or the Stygian *Charon*, which carried thousands of unwitting

Voyage East

Australian tourists to Singapore and, appropriately, livestock for mass slaughter. There was also the ignominious *Elpenor,* named after a bibulous swineherd who fell from a roof while sleeping off an excess of wine and broke his neck. 'The hand of some god was my undoing, and measureless wine,' he was supposed to have pronounced as his own epitaph; it could have been that of many sailors.

Like the men who commanded them, some of these ships acquired their own nicknames. *Ascanius* was known as the *Ashcan;* the *Dolius,* the *Dolly-arse,* and a Yankee pilot had unforgettably christened the *Adrastus,* the *A.D. Rastus.* The Australian dockers called the *Ixion* the *Nine-to-one-on* and their Merseyside brethren referred to the huge, twin-funnelled *Gunung Djati* as the *Jam Butty,* not merely because of the assonance, but because her all-white topsides were bisected by a thick maroon riband. She was unique in the fleet in possessing two funnels and being named after a Javanese mountain holy to Muslims. Built pre-war in Germany as the liner *Pretoria,* she had become the British Government's troopship *Empire Orwell* before Holt's purchased her to fit her for the carriage of Indonesian pilgrims on the Java to Jeddah 'Hajdi' service. This run was one of several foreign routes worked by ships exiled far from the 'mainline' traffic. Often older ships were pensioned off onto these bluewater services, but all bore the distinctive funnels that had distinguished Holt's ships ever since, it was said, Alfred Holt had discovered a tin of blue paint in a coaster he re-engined experimentally at the beginning of his career. With the exception of the Glen and Shire Line names, Holt's had absorbed all their rivals under this splendidly distinctive device.

The clear fresh weather that replaced the rain of joining-day held until the final hatch was almost completed, then disappeared as the last Ford car was rolled over the floor of Guinness cases in No 4 centre-castle deck. As 'the Crowd', the generic name for the deckcrew, secured the ship for sea, a warm front rolled a grey blanket of stratus over the Birkenhead sky. Herring gulls wheeled above us, ridge-soaring the updrafts as the westerly gale slammed against the cranes and sheds and the superstructures of the ships, their gapes wide in the strident half-laugh, half-scream of their cry.

'All old Blue-Flue bosuns,' remarked the Mate casually, glad to see the last dockers off his ship, 'waiting to crap over my decks...' He looked ruefully at the begrimed teak planking and shook his head slowly. 'Go and test the steering gear.'

'Aye, aye, sir.'

Across the oil-slicked and polluted water of Vittoria Dock *Clan Ranald's* lascars were getting her derricks down. She too would be sailing on the evening's high water.

The last dribbles of cargo came aboard, consisting of valuables to be locked away in the ship's strongrooms; the personal effects of a Ghurka officer arrived in an army truck, a single, unspecified crate in a van, delivered by two bewildered, donnish young men and consigned to the University of Singapore.

'What's in dat, den?' asked an inquisitive seaman leaning on his broom as two dockers pushed it behind the massive steel doors of the poop locker. One of the young men stepped forward to explain. It was obviously an enthusiasm of his.

'Hey, Wack, gerron wiv it, eh?' The Bosun's Mate, sometimes known by the ancient term of 'Lamptrimmer', chased the man's unwilling feet along the deck with the jet of his wash-deck hose, making sure I was splashed as I went aft to test the steering gear with the Second Engineer. We spent the forenoon in such tests and checks. Above the bridge the radar scanner had begun to rotate and there were new noises about the ship.

At lunch Captain Richards appeared for the first time, accompanied by his wife and a shy, doe-eyed daughter.

'You know what they say about Welsh girls, don't you?' whispered the Third Mate, nodding in the direction of Miss Richards.

'No, what?'

'Pious in chapel, astute in the market and *frantic* in bed...' His voice was a fair imitation of the Bosun's aspirated accent and his eyes twinkled as we giggled obligingly, attracting a glare from China Dick. The new midshipman, just beginning to enjoy the raw masculine banter, allowed his grin to linger a second too long and coloured violently.

After lunch our dozen passengers embarked and we were occupied with

Voyage East

the inspection, a departure ritual second only to signing-on, but this one a family affair. Senior staff of the Company, including one of the managers, walked round the ship with the Master, the Chief Engineer and the Chief Steward. All three were in spotless uniforms and, similarly attired, we stood respectfully at various points about the ship and shook hands, opened doors or answered questions in deference to those who paid the assembled pipers. If signing-on had been the bureaucratic start of the voyage, this was its spiritual kicking off point.

At dusk the oily water of the dock was churned to a yeast by the appearance of a covey of Rea's tugs. *Applegarth* and *Reagarth* were to attend *Antigone;* the others stopped off the *Clan Ranald.* At 1800 the pilot boarded and we were called to stations by a single long blast of the Mate's whistle.

I escorted the Master's wife and daughter ashore, read the departure draft and dipped the hydrometer in the bucket of dock-water hauled on deck for me by the junior Midshipman. He thought he was doing penance for his *lese-majesty* in the saloon and I explained: 'The density of dock or river water is sometimes less than that of pure sea-water. If we were loaded to our marks, we'd be allowed to submerge them by a calculated amount, so that when we got into the open sea the greater buoyancy of the salt water would raise the ship to her Plimsoll line...' He frowned. The physics lab transposed uneasily to the windswept deck of a ship in the gathering darkness of sailing -day, the bucket of grimy water between us an unimpressive piece of scientific apparatus.

'You see,' I pressed on, 'it takes just over forty tons of cargo to sink this ship an inch in the water. We call this figure "tons per inch immersion", or TPI...'

I waited for intelligence to kindle above the acne.

'But we're not loaded to our marks...' he said uncertainly.

'No, quite right, but we're obliged to record the density of the water in which we read our departure draft and display the form in the mates' alleyway just so that your mother knows that you aren't about to drown.'

'Oh.'

'It's a Board of Trade requirement.'

He frowned. 'You mean a Department of Transport requ ..'

'Smart-arse ... that's what the Government currently call it. Last year it was the Department of Trade, next year it'll be the Ministry of Transport. It's all very confusing, so jack calls it the Board of Trade, then we all know what we're talking about. Okay?'

'Yes sir.'

He had not noticed the last ropes were being let go for he jumped when the Supertyfon siren blasted the news of our departure over the indifferent roofs of Birkenhead. A clatter of pigeons whirred up against a small patch of fading daylight that showed briefly through the thick clouds: shadows began to angle across the deck as the shore lights slid past. The two tugs hauled us out of our berth and then above us, leaning over the bridge-wing, we heard the Pilot.

'Dead slow astern, sir.'

The order was repeated faintly and there came the jangle of telegraph bells, the hiss of the compressed air turning the diesel to ignition and then the rumble of the Burmeister and Wain.

'We're off.'

'Yes sir.'

'Right. Chuck that lot over the wall.' He hesitated. 'Back where it came from,' I explained.

'Yes sir.'

'And for goodness sake say "aye, aye, sir".'

'Yes sir.'

We towed out through the East Float, paused in the Alfred Lock, then continued astern into the Mersey. The dark water of the river was 'standing'; it was exactly high water slack. As we cast off the tugs and squared away to proceed down-stream, a hunter's moon emerged from behind the clouds, briefly silhouetting the famous skyline on the opposite bank: the Custom House, the Cunard Building and the strange, aquiline cormorants atop the Royal Liver Building. It was unkindly said of these that they only flapped their wings when a virgin passed beneath them.

Beyond the waterfront the exciting heart of the city beat with a new vigour quite divorced from the commercial stolidity of the business

Voyage East

quarter. Liverpool had, for a while, eclipsed London as the source of a generation's identity. It was the era of the Beatles and the 'Mersey sound'. We had Liverpool in white-painted letters around our cruiser stern. It gave us a vicarious authority, a passport more potent and better understood than the tired old ensign that tore at its halliards aft. But this was also an era of strikes, of dockside discontent and social malaise. Already, on that evening of departure, the seeds were germinating for Liverpool's sad decline.

A brightly lit Mersey ferry dodged under our stern. We caught a glimpse of long hair streaming in the wind as two girls waved saucily at us. They had a transistor radio between them and the thin strains of Lennon and McCartney came to us before the wind snatched them away.

'Hey, give the judies a wave, then,' said a seaman cheekily, coming aft from his station.

As we increased speed and the shores of Bootle and New Brighton fell astern, we were exposed to the full fury of the gale as it tore across the shallows of Mockbeggar Sands. I dismissed the junior Midshipman and he went off to the half-deck to occupy himself with the newly acquired skill of rolling his own cigarettes. I joined the Mate on the bridge where he had just arrived from the forecastle, his station for leaving and entering port.

'Pour us a cup of tea, laddie.'

On the starboard bridge-wing, behind the bellied stretch of the canvas dodger, Captain Richards and the Pilot leaned on the teak caprail. I took the mug of tea to the Mate, who stood at the wheelhouse door. I sensed a sea-change as profound as the strange transmogrification that had occurred on his first coming aboard. He stared astern, his face a pale oval in the gloom.

'Farewell Lancashire,' he intoned with an exaggerated, melancholic solemnity that I was to learn was characteristic of him, 'where the moors come down from the hills and the whores come down from the mills.'

I knew, for all the crudity of the familiar doggerel, that I was about to share a watch with a romantic.

Our passage seawards was a long curve north and then westwards down the deep-water channel that was maintained by submerged training walls and marked by a line of flashing buoys. The ebb tide was now away, carrying us rapidly downstream and augmenting the power of our thundering diesel-engine. On the horizon the revolving beams of the Bar lightvessel stabbed the darkness. The deck moved under our feet as the ship began a gentle pitching, and spurts of white water foamed out from her bow. Out of the windy darkness the red and white lights of the cutter cruising on the pilot station emerged from the cluster of lights marking the ships anchored on the Bar awaiting berths. *Antigone* did not slow; we would carry our pilot as far as Holyhead.

Pilots never superseded the ship's own staff. They were logged as 'advising' the master; but companies like Holt's appropriated their own pilots to assist their ships in and out of ports like Liverpool, London and Glasgow. These 'Choice Pilots' were regarded by many shipmasters as Company spies, boarding inward vessels to see whether the master was in liquor and reporting secretly to their respective headquarters if they thought him incompetent. Pilots, though experienced deep-water mariners often in possession of master's certificates, had rarely served in a higher capacity than first mate and were therefore viewed with some suspicion by men in command of ships, whose lives were utterly committed to the sea. Pilots were victims of one of those odd, deep-rooted prejudices that flourish at sea, regarded as mere amphibians who had dodged the issue. But caution and Company rules obliged a master to ship a pilot where port regulations did not, and usually their services were sterling.

As the pitching hull of the lightvessel fell astern, the water streaming from her hawse-pipe as she pitched at her mooring, the bridge reverberated to the triple ring of 'full speed away' on the engineroom telegraph. *Antigone* cleared Liverpool Bay and headed out into the wild Irish Sea.

It was Company policy to 'double' the watches until its ships were clear of Ushant. This meant that the Second and Third Mates stood a watch together, while the Mate and I took the next. It was the old routine of four hours on and four off which smacked of sailing ships and hard times, but in the crowded waters of north west Europe with the high incidence of fog, strong winds and fierce tides, two officers on watch were an undoubted advantage. In company with the Mate I was recalled to the bridge at midnight, after a couple of hours below, to relieve the Third Mate.

Voyage East

'Father's still up here,' he nodded at the dark shapes of Captain Richards and the pilot huddled at the rail behind the shelter of the dodger. The ship slammed into a heavy sea, throwing us together, our legs still unaccustomed to the motion.

'Not this dance, sweetie,' the Third Mate lisped. We exchanged the information of course and speed. 'It's getting worse ... be bloody lovely when we round the Skerries.'

We both stared out on the port bow where, beyond the necklace of sparse lights dotting the low coast of Anglesey, the Skerries lighthouse pierced the darkness.

'Yes, I replied, insufficient sleep still stale in my mouth.

'Pot of tea in the chartroom. *Buenas noches* . .

'Night.'

He drifted off with the Second Mate and I skidded across the port bridge wing to take the first bearing fix of the middle watch. Emerging into the wheelhouse again where only the binnacle lights relieved the blackness I found the Mate standing beside the man at the wheel.

'Black as the Earl of Hell's riding boots,' he remarked. I agreed. 'Only whores, thieves and sailors work on nights like this.' It was a gross over-simplification, but I knew what he meant. I had a premonition of philosophical discussion by the time we had traversed the Indian Ocean.

As we approached the Skerries, a granite reef of broken, seascarred rocks that lay off the very corner of Wales, we lost the protection of the land. The south-westerly gale was gusting strongly, approaching storm force, some fifty knots of wind. Around Carmel Head and the Skerries the ebb-tide at its full strength reached several knots in velocity and, in opposing the wind, threw up a heavy, breaking sea. The Mate stood quietly in the wheelhouse, watching the helmsman and drinking his tea while I dodged in and out of the chart-room, plotting the ship's position and calling the diminishing distance to the 'alter-course' position to the Master and Pilot. We had met no opposing traffic in the run from the Bar, but the radar and brief glimpses of her navigation lights showed the *Clan Ranald* ploughing in our wake. As we cleared the lee of Anglesey we saw three inward ships, corkscrewing up from the South Stack towards the Skerries, brief flashes of deck lights on glistening water as the seas tumbled alongside their scending hulls.

Antigone lifted her bow then dropped abruptly into the trough of a hollow sea. The impact shuddered throughout her massive hull as the stern kicked into the aerated and less-dense water of the passing crest. Her propeller raced as her bow crashed, foaming into the approach of the next wall of water and her solid forecastle vanished under a pall that seemed to glow in the darkness.

'Stand-by engines!' snapped Captain Richards, a statue suddenly quickened.

'Stand-by engines, sir!' The Mate swung the telegraph handles and the jangling answer came from below, after which the roar of the diesel in the funnel just abaft the bridge changed its note as the revolutions of the shaft dropped.

'One mile to the alter-course, sir.'

China Dick grunted acknowledgement and we heard the Pilot remark on the difficulties of disembarking.

'Want to come to Gib with us, do you?' Richards's rich mellifluous voice jibed at his fellow countryman.

'Not ploddy likely, Captain.'

'Closing the alter-course, sir . .

'Carry on, Mister.' This to the Mate who acknowledged it and turned to me.

'Okay, La?' he mimicked the Scouse accent, an obligatory accomplishment for every Blue Funnel officer. At this early moment in the voyage I avoided a facetious rejoinder. The Pilot had long ago relinquished responsibility for the ship's safe navigation and, since the Bar, coastal pilotage, 'cabotage', had been carried out by the officers under the watchful eye of China Dick. Now, as we altered direction off the Skerries, critical scrutiny was being directed at my competence. I was, after all, the least experienced of his officers, the weakest link in the chain of his responsibility.

In windswept isolation I bent over the azimuth mirror atop the port bridge-wing gyro-compass repeater. In the prism I could see the reflection

Voyage East

of the softly illuminated notation of the compass card, above the notch of its mounting the glow of the Skerries light intensified twice every ten seconds as the beam swung round towards us. The bearing altered slowly, the compass clicked as the ship yawed in her track, pitching and slamming into the heavy seas that marched downwind towards us in lines regular and bold enough to show as serried ranks on the radar screen. Loose hair flogged my scalp.

'Bearing coming on!' I bawled the intelligence over my shoulder and heard the Mate's soft-spoken order to the helmsman.

'Port easy.'

'Port easy . . .' The ship began to swing, the bow lifted as its angle to the advancing waves changed, the ship climbed then swooped into a dark hole in the ocean that, for a splinter of time, seemed bottomless. I swung the azimuth mirror and collected my tally of bearings: the Skerries lighthouse, the light on the breakwater at Holyhead and the distant single flash of the South Stack; then raced across the bridge for a distance-off by radar, and plotted the information on the chart. The neat intersection of pencilled lines was satisfactorily upon the alter-course position and the ship steadied on her southerly course towards the waiting pilot boat tucked just inside the breakwater at Holyhead. A few minutes later I left the bridge to prepare the ropeladder for disembarking the Pilot. I made a brief stop in my cabin to scribble a final sentence to a letter, sealed it and stuffed it into the pocket of my duffle coat.

From my new position on the centre-castle immediately below the bridge I could hear China Dick conning the ship himself as he slowed her down. The stand-by seaman of the watch was inexpertly helped by the Junior Midshipman, still blinded by sleep as they rigged the pilot ladder. I wondered if he had ever been up at this hour of the night before; perhaps, as an infant with colic.

We hoisted a cargo-lamp over the side to illuminate the dangling ladder and its light threw the surge and suck of the sea into sudden intimacy. *Antigone* rolled and dipped. There was an abrupt pause in the wind-howl, then the sibilant hiss of spray as the icy-cold bite of spindrift struck our cheeks.

'Fuck this!' snapped the seaman, and I recognised him as the complainant of the Birkenhead Shipping Office. His name was Embleton.

The breakwater wall loomed suddenly close, outlined by heaps of white water thundering along it and exploding over its rampart. *Antigone* swung to make a lee for the pilot boat which had appeared out of nowhere and wallowed after us in the comparative calm of our wake. She slammed alongside, her deck-hand staring up at us. The Pilot arrived from the bridge.

'Good-bye, Mister Mate,' he said, grinning cordially and holding out his hand.

'Would you mind, Pilot?' I held out the letter. He turned it to see the stamp and noticed the addressee's unmarried status.

'Certainly not.'

He swung himself over the rail and descended, timing his blind, backwards leap perfectly, and landing on the launch's foredeck to be grabbed round the waist by the waiting deck-hand. For a second he stood illuminated by the cargo-lamp, raising a valedictory hand to China Dick far above.

'Gweld i di!'

Then the two men dived for the shelter of the cabin and the boat turned away.

'Hard a-starboard! Full ahead!' Above us as we hauled up the dripping ladder, China Dick relished his independence at last.

'Lucky bastard,' remarked the seaman as the pilot boat disappeared behind the breakwater, 'he'll be anchored in the lee of Bum Island in half-an-hour.'

'Bum Island ... ?' frowned the junior Midshipman, his eyes hollow with sea-sickness and fatigue.

'Get those bloody men off the upper deck, Four-O!' bawled China Dick, curtailing any explanation.

Men like China Dick, victims of boredom during much of their voyages, were in their element in such circumstances as we now found ourselves. Holt's uninsured ships had the rules for their passing from one port to another strictly set out in the Company's Standing Instructions. China Dick

Voyage East

himself had put up a premium on attaining command, upon which the Company paid him interest unless he committed some adjudged error, when this sum could be docked or trimmed according to the seriousness of the offence. Men's pockets were readier reins upon their conduct than their consciences, but many were well aware of Captain Marryat's advice, that a man who could not write a log-book to his own advantage was not fit to command a ship.

From the Holyhead breakwater the Company's injunction to proceed due west had been faithfully followed by the Second Mate, whose duty it was to lay off all the courses for a passage. This would take the ship well off the land before she turned south-southwestward for St George's Channel and the Atlantic beyond. There was good reason for this. Off the North and South Stacks overfalls occurred, steeper, hollower seas within whose breaking mass serious damage could be sustained, even to ships as sturdy as the *Antigone*. These dangerous seas were a product of the combined forces of wind and tide meeting off protruding headlands. Promontories accelerate the speed of both wind and tide, making a rough turbulence of these 'overfalls' as they fought to resolve their differences. This reaches a crescendo of elemental violence when a spring tide opposes a storm force wind, as was now the case.

But the Stacks, steep-humped islands separated from the buttresses of Holy Mountain by thin, gurgling guts of white water, were steep-to, and could, if a man had nerve enough, be approached within feet. Running close inshore avoided the overalls, the water smoothing somewhat as it thundered against the cliffs and then fell in a backwash of confused crests. These warred with each other, reducing the incoming violence, and were nothing to the white fury a few cables further to seaward. Ignoring the pencilled line to the west, it was via such a route that China Dick took us seaward that wild night.

Free of uxorious constraint, free of the need to kiss the fundament of the Company's hierarchy, and free of a man he suspected of amiable espionage, China Dick was determined to destroy at birth any doubts as to his style of command. We passed the North Stack a few cables from the surge of breakers at its vertical extreme. We clawed out from its brief shelter clear of the thunder of the overfalls roaring and ripping the night apart, into the teeth of the unrelenting gale. Captain Richards followed me into the chart-room I plotted the ship's position. Finishing, I snapped the chart-pencil securely between the twin sides of the parallel rules. His stubby forefinger appeared suddenly on the chart.

'Rub that lot out, Four-O. Courses to be logged 'Various to Master's Orders'. We'll set course here.' He shifted his finger to a spot well clear of all dangers and met my stare with the slightest of twinkles in his deep-set eyes. I was clearly to be trusted.

'Aye, aye, sir.'

According to Marryat's dictum, Captain Richards was eminently fitted to command.

China Dick's bluff was called by the weather.

His order for full speed had to be modified when we finally hauled off the land and set our course for Gibraltar. The moon reappeared from behind the clouds to throw a baleful light on the great streamers of stratus that welled up over the weather coast of Wales and rolled to leeward of the summits of distant Snowdonia. Beneath its cold light the sea churned and spumed, its surface streaked with spindrift, torn away by the violent friction of the wind. Wave-form phased with wave-form to generate huge, coincident seas that came to leeward in distinctive ranks, and we faced the coming day with haggard faces, unseamanlike innards and unsteady legs. As we contemplated what Yeats called 'the murderous innocence of the sea', there was not one of us that night who did not wish he had chosen some alternative profession; except, perhaps, China Dick.

Yet we had not quite finished with our home coast; one last ritual waited to be performed, and it was left to me when the Mate and I next resumed the duties of watch-keeping on a bleak, grey morning with heavy rain clouds massing on the horizon.

This was the matter of Departure, Departure with a capital 'D'. As I stared eastwards, once more bent over the azimuth mirror of the port gyro-repeater, I took a final bearing of the red and white banded column of the Smalls lighthouse, now diminished with distance, to fix the ship's position from 'terrestrial bearings' for the last time. From here we would

Voyage East

calculate our dead-reckoning by traverse tables, work our sights with the aid of sextant and chronometer until we sighted the Iberian coast with its recognisable landmarks marked upon our charts. This carefully plotted position was our Departure ... distinctly a ceremony of navigation ... the technical as distinguished from the sentimental Goodbye ƒ. Who could put it better than Conrad?

The land faded astern; Pembrokeshire rolled itself over the rim of the world and left us alone on the ocean. Out on the port bow a skein of gannets flew west in line astern, two fully mature, the rest wearing the dark plumage of juvenile birds. Sabre-winged fulmars quartered our wake above the tiny, dark, feet-dabbling petrels that eluded all but the sharp-eyed.

China Dick had gone below at last and the helmsman had relinquished the rudder to the Arkas auto-pilot. The Mate came smiling across the bridge and nodded to starboard. The school of bottle-nosed dolphins sliced across our bow at an acute angle, leaping and thrusting themselves through the grey seas at speeds in excess of twenty knots.

Well, laddie, he said in his quiet burr, removing the top bar of formality, are you wondering why the bloody hell you ever came to sea?

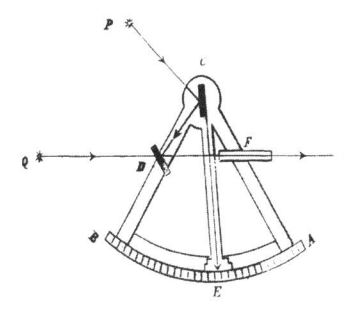

O︎UTWARD BOUND

It was a rhetorical question, not to be answered at that moment by anything more than a grin. I sensed he asked it as a consolation for his present unhappiness and that, like those well-rehearsed crudities of the previous night, it betrayed the shy man he really was. Leaving home was especially painful for the older men, those with wives and families, whose children grew by leaps and bounds during their absence. But the Mate was, untypically, not married. My first instincts proved accurate, for he revealed himself as an incurable romantic and I watched the disease consume him during the coming months. Those snatches of coarseness, the versicles and responses of a ritual catechism, were followed by flashes of greater wisdom, culled from wide reading and a deep intelligence that was constrained by reticence and the romantic's inevitable loneliness. But during that bleak forenoon of Departure we established the footing for our professional relationship. A mutual respect had already sprung up between us, for I kept the Mate's watch once we passed Ushant: his part in the matter would be titular, his presence on the bridge regulated by the navigational formalities and the customary genuflexion to Company policy. He had many other duties to attend to, and I was not without experience; my Second Mate's certificate had grown dog-eared as I accrued sufficient sea-time to sit my examination for the next grade, that of First Mate. With luck, this voyage should be enough.

He leaned beside me at the rail and I realised, with a shock, that he was much younger than I had supposed. His features had a prematurely aged look about them; he had not bronzed well, like so many of us did, and his complexion was coarse. He reminded me of a boy I had once known, the child of elderly parents. He had dark hair and shaggy eyebrows that added to this impression of age and, unknowingly, I had touched on the root of his unhappiness. As though he disliked my thoughts, he suddenly straightened, slapping the palm of his hand upon the caprail.

'Ah, well ...' he said, and drifted away into the chart-room to write up

Voyage East

the log-book from the slates we mere watch-keepers were allowed to fill in with the details of our four-hourly vigils on the bridge.

'It's part of the Welsh Naval conspiracy,' it had once been explained to me, 'a guaranteed market for the export of Cambrian slate combined with the opportunity to modify the true record in time of cock-ups.'

I began to pace the bridge wing, keeping my lookout as the exhausts roared in the funnel behind and above me and *Antigone* pitched and rolled her way south.

The Mate's disappearance left me with his question. The short answer was that I had never seriously considered any occupation other than sea-going. I supposed myself a sufficiently practical fellow, with just enough brain to assimilate the principles of navigation and the theory of ship stability. I felt, too, that I had a sense of responsibility that would not utterly disgrace my parents. Certainly the urge was not hereditary, nor born of a desire to travel; travelling was merely a bonus. Of course, at its start I had no way of gauging the disappointments the life entailed. There was, one quickly learned, a crushing social stigma - best epitomised by the plea of Lady Astor's, that merchant seamen should wear yellow armbands when on home leave to identify them as potential carriers of venereal disease. It was a vile calumny, for though merchant seamen were no better than other men, they learned early that prophylaxis was better than cure.

A child of the suburbs of north London, I knew little about the sea but possessed an insatiable appetite for messing about in boats. The opportunities to do this in post-war, austerity London were negligible. Expeditions in 'ships' were limited to a circumnavigation of the Isle of Wight in an excursion paddle-steamer, which left an indelible impression upon my mind. It had been blustery weather, the rolling decks were wet with spray, the white-capped sea alternately bright with sunlight and shadowed by cloud. In the distance the beaches of Sandown and Shanklin were still barred by their anti-invasion *chevaux-des-frises*. We rounded St Catherine's Point with its crenellated lighthouse to starboard and a school of porpoises gambolling to port. Along the white buttresses of the Needles the seas crashed and foamed with a terrifying majesty and from our spraying bow-wave, little rainbows curved in the patches of sunshine. The memory lodged, to stir the imagination in my journeys to and from a good grammar school where I proved a bad pupil.

If my father had wished me a more sedentary occupation, he compounded the folly of that utterly thrilling steamer trip by another on the *Royal Daffodil,* one of the General Steam Navigation Company's Thames steamers which took tourists round London's Docks. Gently shoving aside the empty, drifting lighters that awaited collection by the bustling tugs, we stared at the great ships that lay in the Royal Docks. Vestey's *Stars* discharged Argentine beef, the big passenger-cargo ships of the New Zealand Shipping Company and the Federal Steamship Company landed Canterbury lamb and New Zealand butter. More meat and bales of Australian wool swung out of the holds of the grey-hulled Port Line vessels and the hatches of the Shaw, Savill and Albion's fine liners. Tea and teak came ashore from the British India ships and the bellies of the dingy cargo liners of the P & O, tucked astern of their huge, white passenger-bearing sisters, the *Canton* and the *Chusan*. At the far end of the King George V Dock where we swung with a great thrashing of paddle wheels, were two modestly elegant cargo-liners, their vast funnels black above red. They had an impressively workmanlike appearance as fitted the successors of the China clippers. The *Glenartney* was discharging tea and rubber, the *Glenearn* loading 'general' for the Far East. I did not know it then, but I was to sail on both of them in later life. A few foreigners were tolerated in this Pale, a single vessel of the United States Line and a former enemy, regarded oddly by many of the occupants of the *Daffodil's* deck, a mail-liner of the Nippon Yusen Kaisha. Somehow these foreigners were a counterpoint. All, all without exception, were heroic to me, opening vistas that stretched vast beyond the airless boredom of the classroom.

The books were chiefly to blame. That first of English novels, *Robinson Crusoe,* and the exciting shipwrecks of Marryat and Ballantyne, led on to more specialised reading. In Alan Villiers I found a mentor more comprehensible than the *magister* who failed to coach me beyond the second declension of Latin nouns. But I had been born too late to cruise on the *Joseph Conrad* and the last commercial barque to fly the red ensign, the *Garthpool*, had been wrecked before Hitler's war. I had once seen the

Voyage East

rusting hulk of a deep-water sailing vessel, a barque named the *Alastor*, decaying in Ramsgate harbour, but she was unseaworthy and the revival of sail training in the UK was, as yet, some years off. What was to be done?

Amongst the debris of war a few battered ex-naval sailing dinghies had found their way into the ownership of the Sea Scouts and the stories of Arthur Ransome stimulated the idea of self-generated adventure. I learned how to use a sextant aboard Scott's tethered *Discovery* and pulled bow-oar in whalers on the tidal waters of the Thames. When a crew was to be found from among British scouts to enter the sail-training race of 1960, my parents generously bent to the seaward blowing breeze and I spent much of my final exam year afloat. After successfully competing in the North Sea race from Oslo to Ostend aboard Hugh Astor's beautiful yawl *Nordwind,* I scraped by some fluke into the indentured employment of Alfred Holt, as a Midshipman. Fortunately Holt's were eclectic in the selection of their trainees. There were young men from Gordonstoun and Wellington as well as from the secondary-moderns of Merseyside. Those from the training establishments of *Conway* and *Worcester,* or the School of Navigation at Warsash, earned remission on the length of their apprenticeships. This made a possible age-difference on entry of between sixteen and eighteen. I was sixteen, with four years to serve. What we experienced in common was a gruelling Outward Bound Course at Eskdale or Aberdovey, where our weaknesses of character or physique were expertly exposed. Only survival of this ordeal with a good report meant that Holt's would accept us.

Like Melville's Ishmael, I found myself accommodated in a twin-berthed room, above the porticoed entrance of the Company's hostel in Liverpool, unaware that occupation of the room contracted certain obligations. In a thoroughly seamanlike manner I had battened the window against the stink of an oil refinery across the river and turned in, uncertain who was supposed to occupy the other bed. My Queequeg turned out to be an angry and very senior South African Midshipman with the name of a Boer general who, after climbing a drain-pipe, expected the window to be open. His return after lights-out from an evening of fornication was marred by my ignorance, and he revenged himself by walking unceremoniously across my bed.

'Liverpool judies know the score, when a merchant seaman walks ashore' went the old sea-song, but neither they, nor we, were indiscriminately promiscuous. Nevertheless, sexual torments were inescapable and how men dealt with them determined their character at sea. Incurable romance was the anodyne chosen by the *Antigone's* Chief Mate; others fell victim to drink; some merely submitted willingly to the great worm of lust. Even staid married men were cankered, and the permissive society of the 1960s undermined many marriages. None of us was a saint and all suffered more or less from the affliction or its remedy.

What then was the lure, as the Mate had asked me? Mere childhood illusions mostly; later augmented by the practical necessity of earning one's keep and, later still, the comfort of the familiar. 'Like habitually drinking in a shitty pub', the Mate was to say to me later in the voyage when we were discussing the matter.

'So you want to be a Blue Funnel master?' the huge, bearded and beer-goitred Second Mate of the *Glenartney* had asked me on my first voyage as a Midshipman.

'Yes sir,' I had replied, astonished by the wild laugh he brayed into the night. I thought I could hear its echoes that windy, grey morning as, free of the lee of Ireland, the Atlantic Ocean heaved beneath our keel. But that *was* the nub of the matter. It has an unfashionable, elitist ring now, this matter of command, but the guts of it were not about the domination by one of many. Most of those who went to sea did not sail as masters, mates or even aspiring cadets. Most fulfiled other functions as engineers, seamen, sparkies, stewards, all ideas of ultimate responsibility far from their minds. The powers of the master were rarely deeply resented, the yoke of articled agreement was freely entered into, and if it gave the master feudal powers in theory, these were in practice rarely invoked and when they were, proved largely empty. In exchange one gained access to two thirds of the planet's surface. Old Men were as necessary as rudders.

For me, command of a ship offered a medium in which my hitherto unrevealed skill might find expression. Seamanship would be my vocation, my own attempt at excellence. Active command of a ship, therefore, was concerned not with domination, but with self-fulfilment. And if this seems overly self-indulgent, it was loaded with such a weight of responsibility that it presented a challenge for, as Conrad put it, 'The genuine masters of their craft ... have thought of nothing but of doing their very best by the vessel under their charge. To forget oneself, to surrender all personal feeling in the service of that fine art, is the only way for a seaman to the faithful discharge of his trust.'

So I thought at sixteen, and so my positive affirmative provoked the mirth of the *Glenartney*'s Second Mate. This sense of pervading disillusion was the first intimation that all might not be quite as I had imagined. Were all those books wrong? Had I read on, Conrad would have provided his own *caveat:* 'The taking of a modern steamship about the world (though one would not minimise its responsibilities) has not the same quality of intimacy with nature, which ... is an indispensible condition to the building up of an art ... It is, in short, less a matter of love.'

Alas, one did not read or understand such warnings at sixteen.

And so *Antigone* rolled and pitched upon her southward way, her new crew full of the sadness of farewell. This the sea embittered with more of her 'murderous innocence', throwing our unsteady bodies about until our heads cleared of the fumes of the taproom and our sea-legs returned.

Below the bridge the Junior Midshipman carried out the duties of mess-peggy, scrubbing out the half-deck for his seniors. Periodically he retched and spewed miserably. The contents of his bucket slopped across the deck and his chief admonished him: 'If you want sympathy at sea, you'll find it in the dictionary between *shit* and *syphilis.*'

By that first noon of the voyage *Antigone* was clear of the land, stretching her course across the maw of the Celtic Sea and the chops of the Channel, with the Atlantic and the Bay of Biscay ahead. Out here in the open ocean, the wind was more regular, a strong airstream of 35 to 40 knots, the Force Eight of Admiral Beaufort's notation. Damp showers of rain swept down upon us, leaching the colour out of the day and rolling off to leeward where the surge of the waves beat on the iron-bound coast of

Cornwall beyond the horizon. It was too overcast for sights of the sun at noon and I contented myself with recording the weather, dutifully writing 'S.W.-8' upon the slate.

'D'you know, laddie,' remarked the Mate in his odd, didactic way, 'he used to sleep with his sister?'

I looked up, uncertain of whom he spoke. 'Pardon?'

'Your Admiral Beaufort.'

He seemed to fix me with his eyes, a man climbing out of the shell of shoreside existence in the same way as China Dick had proved himself in the early hours of the same day. He made me, it seemed, an accomplice to this historic incest; shock treatment, testing reaction.

'Aye, bloody odd lot, sailors,' and he turned to the Old Man who had just entered the chart-room, while I escaped to the open air of the bridge-wing.

The afternoon passed in a state of limbo as *Antigone* continued to roll and pitch through heavy seas. Her motion was a product not merely of the weather, but also of the genius of her designer, for she shipped little water. On her forecastle, her 'pointed' bow was elliptical, though at her waterline below, her cutwater was sharp as a knife. The originator, Holt's chief naval architect Henry Flett, had developed this idea from the successful hulls built just prior to the Second World War for the *Glenearn*-class. Like the 'three-island' hull, the great funnel and the pronounced sheer, it was characteristic of Holt's ships.

Unlike a sailing vessel whose hull, though enormously stressed in other ways, never has to contend with the head-on collision of heavy seas, a steam or motor ship has to be built to withstand enormous forces meeting her bow. The sailing ship cannot sail into the wind and so her motion is more regular. Driven by the same force which moves the surface molecules of the sea, a sailing ship's hull achieves a sympathetic motion, steadier and more rhythmical, despite the fact that for weeks she may heel to leeward. But a power-driven vessel is *forced* forward in any direction. When that direction is to windward, *into* the wind-created sea, she adds to her forward motion an upward and a downward component which is a function of the period of the seas and her length and speed. A fine, razor-bowed ship will slice through such seas, but she will ship water, making her sluggish and dangerous in really heavy weather, so that what advantage she has in initial speed will be swiftly lost as conditions deteriorate. Indeed, this shipping of water may result in more than a loss of speed or damage to her deck fittings and cargo; such a vessel may be overwhelmed and founder. It is therefore desirable that the extremities of a hull, which for obvious reasons taper, also contain some volume, or reserve buoyancy.

Compromise governs the designs of many things, perhaps none more so than a ship which has both to float and move forward to fulfill its existence. Flett recognised the tremendous forces to which a bow, thrust out of a wave and unsupported by anything but air, was subjected. As the hull tipped, the same bow, driven onwards by its motive power and accelerated by gravity, dropped some forty feet into solid water and the breast of the next wave. Such pounding up and down with sudden accelerations and decelerations caused 'panting' forces within the hull. In heavy weather this was quite audible, and clearly even the speed with which the hull allowed this deceleration to occur was a matter of delicate compromise.

Flett's solution was to build an immensely strong hull and provide it with as sleek an underwater body as cargo-carrying capacity would allow, paying particular attention to it at its entrance, that is, the shape of the forward waterline. In moderate weather the hull possessed the virtues of a slim shape. Above this, however, he flared out the bow so that, between the vertical plating at the cutwater and the forecastle bulwarks, the shell plating curved through some forty degrees.

As *Antigone* plunged into Biscay's great seas the bow was slowed in its descent, the frustrated water was thrust outwards, away from the decks which remained substantially dry to all but spray and the twin jets that snorted up her hawse pipes. The great strength of her build prevented damage at the most vulnerable point of a hull, one third of her length from the bow. Here, *Antigone* was strapped with massive butts, five lines of rivets holding them secure.

All these refinements in which we put unthinking trust did nothing to stop the inevitable motion. Of the passengers we had as yet seen nothing, except for one stalwart grey-haired gentleman who had gallantly attempted a few circuits of the promenade deck. The dreary routine of four-hours-on and four-hours-off in such conditions so numbed the brain that it missed all but the most obvious perceptions. Neither the Mate nor I was sorry that the continuing gale and the grey fractus that overcast the sky were going to prevent us obtaining a position by the stars. *Antigone* ran on into the night during the four-to-eight watch on dead-reckoning. Our position was in the northern part of the outer Bay of Biscay, well west of Ushant, and China Dick had decreed that our fortuitous occupation of the watch nicely enabled us to set our proper sea-watches. We would be followed during the eight-to-twelve by the Third Mate. In turn he would be relieved by the Second Mate for the twelve-to-four. Both officers would be assisted by a midshipman. We used no fancy naval terms for our watches, they were known by their hours and went unchanged by any dog-watches throughout the voyage.

The light went out of the west; all was a monochromatic meeting of sea and sky, relieved only where a wavecrest tumbled over. The air was filled with the roar of the gale and the damp sting of salt spray that periodically swept aft over the bridge-wings. In the stays and heavy wire funnel guys it howled a note or two higher, while the crash and hiss of the sea and the thunder of the diesels throbbed below. Beneath our feet the deck see-sawed with the pitch, and oscillated with the roll. These rhythms were interrupted as the bow rose, the screw was forced down into deeper water and the ship climbed against the sky. Then the wave passed under the hull's point of equilibrium and the immutable laws of physics resolved themselves. The bow dipped, sliding downwards in a sharp *dégringolade* to thrust itself into the next wave, sending a great half-moon of white water out round the bow. At the same instant she jerked with a shudder felt throughout her length at the braking force acting upon her and, casting her stern into the air, her screws came up into the passing crest where less-dense, aerated water caused her propeller to race, shaking her other extremity. Such a buffeting speeded up the nervous reactions necessary to reacquire our sea-legs and, as the day faded, most of us achieved this little miracle of evolution. Below the passengers lay, wondering how much of this punishment the ship could take, certain that she was breaking up, that

Voyage East

their doom was imminent, only to be vastly disappointed a day or two later when China Dick declared it had been 'No more than a bit of a blow.'

But the watch-keepers had their first reward of the voyage. Just at sunset a narrow, horizontal fissure split the clouds to the west. It opened for no more than a minute or two, a great rent spreading across the western horizon for perhaps thirty miles. It showed the sky beyond as a red slash of blood, masked almost as soon as it appeared, the winking of a huge, crepuscular eye that presaged a fair tomorrow.

As night claimed us I was kept busy. All day we had seen ships passing north, bound for Liverpool or Glasgow from the Mediterranean, often on the dead reciprocal course to our own that required an alteration of heading to starboard in accordance with the 'rule of the road'. Now we met a drifting fleet of Breton tunnymen, riding out the worst of the gale until they could get their gear over again and fill their fish holds. The bright illumination of their decks eclipsed their navigation lights and we could see the violence of their rolling motion as they corkscrewed wildly, infinitely worse off than ourselves.

The Mate joined me on the port bridge-wing where I leaned on the rail, waiting for my relief and the prospect of eight hours below.

'They're the real sailors,' he said, nodding at a gyrating hull half a mile away. I had been right; the romantic was beginning to show his true colours.

Theoretically, it might be supposed, somewhere aboard a ship labouring in heavy weather there should be a null point, where the motion is least felt. After all, if the bow rises and the stern falls, a natural fulcrum must exist where the hull does neither. Coming below, one fervently wished for that centre of inactivity to be under the pillow on one's bunk. Alas, theory is unhorsed by practice. The ship moves simultaneously on several axes and if such an approximate null exists anywhere it is suspended uselessly in the great void spaces of the engine room.

It is a hallmark of the seamen that he can sleep anywhere and at any time, but so early in the voyage after unbroken nights of shoreside sleep, the habit has yet to be re-formed. After the elemental racket of the bridge, however, one's cabin represented a haven. The deck-officers were accommodated below the bridge, on the boatdeck abaft the Master's suite, their cabins surrounding a communal bathroom and a small central stair-well which led, via the promenade deck lobby, to the saloon on the centre-castle. The rooms themselves were sparsely comfortable. Washbasin, mirror, waterglass and carafe occupied a section of bulkhead next to a small chest of drawers.

Against the outboard bulkhead stretched the settee, or day-bed, provided by a munificent Company for those cat-naps that revived the spirit, and on which one might sit to write at the adjacent table. The other bulkhead was occupied by a high bunk over more drawers, and a small wardrobe. The bunk was furnished with leeboards to prevent one being utterly rolled out.

The cabins were panelled in wood, light oak or mahogany veneers, with walnut in the passengers' cabins. Individual decorations varied. The pin-up was indispensable among the younger men, though other spirits exhibited photographs of wives and many had those of girlfriends, cars or motor cycles, reminders of another life to be regained as soon as the calendar permitted. Among the family men pictures of children proliferated, and these were the most poignant evidence that we lived our lives in fits and starts.

The small bookshelves were usually occupied by a mixture of professional tomes, a few magazines, perhaps a serious work or two and the light reading referred to as 'cunt-yarns'. There was occasionally a sign of a serious hobby, a box of oil paints or a half completed model, and usually a radio or tape-recorder.

The deck officers shared their flat with the Purser, and further aft along the boat-deck, in a four-berth caboose known as 'the half-deck' lived the Midshipmen. Beyond that lay the radio room and Sparks's cabin. Captain Richards occupied a suite running the beam of the ship immediately under the bridge.

Below the boat deck was the promenade-deck, down the starboard side of which were quartered the Engineers and Electricians, the chief of whom

Voyage East

shared a fine forward view with the passengers' lounge. The passengers' staterooms ran down the port side of this deck, a little larger and with better facilities than the officers' accommodation, but scarcely luxurious.

Descending from the prom-deck, one came to the centre-castle deck with the dining saloon extending across it, except for a small cabin on the starboard side where the 'doctor' lived. Ship-owners were not obliged to carry a fully qualified medical practitioner if the total number of certified crew and passengers was below one hundred souls, but Holt's regarded the matter more sensibly and we bore a male nurse on our Articles whose popular title disregarded his lack of status: we called him 'Doc'. The Chief Steward and petty officers like the Bosun and Carpenter occupied the starboard side of this accommodation, the galley and the crew's mess the port. Through this whole block, the upper reaches of the engine room rose in diminishing tiers to culminate high above in the huge funnel. Stores, chilled rooms and fridges lay below the centre-castle, sharing its space with the stowage areas of Numbers Three and Four hatches. At either end of the centre-castle deck was a deck-house. At the forward edge it contained the winch control gear and was called the contactor house, at the after end it was a larger affair, a 'Liverpool House' in which lived the seamen. Right aft, within the poop, lived *Antigone's* Chinese, a small expatriate community with their own cook, mess and galley.

The Mate and I were on watch again by 0400. The wind had dropped, but a thin veil of cloud obscured the sky and time passed slowly. Dawn was a gradual infusion of light that revealed an uncertain horizon and a large, lumpy swell, the residue of the gale. There was a sticky humidity in the air that indicated our steady southerly progress across the Bay of Biscay, and slowly the ship awoke to her first 'proper' day.

Watch-keeping was a ceaseless routine, kept on the bridge, the engine-room and, at specified times relative to GMT and our time zone, in the radio-room. But the domestic life of the ship was carried out by the 'day-workers', a portion of the seamen, the petty officers, cooks, stewards, electricians and sundry other sybarites who had all night in their bunks.

First to be called were the cooks and the stewards, the Bosun and hands (those seamen not helping the watch-keepers by standing lookouts). While the galley was stirring to life, the deck crowd turned to, to wash down and scrub our teak decks. Only the well-decks and the forecastle were exposed steel, and there was much grime and neglect to wash out of odd corners. On the bridge the two junior midshipmen appeared. Their seniors were each on watches, one with the Third Mate and the other with the Second, but these boys had as their especial charge the cleanliness of the bridge itself. They had to scrub out the wheelhouse as well as their own accommodation in the two hours before breakfast, burnish the brass and sand-and-canvas the bridge rail. This abrasive scouring of the teak caprail kept it immaculate and the standards of such things were often the measure of the ship. On these points China Dick and the Mate were punctilious.

At dawn the Mate went below to shave, relieving me for the same purpose around 0700 when the Bosun would come up and they would discuss the day's work ahead. For the first days of the voyage this consisted chiefly of repairing the ravages of a long coasting, but it also contained a component of that long battle with the sea, the maintenance of the ship against the onslaught of rust. For the time being the gale had died, and the smell of eggs and bacon uncoiled itself from the galley ventilators and wafted about the turbulent air around the bridge. By 0800 when relieved by the Third Mate, we had rediscovered both our sealegs and our appetites.

The quality of a shipping company could always be measured by the generosity of its menus. A good ship was, by definition, a 'good feeder'. To eat well was considered part of one's wages and, besides, meals were the focal points of the ship's social life. A ship was 'okay' if you were served two eggs for breakfast. *Antigone* was one such ship, where fruit juice, cereals, a fried breakfast of seemingly infinite combinations, tea or coffee and toast might be finished off with wheat cakes and syrup. We ate like fighting cocks.

By noon the predicted improvement in the weather was confirmed. The overcast broke up, thinning to high altitude cloud that threw no more than a veil across the sky. A watery sun presented itself for the first time since Liverpool and we dutifully assembled on the bridge, lugging our sextants

Voyage East

out to obtain an observed latitude by an ex-meridian sight. We were well west of the Greenwich meridian, so that apparent noon at the ship (that is to say, that moment when, through our sextants, we might visibly see the sun culminate on our meridian, reach its highest point for our latitude, and begin its post meridian descent to the horizon and sunset) would occur well after the ship's clocks registered twelve. We therefore cheated, shooting the sun before its culmination, assuming (pretty accurately) we knew our longitude and making a small adjustment to our readings, to compute our latitude for twelve o'clock ship's time. This juggling of figures is central to what King Charles II rightly called the 'arte and mysterie' of navigation, for it is certainly no science, rather a finely tuned series of compromises that satisfies practical demand to a remarkable degree. This was not the place to examine it too closely, for there were other aids to navigating the Bay of Biscay: radio-beacons and the distant Consol stations at Ploneis and Bushmills. Soon we hoped to raise the lighthouses of Spain and Portugal, and keep the outline of the Iberian Peninsula on our radar screen.

For the time being this noon assembly was not absolutely essential, although in deference to Captain Richards we entered into the spirit of it, each calling our sextant observation in turn, junior first. China Dick decided on a mean value from which we all computed the ship's latitude, signing a chit to that effect and spiking it in the chart-room.

The Mate and I did better at twilight, both of us filing a proper fix, with both latitude and longitude obtained from a rapid-fire series of stellar observations which put us eighty miles off the north west corner of Spain. By the time we came on watch the next morning the loom of Cape Villano lighthouse was fading astern on the port quarter and the rugged indented coast south of Cape Finisterre as far as Vigo was glowing yellow on the screen of the Kelvin Hughes radar. The wind had hauled right round, veered into the north-east, bringing off the land subtle hints of its presence which, before the days of radar and lighthouses, would have been our first intimation of its presence.

We coasted past the needle points of the Islas Berlingas, known to generations of British seamen as 'The Berlings', and the great estuary of the Tagus slipped astern. The cloud cleared, the afternoon turned warm and the sea deep blue. The ship ploughed a white furrow as straight as a rule. She was doing sixteen and a half knots when I took over the watch again at 1600. Cape Espichel and Punta de Sines drew astern, and the sun dropped towards the horizon, a great red ball, expanding as it shone through the increasingly dense layers of dust that encircled the earth. This refraction played strange tricks; the sun's perimeter seemed to ripple and flicker with a scarlet intensity that threw the sea into a jade contrast.

'Are you hoping for the green flash?' The Mate joined me.

'Yes, the conditions are about right.'

'Aye. '

As it neared the horizon the ever-expanding image of the sun seemed to strike a reciprocal frenzy from the sea. The rays of light were so vibrantly refracted that they appeared to boil the surface of the water. Watching, it was perfectly obvious how the ancients conceived the idea of the edge of the world, for was not the setting sun making it molten? In the final moments of its descent the motion of the sun was vertical. Suddenly the orb ceased to pretend it was circular, its lower 'limb' stretched downwards as if striking the extinguishing power of the sea. The whole mass changed shape into a vast mushroom and the glowing ball elongated briefly before it began to sink. From the extremes of the solar equator the edges of the sun's face retreated; the semi-circle broke, as though water had rushed over it and severed its upper part. The trick of the refracted light dismembered the upper 'limb' and it shrank to a lenticular shape, growing ever smaller. At the instant of its disappearance it was bright green.

No wonder the ancients feared the night; refraction had given the impression of the sun's defeat.

'Ah,' said the Mate, straightening up from the rail, 'pretty good, eh?'

He was smiling with satisfaction at the splendour of the phenomenon. 'You'd better go down and have your dinner.'

When I came back half-an-hour later and relieved him so he could eat with his passengers, we were rounding Cape St Vincent. The pink rocks of the sheer cliffs were night shadowed and to seaward there was nothing but the fading day to show where Sir John Jervis had earned his earldom and a certain Captain Nelson had saved the day by disobedience.

Voyage East

Even the Admiralty chart did not let one forget history hereabouts. In the great bight between Cape St Vincent and the entrance to the Mediterranean in which lay Cap Trafalgar, site of the most famous sea-fight of them all, the River Guadalquivir debouched into the Atlantic at San Lucar de Barrameda. Beside the hachured polygon that marked the town on the chart was a note that Magellan had departed from the port for the first circumnavigation of the globe in 1514.

It was a warm tribute and I know of no other such; since the demise of the fathom chart and capitulation to the French revolutionary metre I suspect it is removed. The Mate had a story of his own apprenticeship to mark it.

'I was sent into the chart room by the Chief Officer to look at the chart and locate all the lights I should keep a lookout for. When I got back to the bridge-wing the Chief Officer asked me if I had noticed anything unusual on the chart.

'Yes, sir,' I said, 'it mentions that Magellan sailed for the first circumnavigation in 1514.'

'Bollocks,' said the Chief Officer.

'Sir?'

'Bollocks, it was 1492.'

'Er ... no sir, er, I think you'll find, sir, that 1492 was when Columbus discovered America, sir.'

'Bollocks, I was in Gib bunkering when the bugger sailed past!'

We were off Trafalgar early the next morning, no sky 'blood red reeking into Cadiz Bay' as Browning has it, but a fresh easterly Levanter, warm and humidily cutting up a choppy sea. Our track into the Mediterranean was through the middle of the Strait, to take advantage of the inward set that flowed there. A counter-current drifted westwards close inshore and we would make use of that when homeward bound, but at the moment, despite the contrary wind, the ship was tearing along, pushing seventeen knots as though eager to leave the Atlantic. Shortly after 0600 we altered course off Cape Spartel, close to Tangier. The lighthouse was one of the earliest maintained by international agreement and beyond it rose the toe of the Atlas Mountains. Africa almost met Europe in a mighty wall of precipitous brown rock, its vertiginous fissured face rising 2,750 feet sheer above the Gut to the summit of Sidi Musa, dwarfing the ships below. Beyond this great buttress of rock lay the Moroccan city of Ceuta. To port the white-walled Spanish town of Tarifa, the most southerly outwork of Europe, jutted a ravelin into the Strait, in the angle of which stood another lighthouse. Behind Tarifa the cordillera of Gitano rose thirty feet lower than Sidi Musa on the African shore, shrouded in cloud, as if ashamed of its inferior height. We passed between the Pillars of Hercules, the land fell away on either hand, and then to the north Algeciras Bay opened its bight to reveal the great grey slab of The Rock.

As we reported by aldis lamp to the Lloyd's signal station next to the red and white column of Europa Point lighthouse, we underwent the subtle sea-change which accompanied the knowledge that we had passed Gibraltar and were in The Med. Rounding the Rock meant the voyage was well under way, that the first leg was over; we were reconciled to our part in it now, ceased to think of the past and began to anticipate the future.

As the passage progressed we were soothed by the ship's routine. It was, as Conrad said, 'a great doctor for sore hearts and sore heads ... There is health in it, and peace, and satisfaction of the accomplished round ... He who loves the sea loves also the ship's routine ...' We had washed off the grime of the coasting; the teak decks were scrubbed white, the caprails on the bridge-wings and along the promenade deck had been sand-and-canvassed by the midshipmen. The brass-work was losing the verdigris of neglect and bright spots of red-lead dabbed scuffed paintwork as the bosun rendered first-aid to *Antigone's* superstructure.

We did not see much of China Dick in these early days. He kept to his cabin mostly, his presence marked by the daily ministrations of his personal 'Tiger', Zee Pang Yun, and a steady stream of discarded gin bottles. He made his routine appearances: leading the formal little procession of senior officers on the daily inspection, taking his noon latitude and writing his night orders; but the ship, as far as the upper decks were concerned, was the domain of the Mate, the Bosun and the Crowd.

Voyage East

As I relieved the Second Mate at 1600 that first Mediterranean evening I found the Senior Midshipman coiling up the flex of the aldis lamp. There was an air of conspiratorial amusement I instinctively associated with the battered frigate with the pennant number F437 on her hull that had just passed us, west-bound for Gibraltar. On the poop, the duty seaman of the twelve-to-four watch was belaying our ensign halliards after acknowledging the superiority of armed might by dipping our colours.

'Been chatting to the Grey Funnel Line?' I asked.

'Yes,' the Second Mate nodded, *'Loch Lomond* ... silly bastards, full of Dartmouth bullshit.' They convulsed into laughter.

'What's so unusual in that?'

'Oh, they signalled they had three Old Conways on board and asked if we could do better . . .'

They rocked with laughter again, sharing their private joke. 'And?'

'We replied: "Yes ... none".'

There was more to this exchange than mere sharp wit, for that passing frigate had touched a deep grievance rooted in the psyche of the British merchant seaman. It was a complex matter, due in part to a class-system that conferred status to naval rank and despised those engaged in trade and industry. The very content of the warship's enquiry was evidence of the continued and assiduous cultivation of a *brüderbond* within the Royal Navy, a fact that added piquancy to our reply. Such things, we felt, had no place in the modern world. We were victims of that peculiarly British attitude to its revenue earners; yet in time of war we would not be gentlemen abed in England, but impressed *chair à canon*. It was partly a legacy of the Second World War where the lives of merchant seamen had been squandered with prodigal indifference, and partly a continuing sense of bitterness at the ramparts of privilege that the Royal Navy retained. I sailed with many men whose feeling upon this matter was intense, and the torch of disillusion was handed on to my own generation. On that bright autumn afternoon, as we butted our way into the Mediterranean, the twelve-to-four watch had scored a notable victory for the under-dog.

We had our last glimpse of Europe at sunset; the Spanish coast turned north at Cape de Gata and the Mesa de Roldan stood black against the blood-red sky. The next dawn rose over Africa, flooding the sky with a yellow radiance above the brown coast of Algeria. Cape Tenes was jutting against the glow, lying along the prism of the starboard azimuth mirror. It was a good watch, the four-to-eight, a watch of twilights, sunrises and sunsets, those periods of infinite variety. Dawn and dusk are not sequential reversals of the same phenomenon, they have quite different characters, the first fresh and hopeful, the second weary and melancholic. These moods varied in their intensity, for the visual effects could be quite stunning, or, as we had seen in the Bay of Biscay, the mere monotonous merging of an indistinguishable sea and sky.

We had also the great satisfaction of marking those neat crosses on the chart (evidence of our activity at the crepuscular hour with sextant and chronometer) which indicated our progress from stellar fixes. And added to these natural advantages were the purely selfish considerations of eight hours below during the night, and eight hours of relative liberty during the day.

'Me Dad doesn't work, Miss,' the boy was supposed to have replied to his teacher when asked what his father did, 'he goes to sea.'

The passengers were in evidence as we passed Algiers. Their faces were more cheerful, having lost their waxy complexions. They took turns out of the wind up and down the starboard promenade deck in the sunshine. The first game of deck quoits was played during that afternoon, a tentative affair in which the Chief Engineer gave a lesson in the simple game to Mrs Saddler. She was in her mid-thirties, plumply voluptuous and pleasant looking with hair that reflected auburn lights. She was striking enough to have attracted considerable male interest and her laughter suggested it pleased her. Her husband looked on with apparent indulgence at the attention she was receiving from the Chief.

'There'll be a wee spot o' trouble with that one,' remarked the Mate darkly as he came up from the boat deck, sniffing the perceptibly warmer air after the damp misery of the Atlantic. 'Cape Bougaroni by the end of the watch?'

I laid our 2000 position off the Cape on the chart, handed over to the Third Mate and went below.

'Beer?' offered Mike, the Second Mate.

'Yes. Thanks. I thought you'd be turned in.'

'Tried, but couldn't drop off.'

We sat in Mike's cabin and opened two cans of Tennant's lager that he took from a case beneath his settee, smacking our lips appreciatively. I lit a cigarette. A large photograph of a pensively beautiful woman stared at us. It was the only decoration in the cabin. He followed my gaze and his eyes narrowed.

'Any kids?' I asked, vaguely embarrassed.

'No.' He paused, then asked, 'You married?'

'Me? Good God, no,'

'Foot-loose and fancy-free, eh?' Again that familiar refuge in a cliché.

'No, not exactly ... but nothing permanent.'

'Best keep it that way.'

'You don't recommend marriage then?' I asked, beer-emboldened and staring at the photograph. He too looked at the picture.

'No. Not if you're going to stay at sea.'

'Well, the Mate's not married and he's not what you'd call radiantly happy.'

'No, but he's content ... no worries ... there's a difference.'

'Oh.' An awkward silence fell between us. The woman's impassive stare was putting me on edge. 'And you're intending to stay at sea, are you?' I asked to break the silence.

He shrugged, then bent and took out two more cans of lager.

'What else can one do?' He was twenty-seven and a master-mariner.

'Does your wife work?'

'Yes ... teacher.'

'She's, er, very beautiful.'

'Yes. That's the trouble ... .'

Algeria became Tunisia during the night and we were off the island of Galita at dawn. Among the ships' lights around us were a set coming up astern at a spanking pace. I plotted her on the radar: twenty-one knots, a passenger liner or fast cargo ship. To starboard Africa humped up and out, a salient stretching towards Sicily and the Calabrian toe of Italy. One recalled it as the home of ancient Carthage and classroom memories stirred of Regulus being rolled down-hill in a nail studded barrel: *Carthago delenda est.* The land fell away into the Gulf of Tunis and the fast ship astern came roaring up abeam of us. The Mate joined me on the bridge as we admired her sleek hull and the effects of her bulbous bow. The innovative new hull was one of the first to be built for Holt's, to Lloyd's AI00 + standards and therefore less massive than *Antigone*. She was a precursor of more stringent economic times.

'*Glenlyon,* eh,' remarked the Mate, lowering his binoculars.

'Yes. I was a midshipman on her maiden voyage; joined her at the builders.'

She swept past us without doing more than acknowledge our dipped ensign, her master a little senior to our own and a well-known stickler for rigid bridge routine and radio silence.

'The old bastard,' said the Mate without rancour, turning to the Bosun who had come up onto the bridge for his daily orders. The two men leaned companionably on the rail, discussing the day's work.

The Crowd were called out at 0530 and turned-to half an hour later. Pre-breakfast routine was the same every day the ship was at sea. The decks were washed down and 'barbarised' when required to maintain their whiteness; the junior midshipmen scrubbed out the wheel-house and polished the bridge brasswork, while the Carpenter and his Chinese mate took the daily soundings of all oil and water tanks, chalking the results on the boards on the bridge and engine room, for such matters were of crucial importance to our stability, trim and draught, and the cause of much worry to my watch-mate. At that moment, however, in conversation with the Bosun he was relaxed and the result of their conspiracy became obvious after breakfast.

It began at exactly one minute after 0900, an orchestrated cacophony that lasted, with the statutory interval for Smoke-O, until noon. The thunderous persistence of a Kango hammer was supported by the battering staccato of chisel-peined chipping hammers which varied according to the

Voyage East

energy of the individual operator. The entire Crowd was attacking the fore-deck rust, backed up by the two junior midshipmen who laboured grubbily with the mariners even if they were permitted to eat with the gentlemen. In blue denims and checked shirts, the Crowd dispersed along the scuffed and rusting steel-work under the eagle-eye of the Bosun; they set up a noise that reverberated throughout the fabric of the ship, carried to its furthest extremity by the unique telegraphy of the riveted plates.

Up and down the isolated forward section of the boat-deck immediately under the bridge, China Dick strode ferociously, from port to starboard, to and fro with the measured tread that would eat up five miles in sixty feet laps before he called for his Tiger and a large gin. Above him we calibrated the ship's radio direction finder, using the distant lighthouse on Cape Bon. This was a periodic job, comparing the equipment's radio-bearings with those taken visually as we passed the lighthouse. Errors in radio-bearings were caused by the distorting properties of the ship's fabric. In addition to its conspicuous visual characteristics, Cape Bon was fitted with a radiobeacon, whose signals we could interpret on our direction-finder. It seemed that this metallic refraction was actually audible as the Crowd hammered their way through the forenoon.

There was no chipping or scaling in the afternoon. The time was hallowed for siestas, for watch-keepers' supplementary dozing and passengers' relaxation. The Crowd swapped their keen-edged hammers for paint brushes, and ladled red-lead upon the bared steel; for a night's dew, or a patter of spray would start the relentless oxidisation of the steel again. The ship swung into the Malta Channel and raised the distant blue peak of Pantellaria Island. The wind dropped and by the evening the lights of Gozo and Malta sparkled to the northwards. We laid a rhumb-line course for the Nile Delta and left the land astern.

It would take us two and a half days to transit the Eastern Mediterranean, two and a half days of astro-navigation out of sight of land, pursuing an easterly heading. This made dawn earlier every day, sunset later. Our ship's time revolved around noon, originally the traditional start of the new 'day' and still used navigationally in the 'day's work', that combination of the course and distance-made-good since the previous noon. If ship's officers were shooting the sun for latitude, this had to be done at 'apparent noon', detectable by sextant as the moment the sun's observed arc of transit across the sky culminated on the meridian. This was due south (if one was in the northern hemisphere and north of the sun, as we then were), or due north (if one was south of the sun). For practical reasons this observed apparent noon had to be made to coincide as nearly as possible with twelve o'clock, ship's time, so the *Antigone's* clocks were advanced at midnight. At our present latitude a day's run approximated to a change of longitude of 7½°, and this was a time difference of half an hour. At midnight, therefore, we had been shifting the clocks ahead thirty minutes. The eight-to-twelve and twelve-to-four watches split the difference, the rest of us lost sleep. As we arrived at our various ports of call we should thus automatically be on the local time (zones being an hour earlier than G M T, or U T as it now is, for every 15° of easterly longitude).

    As we approached Port Said we met other ships. A few converging with us, more diverging in the opposite direction, spewed out of the canal in the daily convoys organised by the Suez Canal Authority. We were again overtaken, this time by *Ixion*, a larger, faster, steam turbine driven Blue Funnel ship bound for Australia with thirty-six passengers. We occupied our watches below writing letters and later, turning out to answer the summons of clamorous klaxons that called us to muster at our boat and fire stations. This exercise, known as 'Board of Trade Sports', was a Friday ritual observed by British merchant ships all over the world. The day closed with a wintry northern overcast and spectacular forked lightning through heavy cloud bellying down over Egypt.

    The following morning we sighted Brulos lighthouse and at 0800, off the Damietta Mouth of the Nile, we met *Glenfalloch*, homeward bound and speaking of delays in the canal. Just before noon, nine days out from Liverpool, we dropped anchor in company with thirty other ships off Port Said. To the south the low alluvial coast of Egypt stretched away, broken in its monotony by the lighthouse, minarets and huddle of buildings that marked the northern entrance to the Suez Canal. *Ixion* was already at anchor, though *Glenlyon* had made the previous day's southward convoy. Lloyd Triestino's new cargo liner *Palatino* also lay at anchor, but

Voyage East

dominating us all was the grey bulk of the aircraft carrier, HMS *Eagle*.

'Brought up,' said the Mate on the telephone from the forecastle, indicating the anchor flukes had bitten into the sea bed and would hold the ship.

'Finished with engines, Mister,' responded Captain Richards, his battered old glasses on the aircraft carrier.

'Bloody bastards,' he said, turning away for his cabin.

BLUE FUNNEL

a DISMAL BUT PROFITABLE DITCH

At noon the pilot, a huge bullet-headed, handsome Egyptian, brought *Antigone* through the breakwaters, past the plinth of De Lesseps's memorial. We moored in the tiers on the Sinai side, lying at right angles to the canal. Across our anchored bow, beyond the main fairway, Port Said shimmered in the hot sun. Our stern was tethered to the east bank, where lay the low and less salubrious huddle of Port Fuad. All the south-bound cargo and passenger ships moored within the port. Tankers, returning to the Persian Gulf for crude oil, remained outside, their empty tanks potentially dangerous with the explosive fumes of their last cargoes, objects of cautious handling by the Canal Authority. Only one tanker was laden, a Russian ship, down to her marks with Ukrainian crude oil and partnered by an Odessa-registered cargo-ship: Soviet vessels, like nervous spinsters, invariably travelled in pairs. On our port side lay a gleaming white Greek passenger liner while to starboard our old friend *Clan Ranald* had caught us up.

The missing statue of De Lesseps was the only evidence of the troubled days of 1956. Apart from the natural desire of the near-indigent to rook us, the bum-boat people of Port Said, with whom the ship swarmed during the long, hot afternoon, seemed to bear us no ill-will. On the contrary, they still addressed us as 'McGregor' with a cunning and feigned obsequiousness that seemed a throwback to earlier, colonial times. Their infamous obscene photographs had a dated air, vintage couplings over which the Eighth Army might have tittered, and, with swordsticks, whips, wooden camels, rugs and sandals, as well as common necessities such as soap-powder and razor blades, formed their traditional wares. These vendors came under the auspices of an entrepreneur named 'Rifle-Eye', a man disfigured as a result of some alleged incident with an infantry rifle. One of these opportunist rogues had ventured into the officers' alleyway and accosted me as I returned from reading the ship's draught in the agent's launch.

'Hey, McGregor, what you want, eh? Shufti? Pictures? Spanish Fly? I got very good Spanish Fly . . .'

Voyage East

He was barefoot and villainous-looking under a grubby turban, and wore what might once have been a Dunn's sports-jacket over a ragged robe.

'Very good,' he repeated, waving a small phial of cloudy liquid under my nose.

'Tell him to fuck off.' The Mate appeared from his cabin. 'Go on Ali, fuck off. Take that camel-piss away ...' With a fatalistic shrug, the Egyptian went in search of easier prey.

'You shouldn't encourage the buggers,' he grumbled to me. 'Go and tell those Middies that I want one of them on each watch going through the canal.' He took the draught-chit from me and retreated to his cabin and his interminable responsibilities.

In the half-deck I found the Midshipmen being entertained by the Gully-gully man.

'Gully, gully, gully, gully...'

A small, bewildered and occasionally squeaking yellow chick was disappearing under one of three bronze cups and reappearing under a different one or from the junior Midshipman's nose with bewildering rapidity. The magician, dressed well in light-weight jacket, slacks and casual shoes, was a more urbane and acceptable rogue than the aphrodisiac-seller. He looked up at my intrusion.

'Ah, Mr Mate, how are you sir? I remember you last trip, 'nother ship, *Glenearn* . . .'

He was right, of course. 'Hullo, how are you?'

'I do special trick for you.' He turned to the Junior Midshipman who sat in stunned wonderment. 'You give me coin please? Any coin.'

'Go on, give him something', the Senior Midshipman bullied, affecting a worldly indifference to the proceedings but unable to tear himself away. Reluctantly the boy rose, produced a half-crown and put it in the Gully-gully man's outstretched palm with the bereft air of someone who had unwillingly given away his last crust.

The Gully-gully man pulled out a playing card, gave it to the boy and asked him to mark it with a pencil. Mesmerised, we watched the boy obey.

'Now, I give you money back, you look at money. See, it is same money ... now you fold money in card ... look at card, six of diamonds, okay? Now you fold card tight. Okay?'

The Junior Midshipman followed the instructions carefully, his face showing suspicion, concentration and curiosity.

'Now, hold out hand with card and money...'

'Gully, gully, gully, gully ...' The magician made a series of elaborate passes over the boy's hand. 'You still holding card and money?' The boy nodded. 'Good, now you go and throw over the side.' The midshipman hesitated, looked around at our faces, hoping one of us was going to tell him not to be a fool. At last, without a word he rose, went out onto the boat deck and hurled the tiny parcel over the lifeboat into the water far below. When he had resumed his seat the Gully-gully man produced eggs and chicks from various bodily apertures and then, quite suddenly, there was a crushed playing card, apparently pulled from someone's nose. He held it out to the Junior Midshipman. The boy unfolded the marked six of diamonds, lifted out the silver coin and confirmed it was the same 1953 half-crown. He looked up at the de-camping Gully-gully man with total mystification.

An hour later *Eagle* came in from the roads. The vast grey bulk of the aircraft-carrier with its sinister hum of internal machinery slid across our bows, her upper decks, devoid of aircraft, filled with an untidy milling of her company in their fatigues rig. Clearly her captain had decided against making a show of naval pomp. The ugly, angular shape of her island dominating her asymmetrical hull made an odd contrast to the little schooner that slipped out from Port Fuad in her gigantic shadow. Later we heard the strains of her bugle at sunset and could see, beyond our Greek neighbour, the great white ensign slide smoothly down her staff.

We were still awaiting orders to proceed south into the canal at four the next morning. The Mate and I lounged on the bridge, wrapped in the fragrance of his tobacco smoke.

'I went ashore here once,' the Mate remarked, 'you rode about in an open carriage. Probably still do .. .'

The shimmering water of the canal reflected the lights of Port Said, opposite, periodically obscured by the intervening bulk of the ships of the north-bound convoy as they passed on their way into the Mediterranean.

Voyage East

Running in and out between them the agents' and pilots' launches attended to the final business of the canal transit without slowing the great ships. This bustling activity set the reflections of the lights dancing and it was clear that our own wait would not last much longer.

'I rather like the Gyppoes,' went on the Mate, puffing out clouds of St Bruno. 'Likeable rogues, considering what we did to them in fifty-six.'

He had obviously mellowed since his ejection of the cantharides-seller that afternoon. 'There's no malice in them. I suppose it comes of living on the breadline. When I went ashore here we sat outside a cafe. A wee laddie came up to us. "Hey Joe," he said, "you want jig-a-jig? You want my sister? Only *leetle-bit* syphilis ......'

The VHF radio-telephone squawked into life. We were ordered under way at once, the pilot would board in minutes. 'Wait for bloody hours and then you have to panic,' grumbled the Mate as he roused the ship and we hurried to stations, hoisting up a canal boat and its crew of three men who would accompany us and assist in mooring *Antigone* when it became necessary. Their neat, brightly painted boat hung from a derrick wire, lashed at the rail abreast Number Four hatch while its crew sat on tawdry rugs spread on the hatch tarpaulin, bowing in prayer towards Mecca at the appointed hours. It was already dawn when we finally moved off into the canal. *Eagle* led us, followed by the immaculate Greek liner, her white hull and superstructure on fire from the sudden spread of sunlight, picked out with the traditional blue of her national colours. The intense pride was typical of Greek seafarers and was emphasised by her ensign staff, a barber's pole of blue and white spirals.

We were the next vessel, letting go our stern ropes and weighing anchor, to edge ahead under easy revolutions of our screw and full port helm. Behind us fourteen cargo ships and as many tankers followed us, all these last (except the single Russian) in ballast, bound for the Persian Gulf and the oil terminals of Kharg Island, Ras Tanurah and Mina al Ahmadi. The canal ran dead straight on its first southward leg. To port stretched the seemingly endless eastward vista of ochre sandhills, the shifting *barchans* of the Sinai desert. An occasional nomad on his camel breasted the slope and stared at the passing ships. To starboard a strip of palms and scrub lined the twin arteries of road and railway that accompanied the canal south to Ismailia. The three means of transport seemed to huddle together for company as they assaulted this level and terrible terrain. Beyond, the great lagoon of Lake Manzala was dotted with the high lateen sails of *feluccas* shining in the morning sunshine, reminding us of the presence of the Nile.

It was an odd sensation to stare down from the elevation of the bridge at the road to Ismailia or across the arid and shimmering sands of Sinai. For three hours we steamed steadily south in the wake of the Greek liner, an easier task than might at first be supposed, for the advancing bulk of a ship's hull pushes the water aside, increasing its density and forming a cushion on either bow which helps the helmsman keep the vessel in midstream. The atmosphere on the bridge was relaxed, the pilot giving the occasional order and the officer of the watch adjusting the speed as required. An attentive Midshipman kept a careful record of all engine movements and China Dick maintained a 'presence', coming and going as he thought necessary. We slid past the tower and flag mast at El Qantara signal station, a vital control-point in the days before VHF radiotelephones. Shortly after El Qantara we swung into the New Cut, a five mile long lay-by where, with the help of our boatmen, we tied up to mooring points on the bank and waited for another northbound convoy to pass us.

It is often claimed that the Suez Canal killed the clipper ship by slashing 3,000 miles off the distance to the east, but the truth is somewhat more complex. By dramatically improving the long-distance performance of marine steam-engines, Alfred Holt himself had as big a hand in the murder as the canal. The expansive potential of steam had been recognised as early as 1791 when a certain Jonathan Hornblower patented a device intended to harness it, using the expanding steam vented from one cylinder to drive a larger at a lower pressure and thus increase the power of an engine. The exploitation of this theory foundered on the inability of contemporary boiler design to produce steam at a high enough pressure to harness this 'compounding'. A John Elder had built a compound marine steam engine by adding a high-pressure unit to Watt's design, but it failed to live up to

Voyage East

its promise and it fell to Alfred Holt to solve the problem.

Holt came from humble Lancashire stock, his family migrating to Liverpool, bringing with them a strong Unitarian tradition. Alfred himself was a clever, practical and single-minded man who became first a railway engineer, then a consultant, before finally going into ship-owning in a modest way with his brother Philip. When compelled to sell their little fleet in the face of strong competition in the West India trade, they retained one vessel, the *Cleator,* for experimental purposes. Encouraged by his friend and employee Captain Isaac Middleton, Alfred decided to modify the *Cleator* and in December 1864, having fitted immensely strong and innovative new boilers, succeeded in raising steam at 60 pounds per square inch, three times the then common working pressure. This radical improvement was combined with a new tandem compound engine to give the *Cleator* an increase in speed as well as a reduction in fuel consumption of a staggering 40%. Middleton took her on a proving voyage to France, Russia and South America. It was axiomatic in Liverpool shipping circles that 'steamers may occupy the Mediterranean, may tentatively go to Brazil … but China at least is safe for sailing ships.' To the Holts, such a shibboleth seemed ripe for destruction. In the spring of 1866, under Middleton's command, the brand-new 2,300 ton screw steamer *Agamemnon* sailed for the Far East. It was the very year of the greatest tea-race of them all, when the clippers *Ariel* and *Taeping* entered the English Channel neck and neck after 14,000 miles; three years before the building of the *Cutty Sark* and the opening of the Suez Canal. The Blue Funnel Line was born and the China trade was no longer safe for sailing ships.

It took seven hours for the northbound convoy to pass, seven hours during which a light rain fell and the sudden damp disinterred clouds of mosquitoes whose stings added to the irritation caused by the flies that plague the country. It was dark as we approached Ismailia, named after the Khedive from whom the canny Disraeli purchased shares, so securing Great Britain a controlling interest in the canal. On our forecastle sat the huddled figure of the Electrical Officer, adjusting the beam of the searchlight. The beam picked out the sloping sides of the canal, enabling pilot and helmsman to gauge the midline of the waterway.

The lights of Ismailia slid past and the dark waters of the canal suddenly expanded into Lake Timsah, slashed by the furrowing wakes of the launches attending each ship as we changed pilots. The new pilot boarded first, relieving the old with a few words in English. I shook hands with the departing Egyptian as he swung himself over the rail. Returning to the bridge I found China Dick chatting affably to the new man, an ascetic-looking Russian named Lavrov. In addition to Egyptian nationals there were Russians, East Germans and Poles among the ranks of the Canal Authority's pilots, replacements for the French and British ousted in 1956. China Dick showed no sign of resentment at the Russian's presence; one seaman respected another, political camps notwithstanding. Besides, I suspected our Captain's flinty soul approved of the hard-bitten Russian and had despised the sybaritic lifestyle of his predecessors. They chatted companionably as Lavrov gave his orders in heavily accented English and we made the short leg into the Bitter Lakes.

The Great and Little Bitter lakes were used as a second passing place and here we found another north-bound convoy, only this time it was we who had precedence. The wide expanse of dark water reflected the lights of the waiting ships as we increased speed through the anchorage in rigid line astern. Here, some exegetists maintain, Yahweh divided the sea for the escape of the chosen people from the pursuit of Pharoah. Beyond the lakes we made one long slow curve to Port Tewfik and Suez Bay. Lights from pilots' houses, administrative buildings and the huddle of the township were interspersed with the motionless dark fronds of palm trees; they slid astern as the Bosun lowered the canal boat into the water where it rode behind a massive bow-wave then slipped its painter and curled away into the desert night. China Dick waved Mr Lavrov off as the pilot launch turned away to service the next ship astern.

'Full speed away!' ordered China Dick, setting course. The engine room telegraph jingled in the double-ring that told the engineers below to work *Antigone's* engine up to full power and switch to the lower grade fuel that we used for passage-making. More ships lay at anchor in Suez Bay, coming in to form yet another convoy bound for the Mediterranean and Europe. Ahead of us *Eagle* slowed and turned her huge bulk out of the fairway,

Voyage East

followed by the Greek liner, moving to anchor and re-embark her passengers after their diversion to Cairo and the Pyramids. One could sense China Dick's pleasure in leading the convoy past the screw-pile lighthouse on the Newport Rock and into the narrow corridor of the Gulf of Suez.

We left Conrad's 'dismal but profitable ditch' behind. Being a sailing-ship man he could not be expected to regard it with anything other than a jaundiced eye. For myself, I thought it wholly appropriate that Nasser had nationalised it in the name of the *fellahin;* they had precious little else.

The GATE OF TEARS

Dawn came up fantastically; the shadowed mountains of Sinai striated and fissured in deepest purple, their jagged summits etched hard against the luminous east. To the west a similar landscape emerged rose-coloured in the growing light, while the sea between the two escarpments ran blue, its wave-caps sparkling whiter and whiter in the intensifying daylight. We were launched on one of the world's oldest trade routes, ancient beyond the memory of European history and revived by the cutting of the Suez Canal. The gulf and the Red Sea form part of the Great Rift Valley that runs from the River Jordan to the great lakes of Africa and nowhere is this splitting of the earth's crust more vivid than in the Gulf of Suez, where the faults stand as escarpments and the sunken wedge becomes a sea-filled ria one hundred and fifty miles long. The geological contortions that produced this can only be guessed at: the distant heights of the Hejaz are formed of sea-bed corals and sandstone.

'Have you ever read *The Seven Pillars of Wisdom?*' the Mate asked. 'By Lawrence of Arabia,' he added didactically.

'No.'

'My geography had taught me to expect the desert to be a waste of sand, but a book like the *Pillars* reveals a more complex truth.'

He was given to these odd, professorial aids to my better education. They had a curious effect, irritating my ignorance until I had followed up his hints, sometimes years later. There was an educative quality to the sea-life that extended beyond the acquisition of merely professional knowledge. True, our learning was usually self-acquired and possessed an explosive indiscipline; but occasionally men schooled it either themselves, or under the tutelage of the College of the Sea. The Mate was of the former kind, his knowledge based on wide and indiscriminate reading.

'They reckoned Bernard Shaw helped Lawrence write it,' he went on, 'but that's bullshit. Academic jealousy. You could only write about the desert like Lawrence if you'd had sand under your foreskin.'

Faster ships were overtaking us now. *Ixion*, chafing at being behind us

Voyage East

in the canal, was coming up, and so was the Greek liner. By the time the breakfast gong sounded through the ship and we came below, *Antigone* was passing the lighthouse at Ras Gharib. Exhausted after the prolonged watches of the night transit of the canal, I slept through the morning. By noon the Egyptian coast had fallen back to a low, broken littoral of islets, reefs and rocks dominated by the high, barren island of Shadwan. On the opposite side the Sinai range crowded us, its precipitous spine beetling down and squeezing the racing ships into the narrow Strait of Gubal. We passed through the opening astern of *Ixion*, just leading the *Palatino* and the Greek liner, debouching into the Red Sea which sparkled in the sunshine beyond.

The Red Sea is the saltiest of the world's oceans, at 46 parts per million, and only a degree cooler than the Persian Gulf, the world's hottest, at 34°C, though not in December. But it was the air temperature in which we were interested the following morning, warm and balmy, the first dawn of our voyage to declare a real change of latitude. The northern winter had lost its grip on us; fugitive, we slipped southwards down the long corridor of the Red Sea. I peered into the Stevenson's screen and read the dry-bulb thermometer.

'Sixty-nine, sir.'

'*Soixante-neuf,*' replied the Mate from the wheelhouse doorway. The crude erotic allusion was a measure of our divorce from the society of women, a rueful laugh at our stupidity in following so daft a profession. But, like the 'fuck' that peppered our speech, it was also a carapace behind which we hid our private selves.

'*Soixante-neuf,*' repeated the Mate gratuitously, picking up the voice-pipe to the Old Man's night cabin, blowing into it and then transferring the bell-mouth to his ear. When he heard China Dick's grunts of attention he switched the thing to his mouth again. 'Morning sir. It's six o'clock ... fine morning, yes sir, the temperature is up to seventy ... very good, I'll pass the word.'

I went out to take the 0600 fix, swinging the azimuth mirror round to the distant peak of Jezirat Zabargad, or St John's Island, which lay forty miles off the Egyptian-Sudanese border. We had just turned a page in the

Company's Order Book. Seventy degrees Fahrenheit at 0600, ship's time, meant we forsook the heavy dark doeskin uniforms of high latitudes and broke out the white drill shirts and shorts of the tropics. We were flying-fish sailors at last.

In the northern part of the Red Sea the winds are generally from the north, fading to a central belt of calm before turning and blowing hot from the south as the ship approaches Perim. As the day passed, the northerly wind lost much of its strength, easing to the same speed as the *Antigone*, so that we ceased to feel any breeze over our decks and the engine exhausts climbed lazily upwards into the brazen sky. After breakfast, a meal punctuated by mockery at the sheepish appearance of our white skins, a party of mates and engineers turned to on the forward well-deck to erect the swimming pool. We were encouraged by the passengers, who appeared *en masse* for the first time. The rising temperature, the brilliant sunshine and the change in dress combined with the steady motion of the ship to bring smiles and bonhomie amongst us. Even the crew, chipping and splashing red-lead on the forward hatch-coamings and winch-beds, chaffed us good-heartedly.

'Gerron with that Sec, I wanna swim when I knock off today, not tomorrer.'

'D'you want to jump in before we've filled it with water?' Mike replied, looking more cheerful than he had been. We placed the last wooden planks in their steel frame and dragged the huge canvas bag into the *corrida* we had set up. Finally we lashed a fire-hose into one corner and opened the hydrant.

'When will it be ready?'

Mrs Saddler accosted us as we made our way to Mike's cabin for a cooling beer.

'Oh, give it a couple of hours,' replied Mike. 'Not bad,' he said when we reached his cabin and had opened the cans.

'Just the job,' I replied.

'Not the beer ... Mrs Saddler.'

'Oh. Bit old for me.'

'Rubbish. Many a good tune played on an old fiddle.'

Voyage East

I noticed that the photograph of his wife was missing and I recalled his previous introspection, a mood that the morning's cheerful work had dispelled. It was none of my business.

Our high spirits were short-lived. At noon Sparks arrived on the bridge with a solemn expression on his sallow face. Self-consciously he approached Captain Richards who, sextant cradled, was waiting with the deck officers for apparent noon. The message form rustled in the breeze as the Old Man read it. Looking up he nodded dismissal at the radio-officer, then turned to the meridian, raised his sextant and said, *'Ixion's* lost a man overboard'

Oddly, Mike took it worst. By the time I relieved him at 1600 he seemed very depressed. 'I wonder who it was.'

'We'll know when we get to Aden.'

'I expect it was a suicide attempt ... he could hardly have fallen in this weather.'

'No . . .' There seemed little else to say. I took over the watch and began the preliminary working for stellar observations at twilight. As darkness settled a British tanker with whom we had been keeping company all day finally succeeded in pulling ahead. She called us up on her aldis light: *'Adieu Blue.'*

'Very witty,' remarked the Mate sourly, joining me at the rail where we stood for a little in silence, staring at the stern light of the tanker.

'Too bad about that fellow from *Ixion.*'

'Yes. D'you know who he was, sir?'

'Aye, Jamie Fraser, a Glasgow man, Second Engineer...'

'Oh.' I did not know him, but it was clear the Mate did. Below us the sea hissed past our hull.

'Come and have a beer,' Mike invited as I came below at 2000.

'I was going to have a swim ...'

'Have a beer.' His tone was sharp, peremptory.

'Okay ...' I made myself comfortable on his settee. 'It was the Second Engineer off the *Ixion* ... the Mate knew.'

'Yes. Poor bastard.'

'You still think it was suicide?'

'What else?' He looked at me with what seemed withering scorn, as if I did not understand something that was blindingly obvious to him. I wished I had gone for my nocturnal dip.

'What makes you so sure?'

He was silent and cast down his eyes. It was clear that he had had a few drinks before my arrival. I lit a cigarette and he got up abruptly, pulled open a drawer and threw the photograph of his wife onto the settee beside me. 'That!'

I picked it up and handed it back, aware that I was walking in a minefield. He took the picture, stared at it for a moment and then tossed it aside onto the bunk. 'Have another beer.'

'Last one.' Emboldened by the sudden knowledge that he had got me there to talk, I asked, 'Have you got problems?'

'No fucking mail.'

'Oh ... still she may just have missed the posting date for Port Said. You're bound to get some in Aden.'

'Otherwise . . .' His voice trailed off and I could see his eyes were dark with the intensity of his bitterness; I thought again of the *Ixion's* engineer, with a sense of foreboding. Suddenly he shook off his depression. 'Otherwise Mrs Saddler ...'

It was not only Mike whose attitude was altering, for the sudden onset of tropical weather, the passage of the canal and our change of uniform was another milestone on our voyage, like passing Gibraltar. Except for the separation from home it was now a wholly satisfying experience to be at sea. We made better use of the time. The ship's appearance was trimmer, her paintwork brighter, her cargo gear was being overhauled and made ready for 'the coast'. We occupied our leisure with swimming, reading and sunbathing. 'Bronzey-ing' was pursued assiduously, and certain areas of the ship were set aside for it by tacit agreement. The dedicated few used the after docking-bridge, above the poop-house which contained the Chinese galley and which was well out of the passengers' view. Below us the Chinese squatted on their tiny wooden stools gambling, smoking and chatting over interminable bowls of tea while above, we Europeans spit-roasted ourselves in the burning sunshine. In those first days we aptly

Voyage East

earned the Chinese nickname of *fan kwei:* red barbarians. Not all of us were that keen; for most, half an hour on the salt-bleached tarpaulin of Number Two hatch, conveniently close to the pool, was good enough. Besides, here we rubbed shoulders with the passengers. It was not generally encouraged in junior officers, a relic perhaps of old Alfred's rigid non-conformity, but the society of both men and women from other walks of life was pleasant and stimulating, and whiled away the brief leisured hours of the forenoon.

We were beset by calms now, having run south of the northern wind belt, and the sea bore a pock-marked appearance where light airs ruffled it, then left it quiet again. Flying fish lifted from our hull and glided out obliquely on either bow, drumming their elongated lower tail fin on the water to extend their flights.

'Oh, look!' Mrs Saddler drew our attention as she stood wide-eyed at the top of the pool ladder, her voluptuous figure sending a sudden surge of lust among us. Her plump arm was outstretched and we saw the dolphins coming in from the beam, easily outstripping the ship as they darted into our curling bow wave, breaching and gambolling as we crowded the rail to watch. It was a common enough sight, but Mrs Saddler's enthusiasm was infectious and I found the touch of her arm beside me profoundly disturbing.

'Isn't that wonderful? They're so beautiful ...' She turned to me and I noticed her eyes were warm and brown and a damp lock of hair trailed down on her breasts. 'Don't you think so?' Her skin, I noticed, was lightly dusted with freckles, and this suddenly made her seem younger and infinitely desirable. I nodded stupidly and turned away, making for the pool to escape the effect she was having. Mike remained chatting to her husband who was, I later learned, something to do with the British Council, and then she joined them, lifting her arms and vigorously drying her hair with a towel.

We met the southerly breeze that afternoon, a warm *haboob* that told us we were approaching the end of the Red Sea. On either hand, unseen beyond the horizon, the shores began to close in. The area was littered with dangers: islets, rocks and reefs, most with Arab names but some with the anglicised titles of the Admiralty's hydrographic surveyors. Thus Abu Ail was known as Quoin Island and the narrow and dramatic passage between its precipitous cliffs and those of its neighbour, Jabal Zuqar, was called Hell's Gates. It was an apt enough title, for the rocks and beaches of Jabal Zuqar were black, of volcanic origin, and held upon their sinister sand the remains of an old Liberty ship.

The following morning the lights of Mocha were fading on the eastern horizon and beyond, the Tihamah Plain shimmered in the refracted air while a ghostly dawn broke over the distant Yemeni Mountains. Daylight filtered through a gossamer overcast. Arabia and Africa drew together, crowding our passage and constricting the exit from the Red Sea into a narrow gut, the Strait of Bab-el-Mandeb, the Gate of Tears. Set against the Yemeni shore lay the island of Perim, once an important coaling station, beyond which the Indian Ocean replenishes the Red Sea with an indraught of water. In the main body of the strait the Red Sea chokes out its salty overflow. Less water flows out than in, for it is the high rate of evaporation that causes the dense salinity of the Red Sea.

The strait was crowded with shipping as we rounded Perim, bright spots of colour on the perfect blue of the sea. We swung east, hugging the brown coast of the Aden Protectorate, great ramparts of fissured arid rock whose jagged summits rose 2,500 feet against a sky of cobalt blue. The wind had backed, a cool and welcome headwind fresh from the Indian Ocean that set the sea dancing with white horses. Spirits rose as the temperature on board fell and the prospect of mail from home drew nearer. But our relief was short-lived, for we were ordered to anchor in the bay to wait for a berth. On three sides of us the barren peaks of desolate volcanic rock beat back the brazen sun so that one's head ached with the intensity of it. It was hard to see why the Romans had named this coast *Arabia Felix,* Happy Arabia, even though the comparatively moist ocean breezes stimulated the growth of vegetation, particularly coffee. For us the heat was terrific and it seemed that, if we waited long, we would share the fate of the *Esso Norway* lying less than a mile away. She had suffered severe fire damage following an explosion. Her boats were missing except for one which hung forlornly from a single davit fall; her rudder was gone, torn off when, to save her,

Voyage East

she had been beached. This was corroborated by the marks of a waterline that ran obliquely up her sides from her forefoot to her afterdeck. She was quite a new ship, the pilot said when he boarded, but was to be scrapped.

'Anyone killed?' asked the Mate.

'Yes. Three men.'

That made four deaths we had heard of within a few days.

By late afternoon we had secured to a bunkering pontoon off Steamer Point under the peak of the great volcano. Although we had a few cases of cargo for Aden, we had come for fuel oil. At 16 knots we averaged 384 nautical miles per twenty-four hour day at a consumption of 30 tons, and replenishment was a matter of importance. *Antigone* carried all her oil, fuel and fresh water in double-bottom tanks; these heavy weights placed low in the ship improved stability and were in an area where the structure of the ship consisted of webs, intercostals and frames which served to minimise the 'free surface effect'. This, which might better be described as a cumulative sloshing, was a potential danger if not restricted. Unrestrained liquids, free to slosh back and forth under the inducement of a heavily rolling hull, can suddenly rush to the low side, producing an abrupt shift in the ship's centre of gravity, increasing the list which in turn throws more liquid to the low side, exerting a violent capsizing moment unless slowed and subdivided by barriers. The whole bottom of the ship was doubled, and in these spaces, criss-crossed by bulkheads and the internal framework of the ship, the lifeblood of *Antigone* was stored until wanted. Oil and water tanks were separated by narrow void spaces called 'cofferdams', so that the two commodities could not be mixed, and a substantial reserve was always maintained.

For the Chief Engineer, Mr Kennington, bunkering was a 'workout', a feverish rush of activity to fill one tank to the brim and switch to the next so that no overflows took place but the pumping rate was undiminished. Since each tank had a narrow breather-pipe to the upper deck, overflows could be messily polluting, staining immaculate teak decks and stirring the old antipathy between engine-room and deck departments. Kennington and his staff were therefore on their mettle under the broiling sun, aware that China Dick disliked delay. The rest of us haggled with the bum-boatmen, for Aden was a free port, full of those cheap Japanese consumer goods just then reaching western markets and signifying the beginning of Far East industrial ascendancy. Perhaps we were among the first to recognise their quality; that they had ceased to be a joke. A junior officer like myself on about £90 per month could not afford a pair of Barr and Stroud binoculars, but a serviceable pair of Japanese glasses could be had from the bum-boatmen of Aden for a fiver. Or, one's cabin could be fitted out with an Akai stereo-system for a modest outlay. What was more, the bum-boatmen would barter odds and ends of currency, so that one could purchase in Straits, Hong Kong or U.S. dollars, European notes or Japanese yen. It was odd to watch such modern goods being bought and sold in so primitive a manner for, unlike the vendors in the canal, the Aden Arabs did not come aboard unless it was with a knife in their hand to settle-up with someone trying to cheat them. For the most part they bobbed alongside in their boats, opened cartons of radios and cameras and awaited trade with the aid of a little self advertisement.

'You want, Johnnie ... hey! You want? Camera? Binocular? Hey! Special for you Johnnie ... radio ... very good radio ... I make for you special price!'

'Okay. How much?'

'No. You have look-see.'

I leaned over the rail and caught the line thrown over the after well-deck rail. Next to me Zee Pang Yun, the Old Man's personal Tiger was arguing over a pair of binoculars. I pulled on the line, half-way along which was secured a large rush basket. The radio was inside and I pulled it out and turned it over. Despite myself, I noticed the numerous wavebands, the fine-tuning and the tone control. It would make a welcome addition to the sparse furnishings of my cabin. I leaned back over the rail. Below, the bum-boatman, still holding the other end of the line, looked up.

'How much?'

'Twenty pound.'

'No.' I shook my head vigorously and replaced the item in the basket, lowering it over the rail. The Arab made no attempt to pull his end of the line and the disputed radio swung between us.

'What you pay? Eh? English money? Straits dollar?' There was an edge of aggression now. I knew I had to take the offensive.

'English money. Hey, you say you make me special price. Twenty pound is not special price.'

'How much you pay?'

'Eight pounds.'

There was a disgusted tugging on the line and recognisable Anglo-Saxon floated up amid a torrent of Arabic abuse. Next to me Zee had reached a similar stage in his negotiations. He was swearing in Cantonese, leaning outboard and grinning as he shouted 'Too fucking much, savvy? Fucking Arab robbing bastard . . .'

'Hey you fuck me, eh? I fuck you, bastard Chinaman …' It was a great comment on international relations that we were driven to such extremes, but there was little real malice in it, rather a series of ritual posturing. My own line jerked tight. I still wanted that radio and the bum-boatmen knew it; he could afford the Parthian shot.

'American ship comes tomorrow. I sell everything…'

'Okay you give me special price in English money.'

'Fifteen pounds.'

'Too much!'

We compromised at twelve, both affecting disgust yet both having done well, the Arab probably better than I. Zee was less easily satisfied and stopped frequently to report in asides to his countrymen, who were milling about in vests and thin cotton shorts, their feet in sandals that flapped on the hot steel deck.

'Ay-ah …' Zee consulted his friends for a last time. His broad face cracked into a mirthful grin, revealing his gold fillings; he had reached a last price and hoisted up the binoculars again. I was busy sending down twelve pounds in my own basket.

We took less than six hours to bunker, three of them in the sudden, surprising chill of the desert night. That evening the Mate announced that China Dick intended breaking with tradition to the extent of altering the watches. The Mate himself was going on daywork, office hours, the better to supervise the maintenance work that could be undertaken during the nine days' run across the Indian Ocean. The Third Mate was to stand the twelve-to-four, the Second Mate the four-to-eight and I was to have the eight-to-twelve. Each of us would be assigned a Midshipman, in my case the young greenhorn whose acquaintance I had first made over a hydrometer and a bucket of foul water from Vittoria Dock.

We went to stations and slipped from our berth, discharging the pilot and swinging eastwards round Ras Marshaq. It was nearly midnight when we took our departure and China Dick watched me plot the position on the chart and the abbreviation 'Dep' in squared brackets next to it.

'Well, Mister, you'll be keeping the eight-to-twelve then.'

'Yes sir.' I turned to face the portly figure in the white drill shirt with the four gold bands of ultimate responsibility upon his epaulettes.

'D'you think you can teach that young man some navigation?' He nodded to the pale figure of the Midshipman wandering uncertainly on the port bridge-wing.

'I'll do my best, sir.'

'Well you'd better go and teach him how to keep a bloody lookout while I write up the night orders.'

He lifted his glasses from around his neck and laid them on the chart table. I recognised them as the pair Zee Pang Yun had bought that afternoon at Steamer Point. I wondered how much the Old Man had had to pay for them.

The Third Mate and his Midshipman relieved us at midnight. When Bob had acquired his night vision and noted all the ships in sight I lingered for a few moments' gossip.

'Mike's a bit pissed off,' he said, stroking his new and itching beard.

'Didn't he get any mail in Aden?'

'No.'

Voyage East

fLYING FISH SAILORS

Before us lay a nine-day ocean passage of some three-and-a-half thousand miles between Aden and Pulo Penang. Initially we shaped our course obliquely across the Gulf of Aden, raising the grey bluff of Cape Elefante the following day. The Somali coast to the eastwards of this mighty rock hummock was high, a vast upland plateau extending to Cape Guardafui, beyond which lay the Indian Ocean. Refreshingly strong katabatic winds streamed down from the Horn of Africa, relatively cooler air drawn off the land to replace the rising updraughts of the sun-warmed air at sea level.

Cape Guardafui, the Cape of Spices of the ancients, was marked by a lighthouse, extinguished on that first night-watch as I stood the eight-to-twelve with the young Midshipman.

'I wonder if they've been eaten,' I remarked, giving up the search and putting my binoculars into the bridge box.

'What?' asked the Midshipman incredulously.

'Eaten,' I repeated. 'Soon after the Italians built the thing, native tribesmen attacked it and were supposed to have eaten the keepers.'

'Bloody hell.'

I went into the chart-room, where the high cliffs of the Cape glowed hard-edged on the radar-screen, and fixed our position, recording the fact on the slate and adding the symbol <R> alongside to indicate a radar-derived position. After checking the positions of three other ships within ten miles I returned to the Midshipman and began my lectures.

'Astronomical navigation,' I began bravely, 'is based on the pre-Galilean misconception that the earth is the centre of the universe.'

I could almost hear his brain coping with the acceptance of this great lie as we leaned on the rail and stared at the horizon. Above our heads the vault of the sky was a mass of stars, a perfect night for the elucidation of the great nautical mysteries.

'As you can see, all the heavenly bodies - sun, moon and stars can easily be imagined as moving relatively on the inside of a vast sphere, which we call the celestial sphere. Okay?'

'So far, sir.' I sensed a wariness that it was not all going to be so easy.

'Good. Now just as our position on the surface of the earth is located by latitude and longitude, so it may be on the celestial sphere. Up there!' I pointed dramatically overhead. 'It's called our Zenith, and is point Z of the P Z X triangle.' I could see the starlit frown smooth with the realisation that the thing had no visible existence.

'And if we extend the earth's axis through the poles to a point above them, then we have the P of our triangle. Point X is the sun or star which we observe with sextant and chronometer, and the solution of one or more of the component parts of the P Z X triangle helps us to determine our position.'

My arm swept across the great blackboard of the sky from our zenith to a point close to Polaris and out towards the great coruscating glow of Canopus low on the southern horizon, where the refraction of low altitude was producing spectacular flashes of blue and red from its ice-water centre.

'But, just as a single line of bearing, such as that radar bearing I took off Cape Guardafui, will not give you an exact position unless crossed with another piece of information such as a second bearing or, in the case we have just taken, the distance off the Cape by radar, so a single observation of a star will not give you a position.'

'Then how do we … ? I mean you get one at noon, don't you?'

'Ah. Good question. That is a piece of legerdemain, a nautical conceit which we can look at later, but it is conditional upon a good observation of our longitude early in the morning. We make an allowance for the run between the morning longitude and the noon latitude and, hey presto! A noon position to use for calculating the day's run to keep the passengers happy. It's not perfect, but substantially accurate. The best fix is obtained by stellar observations at twilight …'

'When you shoot more than one star at the same time?' He was a quick-witted lad; I would have to watch myself.

'Except that we "observe"; "shooting" things is strictly for Hollywood.'

'Oh.'

Voyage East

'Well, that's enough for tonight. It's nearly one-bell. Nip down and call the next watch.'

He left me alone for a few minutes. Ahead the pale half-moon of the forecastle bulwarks showed the dark shape of the lookout pacing his lonely grating in the very eyes of the ship. Beyond, the horizon stretched away dark and empty now. I went into that chart-room to complete writing up the log-slate.

'Okay dere, Fourth, I got de tea.' Wakelin, the second man in my watch, brought the pot of tea onto the bridge. He had stood the first two hours of the eight-to-twelve as look-out, the second two hours in the seamen's mess on stand-by.

'Thanks. Nip down and see if the Middy's put the Third Mate on the shake.'

'Okey-doke.'

After the change of watch I came off the bridge to make my round, a quick, torch-lit tour of the upper decks to see that all was well, reporting the fact from the gyro-room where our Sperry master gyro compass hummed and from which we regularly verified the readings of the bridge repeaters. I made my way back to the boat-deck, exchanging a few words with a passing engineer and avoiding the passengers, still revelling at the bar. I was pleasantly sleepy and almost bumped into Mrs Saddler leaning alone on the promenade-deck rail.

'Hullo,' she said coolly, turning and leaning back, her elbows on the rail. She wore a thin white crepe dress with a stole of the same material, caught on her shoulder with a brooch. The noise of male laughter came through the jalousies of the adjacent Chief Engineer's cabin.

'Oh, hullo.' I paused briefly as she smiled.

'They're all drinking,' she said in answer to my unasked question. 'D'you have a cigarette? I don't like to go back and disturb them.'

I fished the packet from my breast pocket and a lock of her hair brushed my hand as she bent over the lighter flame. She caught my eyes on her cleavage as she smiled her thanks and her perfume completed my confusion. She turned back to the rail and stared out over the sea while, I, hesitating, lit a cigarette and leaned beside her. Beneath us the wake rushed, hissing past.

'I'm sorry if I embarrassed you all the other day, when we saw those dolphins.'

'Oh.' I recalled the incident. 'Were we embarrassed?'

'Well, I said they were beautiful. I suppose it was a silly thing to say to a lot of men.'

'Why? We're not all boors.' I thought of the Mate and the sensitive person beneath the professional carapace. 'Just a bit different, I suppose.'

'I suppose so.'

I could not tell her that her physical presence aroused us; that every day the voyage lasted she became increasingly desirable. I felt her elbow brush mine. Or could I?

'And by drawing attention to the beauty of the dolphins, you naturally drew attention to yourself.'

She remained staring at the horizon. 'That's rather a bold speech.'

'Not intended to offend.' I straightened up as if to go, uncertain if a note of coldness had entered her voice, but she turned and looked at me.

'It didn't,' she replied reassuringly. 'You're just going on watch, are you?'

'I've just come off. It's past midnight.'

Guffaws of laughter came from behind the jalousies and I recognised her husband's nasal accent.

'So you're off to bed.' She smiled again and I lingered, finishing my cigarette. 'Don't you get fed up with this?' She motioned her head at the surrounding darkness, and I was leaning beside her again, aware that I was being seduced.

'No ...'

I felt her fingers cool on my arm. 'Don't you miss ...' The dark eyebrows arched and the bare shoulders lifted in a gesture of unmistakable suggestion. I had begun to turn when she suddenly pointed: 'Oh, look!'

Half-relieved, half-regretful, I did as I was bid. It was as though the sea had caught fire. The breaking bubbles of the bow-waves, the hissing rim of foam that tumbled outwards from *Antigone's* bow were suddenly luminous. And beyond the disturbance of the ship's advancing hull it was as if every breaking wave was visible for miles.

'It's magical ... what is it?' Mrs Saddler had straightened up, her eyes as wide as a child's, her lips slightly parted.

'It's called a milk-sea, caused by phosphorescence due to the presence of plankton.' I paused, unwilling to bore.

'Go on' she prompted, never taking her eyes from the brilliantly luminous surface of the ocean.

'Well, it could be a protozoan called *Noctiluca,* or there's a luminous shrimp called, I think, something like *Meganictyphanes ...*'

'But it's so ... so eerie' she broke in, 'almost unbelievable.' She shivered slightly and I could see goose-pimples raised on the bare skin of her shoulders.

'It could also be sinister.'

'What do you mean?' She asked, turning with a look of alarm on her face.

'There's a little plant, a dinoflagellate, I can't remember its name, which contains a terrible poison that makes shell-fish toxic during certain seasons; the stuff reacts on the nervous-system like strychnine.'

'Oh, how horrible. I really *won't* eat lobsters when there's an R in the month.'

'Now look!' I said, pointing. It seemed that among the random glowing of the tumbling water a molten stream was running, undulating through the depths. Following this thick line of luminiscence were faster, thinner trails, darting in and out, harrying the steady flow of the stream into sudden swirls of disturbance; fiery lines that wove a pattern of depredation and then rose upwards, faster and faster until, right beside our rushing hull, the dolphins surfaced for air, gasping as they breached, ignoring us in the wild ecstasy of the hunt as they savaged the shoal of fish. We watched for several minutes, the answer to her question about boredom spectacularly answered for me.

'What the hell are you doing?'

I turned. Captain Richards stood in the adjacent doorway, flanked by the Chief, the Mate and Mr Saddler. I realised my hand was on Mrs Saddler's arm, put there in my eagerness to point out the dolphins.

'He was showing me the phosphorescence, Captain. It's absolutely *beautiful.* Look, Darling,' she stepped forward and drew her husband out from behind China Dick, who grunted and never took his baleful eye from me.

'Time you were turned in, Mister.'

The Indian Ocean is dominated by the sub-continent in more than name alone. Although it merges imperceptibly into the Southern Ocean where the westerly winds of the Roaring Forties blow interminably round the globe, and although it possesses the characteristic Trade Wind belt of the southern hemisphere in conformity with the global pattern of oceanic winds, its northern wind system is influenced by the presence of Asia and the salient of India.

During the hot summer months, between May and October, rising air over the land draws in warm damp air from the ocean to cause the South-West Monsoon, the rainy season for India and a period of thick, boisterous weather in the Arabian Sea and Bay of Bengal. We, however, were making our passage in the fall of the northern year, when the low pressure over the ocean and the higher pressure over India forced the air south-westwards again. It was a lighter wind, this North-East Monsoon, with fine, clear weather.

The morning following my encounter with Mrs Saddler the summits of the mountains of Socotra were just visible to the far north. Curiosity about this remote island was swiftly quelled by the information in the Admiralty Sailing Directions for the Arabian Sea. The island was inhabited by 'unfriendly' persons who had attacked watering parties from naval survey ships. Unlike those of the Pacific, the islands of the Indian Ocean were then largely unexploited. The Maldives, the Laccadives, the Andaman and Nicobar archipelagos were inaccessible to tourists, only visited by seamen and the occasional intrepid traveller. As we steamed east-south-east, heading for that gap in the island chain west of India known as the Eight Degree Channel, the fresh north-easterly wind was on the port bow, curling the sea into a vista of white-caps beneath a sky of blue dotted with the puff-balls of fair-weather cumulus. Flying fish darted from our passage, sometimes pursued by an albacore or the leaping shapes of long-beaked

Voyage East

dolphins. These, of the genus Stenella and notoriously difficult to identify specifically, would rush in from our beam to bow-ride under our forecastle, sensing the point of equilibrium where the forward thrust of *Antigone's* hull balanced the drag on their bodies. For this purpose they were able to alter their physical shape, enabling several of these beautiful creatures to bow-ride together. Capable of speeds well in excess of twenty-knots, they could sometimes be seen accelerating alongside in spectacular fashion, but to distinguish a bottle-nose, a bridled, a common or a spotted dolphin from the other members of their genus was almost impossible, for their leaping acrobatics were unpredictable and they always foiled the most dedicated photographers waiting to record their grace and agility.

Occasionally a whale spouted, though too distant to identify, and a few pelagic birds, boobies and the like, wheeled about the ship. After taking my morning sight for longitude seemed an appropriate time to hector my young watch-mate and we settled down on the starboard bridge-wing, eyes mechanically scanning the horizon ahead. Below, Captain Richards, formidable in white shirt and starched white shorts, led the senior officers on their daily rounds.

'We talked last night about the P Z X triangle . . .'

I led him into the complexities of spherical trigonometry where both sides and angles are expressed in degrees, and Euclidean ideas about plane triangles can be forgotten. We discussed the component parts of the P Z X triangle, talked of hour angles, polar and zenith distances, co-latitudes, azimuths and the broad theory of position circles.

As I talked I watched Mrs Saddler on the forward well-deck climb the short ladder and poise herself to dive into the pool. She wore a one-piece bathing suit of black and her figure was stockily handsome. She rolled over at the far end and gave me a playful little wave. Beside me the Midshipman waved back.

'D'you understand what I've been saying?' I asked sharply.

'Er, yes. I think so, sir.'

'Good.'

Below us there was a loud grating noise as of someone clearing his throat. After completing his rounds, China Dick was taking his morning walk across the deck immediately below us. I wondered if he too had waved at that voluptuous figure.

'Okay, so you know the theory. The problem is how do we turn this into practical use. After all, we're on the bridge of a ship, not at the centre of the earth. When we use a sextant to observe a heavenly body . . .'

'Talking of heavenly bodies . . .'

Mike joined us, having just completed his morning sight. He stared down at Mrs Saddler swimming vigorously up and down the short length of the pool and turning with a swirl of exposed buttocks, then he too spun round and abruptly left us. A few minutes later his lithe form had joined her.

'But these calculations, sir, how do you *do* them?'

'Eh?' The question brought me back to the present. 'Oh, they're based on something called the haversine formula, proof of which is deeply boring and not a patch on watching the buoyancy of Mrs Saddler's tits. Did you know women stay afloat longer than men? Anyway, you need to understand something called the Reduction of Altitudes first, and we'll save that for this evening. It's time you did an hour on the wheel.'

My watch below in the afternoon took in a swim, but there was no sign of Mrs Saddler, though I saw her briefly at boat drill. We were in the throes of this Friday ritual, held at 1615 ship's time, when *Menestheus* passed us, homeward bound. The bright spots of orange dotting her boat deck showed she too was performing this rite and we dipped our ensigns in mutual salute before dragging fire hoses along the decks and squirting fire-extinguishers over the side in order, the Senior Midshipman claimed, that he could fill them up again. The Mate joined us briefly during the evening watch. I did not think he enjoyed the hearty drinking in the Chief Engineer's cabin.

'Ah, laddie,' he said, stretching himself before leaning beside me on the rail while the Midshipman sensibly beat a hasty retreat to the other wing, 'there is no entrance fee to the starlit hall of the night.'

It was years later that I discovered the source of that quotation and odd that it stuck. Perhaps it echoed my own pre-Galilean assertions of the previous evening, imposing comprehensible limits on the infinity of the sky. I do not think the Mate saw this in his repetition of Axel Munthe's words, but his next remark suggested that he might have.

'I always think the tropical sky offers a paradox.' He paused and then resumed, 'you either feel incredibly insignificant when contemplating it, or immensely privileged to be here, aboard this steel speck on the ocean.' And then, almost without drawing breath, he added, 'you be careful ...'

'What about?' But I sensed it coming.

'China Dick doesna like his officers misbehaving.'

'Mrs Saddler?' I was incredulous.

'Aye.'

'But . .

'She was on the bridge at midnight, throwing snowballs at the moon,' he muttered, 'She said "I've never had it," but she spoke too bloody soon ...'

I thought better of further reply. The doggerel and the euphemism 'misbehaving' belied the seriousness of his warning. Passengers were *Verboten* and the Mate was a bachelor; perhaps he had a better right to contemplate adultery than I.

'*Droit de seigneur,*' I muttered resentfully at his retreating figure. He paused at the top of the ladder.

'There's a light coming up astern,' he said. 'Probably the *Ashcan...*'

The Mate proved right. It took her all the next day to overtake, but the *Ascanius* had the advantage of a fraction of a knot over *Antigone*. Her proximity provoked messages by aldis lamp, signal flags and radio telephone, mostly of a facetious nature and, as the day wore on, pretty thin on wit. During the afternoon I watched her occasionally from the lifeboats where, with the assistance of two Midshipmen, I was checking the stores, the barley sugar, biscuit, water and condensed milk that would sustain us if disaster struck. Mild fantasies of being alone, adrift with Mrs Saddler, played upon my imagination. As I turned over the watch at midnight, *Ascanius* could still be seen, a faint glimmer on the horizon ahead.

Although I followed the same itinerary on my rounds and the laughter from the Chief's cabin betrayed the establishment of a 'school', there was no lonely figure on the promenade deck nor, as I half-dared to hope, on the shadowy boat-deck.

'Looking for somebody?'

Sparks was locking up the radio room, his statutory watch finished.

'No,' I lied, adding defensively, 'fancy a beer before turning in?'

We sat in my cabin and I sensed his loneliness. Younger than the Senior Midshipman, he was denied the rough bear-pit atmosphere of the half-deck, separated by convention, pride and unfamiliarity.

'How are you liking it so far?'

'Great,' he answered insincerely. 'I've been talking to Mauritius tonight, as well as the *Ascanius.*'

'I expect you miss your girl-friend, don't you?' My mind was running along a predictable track of sexual deprivation.

'Yes. We've been going together for over two years.'

Such fidelity was quite unknown to me and made his presence on board the more inexplicable.

'What made you come to sea, then?'

It was obvious he had no answer. He was too young to be one of those who had chosen the Merchant Navy in preference to National Service in the armed forces.

'My uncle was Chief Engineer with Ellerman's.'

'Where d'you come from?'

'The Wirral - Bebington actually.'

With such a background, the Merchant Navy would have seemed so obvious an option, like the mines to a lad in the Rhondda; perhaps the only option.

'Well, cheer up. You'll enjoy it when we get to the coast. Sparks is usually the only one of us to get any decent shore-leave. Here, have another beer.'

He seized it with the avidity of an incipient alcoholic and I realised that here was a potential family man treading the knife-edge of self-destruction. He achieved a curious kind of vicarious authority the following forenoon, ringing the bridge and speaking in a tone pregnant with self-importance. I sent the Midshipman down to collect the message and, having read it, despatched him at once to Captain Richards.

Voyage East

Below, in the pool, Mike and Mrs Saddler waved at me. I waved back, beaten.

China Dick puffed up onto the bridge, wearing his hat in readiness for his daily inspection, and disappeared into the chart-room. Five minutes later he emerged, ignored me and went below.

'What exactly is it, sir?' asked the Midshipman.

'There's a cyclone generating in the Bay of Bengal.'

'A cyclone?' The boy frowned.

'Yes,' I answered irritably, trying to ignore the salacious horseplay in the pool below, 'a T R S - Tropical Revolving Storm - known in the Bay of Bengal as a cyclone, and in the West Indies as a hurricane. The Chinese call it the Great Wind: *Taifun*.'

'A typhoon!' the boy exclaimed excitedly. 'Have you ever been in one?'

'Yes. Not a really bad one, but bad enough. In the Taiwan Strait. You'll find Richard Hughes's book *In Hazard* in the library. It's based on fact, about a Blue Flue caught in a West Indian hurricane. She lost her funnel and her boats.'

'Bloody hell.' The boy looked aft and upwards at the massive steel column and its wire guys.

We were traversing the Eight Degree Channel by noon. Away to the northwards a smudge of pale golden sand, fringed by white breakers and topped by the waving green fronds of coconut palms, marked the atoll of Minicoy. From the midst of the grove of palms rose the white column of its lighthouse. The dark parallelograms of a dozen sails dotted the ocean, the outrigger hulls of tiny, half-waterlogged fishing boats. We could see the dark skins of the Tamil fishermen and the sudden flash of their catch as they hauled their nets. The gentle timelessness of a subsistence way of life exerted its brief, spurious attraction. Minicoy exported coir in exchange for rice, the cargoes carried still in three-masted *dhonis* plying to Tuticorin or Cochin; we spotted one later that day, the very last of the true deep-water sailing ships.

My thwarted concupiscence sent me in search of literary consolation, for a long sea-passage was an ideal opportunity to read. One discovered strange companions of like mind in the ship's library. I found the Cook from

Swansea, who proved to be an authority on Guy de Maupassant.

'*Du*, no-one writes about women like Maupassant, can't fault him, like.'

'I thought Hardy was supposed to be pretty good.'

'Jesus Christ no, Hardy's crap compared to Maupassant. Got his complete works at home, Maupassant that is ... wouldn't give a toss for Hardy.'

'Well, there's no Maupassant here,' I said looking along the shelves, which contained a comprehensive collection of the newest novels, works of recent biography, history and travel.

'Try that,' said the Cook, pulling out *The Apprenticeship of Duddy Kravitz* by Mordecai Richler. 'You'll enjoy that.'

I took it and added *The Lotus and the Wind* by John Masters, sitting to decide which I should read first. While I sat browsing in companionable silence with the Cook, two figures went past the open door: the Chief Engineer and Mr Saddler.

'Well, she can't have gone far.' I heard the Chief say. The Cook and I exchanged glances.

The following morning the wind had backed a little and freshened to a near-gale. Although the barometer remained steady, there was an oppressiveness in the atmosphere. The sky had become overcast and the sun was surrounded by a halo. We had expected to sight the coast of Ceylon that afternoon, but at noon China Dick decided to avoid the path of the cyclone and our course was altered drastically to the southward. During the day the strong wind continued to back, indicating the centre of the intense low pressure was passing well to the northwards of us, but in response to its disturbance *Antigone* began to roll and pitch, lifting easily to the swell.

I almost shared the Midshipman's disappointment, for such a storm was an awesome sight, but I consoled him by taking a lunar sight and showing him the method. It proved to be a mistake. When Captain Richards came onto the bridge to write up his night orders he saw the columns of pencilled figures and summoned me to the chart-room.

'What's this?'

'Observed intercept of the moon, sir. For the benefit of the Midship...'

Voyage East

'The only thing you're supposed to teach the Midshipman is how to keep a bloody lookout. What bloody good is this?' He flicked the page of my sight book contemptuously, forgetful of his injunction to instruct the young apprentice. I held my peace. Initiative was something to be encouraged in aspirants under training, but squashed in junior officers. It was a paradox of the sea-life and I was half-expecting what followed. 'And keep away from the passengers.'

'Aye, aye, sir.'

I took myself back to the bridge-wing, exiled the Midshipman to the other side and sulked. China Dick had no time for the unorthodoxy of others.

'That cyclone,' said Sparks as we enjoyed a beer in my cabin after midnight, 'passed over Trincomalee.'

'Is that fucking so,' I said unkindly.

When I relieved Mike at 0800 the following morning he was singing, a trifle obviously, I thought.

'I've got a ticket to ride - I've got a ticket to ride - and I'm okaaay . . .'

The misquotation and the coarse pun advertised his triumph.

'You bastard,' I said. 'The Old Man thinks it's me.'

He handed over the watch and went laughing to his breakfast. It was a glorious day, the breeze light and only a low swell rolling ominously out of the north-west where the cyclone had beaten upon the beautiful coast of Ceylon. The sea's population seemed to revel in the passing of the great storm, for myriads of flying fish rose around us, extending their gliding flight by beating the elongated lower halves of their fail-fins against the surface of the ocean. The action left expanding chains of concentric rings on the smooth water.

On deck the splashes of red-lead had disappeared under successive layers of under-coat and gloss, while a second task supervised by the Mate, had resulted in the after deck being covered with loose coils of derrick wires, drawn off the winch barrels for greasing. From the heads and heels of the steel derricks the blocks had been unshackled, the pins knocked out and their sheaves removed for greasing and an inspection of the bushes. Much sloshing of grease had been evident and each block on reassembly had the date of the examination stamped into its steel cheek, the numerals picked out in white lead. Such were the preparations that occupied the Crowd, hatch by hatch, in preparation for the ports we were about to visit. Most were without cranes and many were devoid of wharves. We would work our cargo in and out of our holds by means of these derricks and their complex rigging.

That evening I showed the Midshipman a simpler mystery of navigation, the taking of an azimuth. It was a much easier procedure than a sight, merely a compass bearing of a prominent star taken through a prismatic instrument mounted on the compasses. This azimuth was compared to the calculated bearing of the star worked from our dead-reckoning position. The infinite distances of the stars and the comparatively crude calibration of a compass made the accuracy of our position less critical than might be supposed, and our dead-reckoning was rarely far out. The result showed the small instrumental error in the gyro-compass, but it was the comparison with the standard magnetic compass that was important, for one never knew when a power failure would throw one back on this primitive instrument. The total error of a magnetic compass was compounded by the earth's 'variation', that is the influence of the planet's magnetic field (which varied from place to place), and the ship's local influence, known as 'deviation'. Deviation was complicated by being almost infinitely variable, depending upon the ship's heading, upon her cargo and the amount of soft iron or steel therein, even on whether the derricks were topped up or stowed for an ocean passage. A close record of all its values was therefore desirable and at least one of these 'compass errors' was expected for every course steered and during every watch, unless other demands (such as fog or dense traffic) prevented the officer-of-the-watch from attending to the matter.

Next morning was Christmas Eve and as I sipped my coffee at four-bells, China Dick arrived with a surprise.

'Emergency boat-drill, Mister. Sound the alarms and stop engines. I'm going to lower the motor boat.'

I did as I was bid, mustering on the boat-deck as *Antigone* slowed in the pellucid blue water. The Mate told me off to command the boat and I

Voyage East

sensed victimisation, scowling at Mike who grinned infuriatingly back. Scrambling into the boat as it was swung out on the tall arms of the luffing davits, I shipped the rudder, aware of the ocean fifty feet below. Others were joining the boat as it lay griped in, level with the boat deck: a pair of Midshipmen, three seamen and the Lamptrimmer, the Fourth Engineer, two Chinese greasers and three Chinese stewards. Sparks came too, crouching proprietorially over the emergency radio.

I checked the plug was in the boat's bottom as the Mate ordered the gripes slipped and the winch-brake lifted. The boat began its long descent, swinging with increasing oscillations on the ever-lengthening span of the wire falls and bumping *Antigone's* side as the ship rolled with an easy motion, striking sparks from the metal skids that wrapped the bilge in an effort to protect the boat's planking and facilitate a launch against an adverse list. We struck the water with a thumping splash. The boat rose, the suddenly slack falls looping dangerously inboard then jerking tight again, snapping together as *Antigone* rolled away from us.

'Unhook! Ship crutches and toss oars!'

Mindful of their fingers, two seamen cast off the heavy blocks and pushed them over the boat's gunwhale. I put the tiller over, allowing the residual way of the ship to ease us off *Antigone's* unforgiving plating as we towed alongside.

'Leggo the painter ... Down oars!'

We were on our own, crabbing awkwardly off the black cliff in a shambles of missed strokes, of curses as oar-looms struck the back of the next man, a tangle of blades and knocking of crutches. High above us the passengers stared down from the promenade-deck and I saw Mrs Saddler laughing beside her husband. Above them, hands on hips in disbelief, the Mate shook his head over us, while from the bridge a stream of advice, or perhaps it was abuse, came from China Dick.

Clear of the ship we got our oars inboard, the men gasping as they watched the Fourth Engineer bend over the engine. At the tenth despairing swing of the handle it fired amid a cloud of black smoke and we chugged shamefacedly away from the ship.

'Right fucking game this is,' muttered the Lamptrimmer, while the

Chinese chatted amongst themselves, unconcerned by western preoccupations with smartness and efficiency. The intimacy with the surface of the sea was pleasant, the true magnitude and power of the swells that rolled the diminishing ship now obvious to us as our grab-lines trailed in the white foam that rolled back from our bluff wooden hull. A dozen flying fish lifted from the sea and we saw them clearly, the sunlight glancing from their armoured sides, their eyes wide with the terror of our strange intrusion. Borne on the huge undulating surface of the sea we opened our distance from the ship to a mile, so that only her upper-works, masts and funnel were visible in the troughs, then eased to a stop.

In the stern Sparks had been preparing the emergency radio, a hand-cranked apparatus with a small aerial. He bent over his key and, after some experimental twiddling, announced he had contacted the Purser on the ship. After a little he raised his head smiling.

'Message reads: "Come back to mother".'

'Okay. Acknowledge it.' I nodded to the Fourth. 'Give her full ahead, Billy.'

Half a mile from the ship the engine faded and died. Eighteen swings of the handle and Billy collapsed, swearing it was moribund: 'The fucking fucker's fucked.'

'Shit ...'

The groan went up and down the boat. Leung Yat, the Number Two Greaser swore a rich, descriptive Cantonese oath.

'Out oars.'

I determined to make a better show of our return. 'Come on. When I say "Pull!" put your backs into it.'

I stood in the stern and urged them on. To their everlasting credit, we made a show of it, backwatering neatly in under the falls and hooking on without mishap. A little flutter of applause came from above and I saw Mrs Saddler clapping. We rose dripping past the row of curious faces on the promenade deck.

'Not bad - for beginners,' I heard one of the men remark facetiously.

'Bollocks,' came the reply from one of the seamen bent over the plug, and then we were drawing level with the boat-deck and scrambling out of

Voyage East

the boat.

'Practice makes perfect,' Mike said, grinning as he supervised the swing inboard and onto the chocks.

'Bastard,' I replied, grinning back.

'Two of your men had their fingers on the gunwale as you came alongside,' admonished China Dick when I reported to the bridge, pricking my bubble of pride.

'Bastard,' I mouthed at his stocky back as he left me to my watch. *Antigone* gathered speed and along the boat-deck a group of engineers gathered round the recalcitrant boat-engine.

'Hit the fucking thing with a hammer,' advised the Bosun as he saw the last of the seamen below.

It was not much of a Christmas. The cyclone thrashed itself to death on the Coromandel coast and night fell in a downpour of torrential rain. After the days of clear weather and empty sea, we ran into traffic and, blinded by the rain, were driven to the tedious expedient of avoiding collisions by radar plotting. In such conditions we passed the northern tip of Sumatra. The rain continued intermittently all day and we passed the lonely, bird-limed islet of Pulo Rondo as we assembled for pre-lunch drinks. It proved a mirthless occasion, as was the more-than-ample Christmas dinner in the saloon, eaten with the passengers under a cloud of forced bonhomie from China Dick, causing brittle laughter from the ladies and insincere guffaws from his officers. To be absent from home at Christmas was bad enough, but to be at sea, under way, was terrible. At least in port the yoke of duty could be eased, but at sea the ship's routine went remorselessly on, though those on day-work knocked-off. The ship's company fragmented, drinking schools assembled in hidden places, dominated by maudlin sentiment and occasionally deteriorating into a scrap. On the whole it was better to be on watch and pretend the whole thing was a normal day. Perhaps Sparks was the most fortunate, kept busy with a stream of incoming and outgoing telegrams. I wondered if Mike had either sent or received one. He did not say, merely wore the stupid grin of gluttony and lust.

By 2000 the ship had sunk into inertia, only the watch-keepers awake. For us on the eight-to-twelve there was a spectacular consolation; a massive, soundless electric storm illuminating huge cumulo-nimbus clouds that rose over the distant mountains of Sumatra.

Dawn showed the dark, jungle-clad shoulders of Pulo Penang ahead. Before breakfast the Crowd were out, topping the derricks, while Chippy and his mate worked along the hatch-coamings, knocking loose the wedges in preparation for opening up. As we rounded Muka Head and picked up our Chinese-Malay pilot, the pool was coming down; half an hour later we were edging alongside the wharf, under the ramparts of Fort Cornwallis. The halcyon, flying fish days were over; it was this for which *Antigone* was called into being.

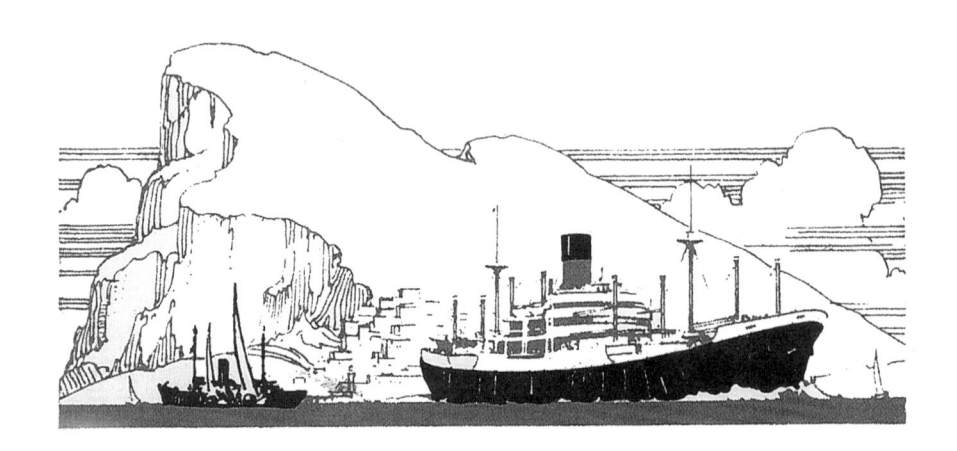

Voyage East

Orestes

Prometheus

BLUE FUNNEL

Tydeus

Teiresias

Voyage East

Alcinous

Aeneas

BLUE FUNNEL

Clytoneus

Anchises

Voyage East

Dymas

Astyanax

BLUE FUNNEL

Centaur

Idomeneus

Voyage East

Cyclops

Eurymedon

BLUE FUNNEL

Antenor

Memnon

Voyage East

THE SMELL OF MANY MORNINGS

Alongside at Penang in Malaya *Antigone* underwent a transformation. The spot where Mrs Saddler had with outstretched arm pointed out the leaping dolphins and aroused our lust, was unrecognisable. The decks were no longer neat but littered with the tarpaulins, hatchboards and beams that had kept the sea out of our vast and vulnerable holds, removed by the swarming gangs of labourers who seemed to have taken the ship over and were busy erecting sun-shades of dunnage and coconut matting over the winch-control positions. Under the jutting derricks, these odd excrescences gave us the appearance of a native *kampong*. Malays and Kling Tamils moved about the ship with familiar ease, shouting and gesticulating, crouching around the dangerously yawning holds in the simian squat that allowed a man to keep cool. In shirts and sarongs, their dark hair neatly plastered above their impish faces, they began the business of discharge. Tally clerks of Chinese blood, many wearing pith helmets and the concerned expressions of responsible men, began to check out the consignments of cargo as the derrick wires started to sing over the metal rims of the coamings and the first slings rose from our 'tween-decks.

Beyond the stucco-white walls and tiled roofs of the town, lush green jungle rose up to the island's peak. The scent of peepul, tamarind and banana came down from the groves of trees that covered the hillside, taunting us as we laboured in the heat, for we came not as tourists but as men with work to do. Across the strait dividing Penang from the old sultanate of Kedah, junks and sailing barges moved among anchored ships with a ponderous, wind-driven beauty. There too the green of the jungle seduced our eyes, too long starved of its colour. Beyond, sensed more than seen through the steaming cumulus that hung over the rain-forest, rose the blue foothills of the Cameron Highlands where the rubber plantations lay, and from which ran the tin-laden rivers that enriched this hinterland.

But our true horizon was more circumscribed, bounded by the quay to starboard and the waiting lighters to port. We had exchanged the whites of parade for the khaki of battle and, amid a bedlam of noise, sought to supervise the discharge of the cargo, to avoid accidents and breakages, to deter pilferage and to oil the complex works with our presence. Already the decks were no longer white. Gobbets of spittle reddened with betel-juice disfigured the teak, and chipped paint flew from the superstructure where hatch-beams from the lower 'tween-decks struck it, unheedful of the crew's careful maintenance.

'Oh, fucking hell,' growled the Bosun despairingly, 'you'd think they'd just try a bit harder not to be so fucking careless, wouldn't you, eh?'

'You'll have to paint it again before we get back to Liverpool, Bose,' I offered philosophically.

'*Du*, that's a fine lot of encouragement. Bloody Company cut my allowance of white gloss and the Mate still wants us to look like our kid's yacht ...' he went off grumbling.

'Third Office, Third Office.' The foreman wore a worried frown beneath his helmet.

'I belong Fourth Officer...'

'Okay. Please you lower foreside derricks, Number Two hatch.'

'Okay. Bose!' I arrested the Bosun's retreat. 'Get the derrick gang along to Number Two and lower the forrard derricks.'

'Aye, aye.' He waddled off and I went forward with the foreman.

Our derricks were rigged 'yard-and-stay', terminology left over from the days of sail. Arranged in pairs, their wires joined, one derrick plumbed the hatch, the other the wharf or an overside lighter. The married wires, known as a 'union-purchase', were controlled by one man, sitting beneath his coconut matting and driving two winches, deftly using one to lift out of the hold, then transferring the weight to the other, veering on the first and allowing the sling of cargo to slide horizontally and then down into the waiting lighter or onto the dusty wharf.

Movement on the decks, already impeded by the piles of hatch-boards and beams, was now further endangered by traversing loads, swiftly followed by the slack wires which draped innocently across an unsuspecting back and could, just as easily, draw suddenly tight, rising across one's path like a trip-wire. All this activity was accompanied by shouts and chatter so

Voyage East

that the movement, the heat and the noise fused in one stultifying oppressiveness.

Cars lifted over the rail, revealing a floor of Guinness cases which were swiftly followed by cartons of Brand's Essense of Chicken, held, I was assured, in high esteem as a potent breeder of children.

'I thought Guinness was good for that,' I said to the foreman. 'They speak one son in every bottle.'

'*Aiee-ya*, Guinness plenty good for man ... Essence of Chicken more better for woman.'

We were to revert to our normal watches at noon, which only gave me four hours respite from this bedlam, so I wrote letters and heard on the radio that Trincomalee had been reduced to a ghost-town by the Christmas cyclone. At 1600 I returned to the continuing chaos of the deck until 2000 when, standing in the shower, I was disturbed by the Fourth Engineer.

'Coming ashore?'

Night had fallen, the seductive night of the tropics. The invitation was irresistible.

'Yes. Five minutes.'

At the dock gates we piled into waiting *trishas*, a cross between a tricycle and a pushchair, with the simple command: 'Bar!'

There were six of us, the Senior Midshipman, the Third and Fourth Engineers, the Sparks, a junior Engineer and myself.

'How's it going, then?' I found myself in a *trisha* with Billy, the Fourth, a North-Country lad from Preston, whose humiliation in the recent boat-drill had turned into friendship.

'Bloody hot.' I was already sticky, despite my shower.

'You should have been down the engine room. Over a hundred this afternoon. The bloody Chief had us stripping down a genny ... the bastard's talking about doing a unit in Singapore. It's going to be a bloody work-out.'

'I expect he thinks he's done his bit in Aden.'

'Yeah. I heard he thought that manual labour was a Spaniard . . .' We piled out at the bar. It was on a corner, the wide monsoon ditch where a European gutter would have been. The raised sidewalk was arcaded, stucco pillars rising to the jutting first storey where jalousies stood open against the faintest whisper of a breeze, the ceaseless hum of oriental life spilling out into the warm night. The open bar was bright and cool under a revolving punkah.

'Six beers, please ... .'

A couple of Chinese smoked and drank in one corner, but otherwise the place was empty. We sat noisily around a central table and thirstily drank our San Miguel beers. Drunkenness is part alcoholic intake, part state of mind and we were in high spirits, released from the artificial confinements of the ship. It was not long before someone called for a woman. It was a half-hearted joke, bravado prompted by that quickening of impulse provoked by several swift drinks. The Chinese proprietor came over and gave us a distasteful look. 'You want woman?'

'Yes! Yes! We want woman.'

The man shuffled off. Rather shamefacedly we continued drinking and gossiping. 'Hey, is Mike really knocking off that passie? Mrs Saddler?'

'I don't know,' I answered evasively.

'Of course he is,' said the Senior Midshipman knowingly. I recalled they were on watch together. The conversation turned enviously on Mike's adultery. We had forgotten our demand. Nobody expected anything to happen. This was just an ordinary bar.

But she came, a Chinese-Malay girl of the Peranakan, sheathed in a cheongsam of pale blue cotton. She had short black hair above a pleasant face which was marred slightly by smallpox. Expressionlessly she sat down facing us, on a chair drawn from an adjacent table. She met our several stares as a sudden, animal pervasion filled the air. Who was she? The proprietor's daughter? His sister? Wife? The local prostitute, called on the telephone and hurried here by trisha?

The cool bar in the heat of the evening was possessed of a strange stillness. Prostitution, it is claimed, exploits women; but that is not wholly true, for the thing cut the other way. We were the victims of our own urges; looking at her we were each stirred.

The Third Engineer rose. We all stared at him; the powerful physique, the tangled hair bursting out of his open-necked shirt, his dark, flushed face. The girl looked up too, uncrossing her legs and standing to face him.

Voyage East

They exchanged glances, striking only in their total impassivity, and she turned and led him away.

The rest of us sighed, a noise of lust cheated, but also of relief. We avoided each other's eyes, picking up our beers. The man who had first half-seriously called for a woman coughed.

'What about another round?'

'While we wait ..!'

We thought of the bodies coupled in the adjacent room. The proprietor swabbed the bar, above us the punkah revolved and a gecko chased a late fly to its doom.

'Hey, five more San Migs; please...'

There was about the whole sordid little episode an effect rather akin to that which commonly accompanies the viewing of a cream cake. Once someone else has taken it, gluttony disappears and one basks in virtue, by default. The Third Engineer returned twenty minutes later. No-one asked him if the earth had moved.

With our derricks still topped but swung inboard we sailed from Penang the following noon. Embleton, one of our able-seamen, had gone missing and China Dick was furious. 'First bloody port ...' I heard him hiss to the Mate.

On deck the sailors tore down the shelters erected over the derrick controls (a futile act of demolition for they would be re-erected at Port Swettenham) and drove the accumulated debris of our brief stay in Penang out of odd corners with the wash-deck hose. Here and there slings of dunnage remained on deck. Pulo Penang, dark under its dense mantle of vegetation, fell astern and the smooth, calm surface of the Malacca Strait opened before us.

Lying between the Malay peninsula and the elongated Indonesian island of Sumatra the Strait was peppered with islands and dotted with fishing craft of every size, from small *praus* and *sampans*, to *lorchas* and junks. Often unlit at night, these craft would be a hazard and occasionally fell prey to Indonesian raiders, for this was the period of 'Confrontation' between

Malaysia and Soekarno's Indonesia, a phoney war which flared along the jungle borders of Borneo and among the conflicting interests of rival fishermen who met on the high seas. The Royal Navy were much in evidence; the old Battle-class destroyer *Corunna* had been at Penang and that morning we passed a flotilla of gunboats, led by the diminutive HMS *Ickford*.

Due at Port Swettenham at daylight the following day we ran down the Malay coast at reduced speed. As darkness closed in we were witness to another electric storm over Sumatra. Huge, thunder-headed cumulo-nimbus clouds rose over the jungle a hundred miles away. Starting from a cloud base of about 1,500 feet these developed vertically to 35,000 feet where their heads were torn to leeward by the jetstreams of the upper atmosphere, distorting their turbulent curling appearance to that of a great anvil. Although rising with a ponderously slow majesty, within the clouds unstable conditions produced rapid vertical movements, whirling water droplets suspended in the warm rising air into sudden contact with ice-crystals, super-cooling the water to temperatures as low as - 40 ° C, so freezing them instantly. Then, too heavy to be supported by the updraughts, huge hailstones drove groundwards with destructive force.

Not all the droplets froze, some split, producing a negative charge, although that of the individual drops remained positive. Despite this, the general charge within the cloud-base was negative, while its head became positive. Potential difference between cloud-base and peak, or between adjacent clouds, caused discharges of lightning, great flickering flashes that illuminated the cloud from within, throwing its heavier, whorling flanks into shadow and bursting brightly through its thinner sides. At the distance from which we observed this stunning show no thunder was heard, yet the titanic flaring was bright enough to cast shadows about the bridge and the Mate and I watched in silent wonder as it climaxed, died, then flared again in a display that lasted two or three hours.

Set behind islands of dense mangrove swamp, the approach to Port Swettenham from Penang was through the North Klang Strait, a narrow stretch of thick, green water that lay flat as sheet-lead. The view from the bridge was of a low, monotonous sea of foliage, here and there enlivened

Voyage East

by the brilliant flash of a parrot or the half-glimpsed, flying form of a monkey. Behind the swampy island barrier the river estuary, opened out into a lagoon where several ships lay anchored, awaiting berths at Deep Water Point; beyond, the river wound inland to the town itself. Even at eight in the morning the sun was high enough to cause a sizzling glare off the concrete of the new godowns. We slowed, sliding past *Glenogle,* anchored and waiting to load latex in bulk, and made fast astern of *Ascanius.* Ahead of her were a Norwegian ship and Jardine Matheson's *Eastern Moon.*

It fell my lot to spend the afternoon on deck. It was blisteringly hot, though periodic showers swept over us, prefaced by the Malay announcement of rain: '*Hujan! Hujan!*'

To close the hatches quickly and prevent the cargo from spoiling, huge canvas tents were hooked onto the derrick wires and guyed out with lashings to any suitable fastening point. In theory the water should have run off into the scuppers and over the side, but in practice the weight of a downpour soon formed heavy pockets of water in odd corners of the tents. Running up to the half-deck, I turned out the Midshipmen then called on the derrick gang. Reluctantly they appeared with buckets and we baled the tents while the rain stabbed down like stair-rods, soaking us instantly, but infinitely cool and exhilarating.

'Best use a six inch nail, Jimmy,' said one of our AB's, a thin, middle-aged man with a once handsome, dissipated face.

'Belay that Roberts ...'

'It'll only fill up again, Fourth.'

'Then we'll bale it out again.'

'Logical bastard.'

If we did not attend to the matter, when the rain stopped, the guys would be cast loose and water cascade below. Alternatively the tents might split under the load. Then, quite suddenly, the rain did stop, and as if mechanically controlled, the sun blazed down again. I was relieved at dinner time, for we were working six-hour deck watches, and went gratefully to the trough.

The new wharf was some distance from civilisation and I joined a party of officers sitting on deck drinking beer as darkness settled over the ship. Mike was there and the conversation had turned on the morality of prostitution, the Third Engineer's sexual indulgence having fired the subject.

'Any spots yet, Third?' one of the juniors asked pruriently.

'He squeezed and he squoze and a bubo arose,' intoned Mike and I realised he had been drinking before dinner.

'Look,' said the unashamed Third Engineer, 'when you've got to go, you've got to go . . .'

'Yes,' said Sparks, still the most ingenuous of the group, 'but what about the girl?'

'*What* about the girl?' They all looked at him.

'He's going to ask if she enjoyed it!'

'She ought to have done,' said the Third philosophically, 'she got fifty dollars!'

'Yes, but it's degrading ... I mean to have to sell your body...'

'She didn't *have* to sell it, Sparks. Not in Penang. Wait till you get to Bangkok ...' An expression of gleeful anticipation appeared simultaneously on the ring of sweating faces.

'Hey, you're not a cherry-boy, are you, Sparks?'

'A what?'

'A cock-virgin'

Sparks blushed and shot an appealing look at me. 'He's in love,' I put in, 'got a girl-friend . . .'

'Oh, well ...' They swallowed their beers direct from the can, replacing the empties from the case round which they sat, lonely men most of them, frustrated, drinking because there was little else to do.

'I don't think it wise, Sparky,' said Mike with careful solemnity, 'to take a moral stand. Just remember, a standing prick has no conscience.'

'You should bloody know,' mumbled someone.

'Now don't be jealous,' replied Mike.

'It's all right for you, you bugger, you've got your bread buttered on both sides.'

'You mean I'm married?' A dangerous gleam came into Mike's eye.

Voyage East

'Yes.' It was odd. Most of these men, discussing casual sex with such frankness, knew that what they most wanted was a stable relationship. But at home a new freedom was releasing girls from ideas of fidelity and this knowledge had undermined many relationships. Mike swallowed his beer slowly and we waited fascinated as he turned to his accusers in this kangaroo court of morality.

'Marriage,' Mike began, belching fatuously and waving a new can of lager so that it sloshed out, 'is legalised prostitution ... you pay for the woman ... keep her in clover, and in return, you have your hole.'

'Delightful expression.'

'It's true.'

'I'm not arguing.'

Sparks looked at me, an expression of despair on his face. I shrugged and lit a cigarette. 'Stick to your bird at home.'

'Too right.'

We were five days at Port Swettenham, seeing in the New Year there. Towards midnight we gathered in the smoke room then, by invitation of China Dick, made our way to the passengers' lounge. Mrs Saddler made a great fuss of us as her husband drank quietly by the bar with the older man who had first attracted notice by walking the deck during the Atlantic gale. Another married couple rather distantly observed our antics, he tall, rather distinguished looking and obviously an old Malay hand; she equally obviously a long-time resident of Singapore, but run to seed, colourless, thin lipped, wide haunched and exhausted.

The skirl of pipes came from a tape recorder over which the Mate stood proprietorially, his feet tapping and a rapt expression on his face. He winked at me once and then became lost in his own thoughts. I envied him his amazing self-possession. China Dick was holding court, moving among the slightly embarrassed groups, his short, barrel figure tight-buttoned in the high neck of his Number ten patrol jacket. Both he and the Chief Engineer wore the formal tropical rig. They needed only feather-plumed white pith helmets and swords to look like a pair of colonial governors, but they were affably pleasant, topping up drinks and making light asides designed to put us at our ease. It proved a pleasant contrast to Christmas.

Mike sat on the whistle handle at midnight while the Junior Midshipman, escorted to the forecastle by a posse of well-wishers, rang the traditional sixteen bell salute to the new year. Along the quay and off at the anchorage other ships were doing the same. One, a tiny, woodbine-funnelled antique vessel, the *Impala*, was whooping an ancient steam-whistle. The lounge party broke up after this. Down aft, in honour of our new year, the Chinese let off a sputter of fire-crackers and I saw Zee carrying three bottles of Johnnie Walker Scoth whisky aft with a broad grin on his face.

'Captin belong velly good, number one,' he slurred, his lambdacism too obvious for sobriety.

'Be careful on ladder. No drop bottles.'

'Ya, Ya, be careful.. Johnnie Walker velly good, number one first class.'

For us the evening ended with a darts-match in the seamen's mess-roorn. The Fourth Engineer from the *Ascanius* was narrowly beaten by the missing Embleton who had turned up that afternoon, put on a train by the agent in Penang.

'Like a bad bloody penny, you are,' growled the Bosun, a disappointed runner-up.

There was a brief flurry of activity when we sailed that afternoon. The tug heaving our stern off parted her tow-wire and there were fears that it had fouled our screw, but it pulled clear. We swung away, increasing speed as we entered the long, viscidly green corridor of the South Klang Strait. By the time the dinner-gong chimed through the ship we had crossed the Pintu Bar and were headed south-east. We ate breakfast the following morning anchored in Singapore's Western Roads.

At that time the combined trade of Penang and Singapore almost equalled that of the whole of Australia, for both were entrepôts. Singapore, even under the constraints of Confrontation, was a booming port, hence our wait for a berth. Both the Eastern and the Western Roads were full of shipping of every description.

In the wake of the agent's representative and his welcome bundle of mail we were invaded by a swarm of oddly assorted people eager to trade with

Voyage East

us. Elderly Chinese women in shapeless black *samfoo* pyjamas, their splayed feet bare upon our decks, their grey hair drawn back to reveal the alopecia of age and their rheumy eyes peering through steel-rimmed spectacles, whispered the cry of their trade as, with baskets on their arms, they shuffled along the alleyways.

'Sew-sew, sew-sew . . .'

They would undertake any task of sartorial repair for a few coins, darning with the finest of stitches even the most decayed article of clothing. Tall, turbaned and bearded Sikh fortune-tellers prowled the accommodation, dignified men who dealt with recondite matters far above the bodily, elbowed aside by eager Chinese tailors and the lithe Chinese laundryman who, certain of business, collected our soiled tropical whites. Another Chinese laid out his wares for us to see (from Pasternak's *Doctor Zhivago* to toothpaste) in a shady corner of the centre-castle, and a barber solicited trade. I submitted to the barber as he opened his briefcase and showed me his testimonials in the lid.

'This one from Chief Office of *City of Durban* . .'

Wong will cut your hair for $2.50 and make an excellent job, the Ellerman Line officer had written.

'This one from Captain of P&O ship *Salsette*.' Wong produced his ace card.

Wong cuts hair like I cut corners. On your own head be it.

'You savvy English, Mr Wong?'

'Oh, yes, sir. Wong number one barber Singapore-side.' With this *non sequitur* he produced his clippers, comb and razor.

Best loved among these visitors were the milk-girls. One among them was a tall, erotically figured Malay girl named Rose, who invariably wore tights and a low-cut tee-shirt. With a large basket of fresh milk and fruit squash supported on a jutting hip, she gathered men like moths round a candle. Crop-headed and hot from beneath Wong's cotton cape I bought a bottle of squash.

'Who the hell cut your hair?' asked the Mate as I made by way back to my cabin clasping my bottle of Fraser and Neave's orange.

'Someone with a sense of humour,' said Mike sardonically from his settee. I had the fleeting impression he was reading a letter.

The pilot came aboard as the dinner gong sounded. 'Why is it we always go on stand-by at chow time?' Mike asked, making for the bridge ladder; then he stopped and said, 'Bob's doing the evening on deck, you coming ashore?'

'Where are you going?'

'Drinking, where d'you think?'

'Should be great. Okay.'

Keppel Harbour was a long half-moon of quay, backed by godowns. Along this great crescent lay the ships of all nations: smart Dutch liners of the Royal Inter-Ocean Line, two Norwegians and a Swede of the Swedish East-Asia Line; one of A. P. Moller's Maersk Line with her bright blue hull and Danish ensign; three Panamanians, a French vessel of Messageries Maritime, an American ship and the high white hull of P & O's *Chitral*. There were two of the same company's drab cargo-liners; one was the *Salsette*, and I wondered if she were still commanded by the master who wrote Wong's testimonial. From Madras had come the ancient and creaking hull of British India's *Rajula*, one of the oldest ships then flying the red duster, and astern of her a Jardine Matheson ship, *Eastern Glory*, flying the old *taipan's* house flag of a St Andrew's cross. Further down lay the *Anshun* of John Swire's China Navigation Company, an old rival of Jardine's, and two of Ben Line's ships, our chief and sharpest competitors in the trade.

In addition, there were our own Company's ships, Bluies and Glens, inward and outward bound, held briefly at this focus of international trade, loading, discharging and trans-shipping cargoes. Some came from beyond the Java Sea, loaded with the produce of Indonesia, their crews half-native from three months on that coast; the austere *Glens* on the main-line run to Japan, the *Cyclops* on the Borneo and Philippines service; the *Ascanius* bound for Japan and the United States, ourselves ...

And all these vessels formed only the arterial traffic. In the roads at lighters, or tucked away in Empire Dock, the smaller 'feeder' ships came in from the Natuna Islands, or from Kuching or Labuan, Songkhla or Ko Phukit with their coconuts and copra, their rubber, tin and timber to feed

Voyage East

the holds of ships like ourselves. In all, perhaps two hundred vessels, and the number constantly varying as arrivals and departures took place against the sun bleached back-ground of the Lion City, a city that had grown from the foresight of a single Englishman and now teemed with the industrious Chinese who formed the majority of its population.

We berthed ahead of *Cyclops*; beyond us lay the grey hull of Isbrandtsen's *Flying Architect,* the Stars and Stripes over her stern. Her crew had been painting her hull and two negroes were knocking off, climbing up from the staging rigged under her ensign. They had been picking out the lettering of her name and left the task unfinished for the morning.

As arranged Mike and I went ashore after dinner. We were joined by Sparks, who had attached himself to us for motives of his own which included, I suspected, a mixture of reticence and prurient curiosity. Mike, the rake-hell and rollicking sailor, rather fascinated him and he had marked me down as a confidant. It was hard to shake off such a trust so we accepted him with a good grace.

We taxi-danced at the Straits Cabaret and Toby's Paradise Bar, sailors' haunts off Anson Road and within staggering distance of the dock gate. Mike's mood was brittle, a feigned exuberance overlying the ambiguous emotions left by Mrs Saddler who had disembarked that afternoon. There was too, the matter of that letter.

'He's no innocent,' said Mike, watching Sparks dance with a Chinese girl.

'I told you, he's got a steady girl at home. I think they're engaged.'

'Why the hell did he come to sea, then?'

'Romance . . .'

'Bullshit. You should know better than that.'

'Don't be so cynical. We all have to unlearn the lessons of our education.'

'Disillusion instead of a degree, eh?'

'Something like that. More beer?'

'Why not . . .'

We ended the night at Bugis Street, an area of open-air eating places. It was long past midnight and the clientele were almost all drunk. A few sober people had emerged from the popular midnight movies, but most were seamen from the merchant ships, matelots from the naval base at Sembawang, airmen from RAF Changi or squaddies from the garrison who still maintained a supporting role for the government of Lee Kwan Yu in his Confrontation with General Soekarno. Blue Funnel officers patronised the tables run by a short sighted, thickly bespectacled Chinese known to us (without malice) as 'Four-Eyes'. We made quite a party; next to us were two old shipmates of mine from *Cyclops* and one of Mike's then on the *Ascanius*. They had a drunken Norwegian in tow.

'You from Blue Funnel ship, Ya?'

'Yes . . .'

'My name Per, I come from Trondheim. I too work on ship with blue and black funnel. We say "Black and blue, nothing to eat and plenty to do", hey? Ha, ha!'

'What ship?'

'*Talisman*.'

'Ah Willie Wilhelmsen, eh?'

'Ya, Bastard Wilhelmsen, no focking good. British ship good, eh?'

'No ship good, Per,' said Mike. 'All ship's focking bad, okay?'

'Okay, *Skol*...'

'*Skol* . . .'

This conversation was shouted above the general din as we fought off a succession of ploys to separate us from our money. Toy-sellers, taxi-touts, shoe-shine boys and watch-vendors (from whom a superb looking 'Swiss' watch could be obtained for 12/6, [62½p]) pleaded their respective causes. Flower sellers and Indian palmists importuned us and we were plagued by small Chinese boys who, for loose change, would thrash us at noughts and crosses.

We ate ... God knew what we ate, but we told Sparks it was steak and we were past caring. So was he, for he could hardly take his eyes off the silk-clad visions who wandered among the tables soliciting outrageously. Their faces were painted, their breasts jutted provocatively and their long legs flashed through the slits in their cheongsams. I knew Sparks was drunk enough to succumb.

'D'you fancy them?' Mike asked, halting one of them beside our table. 'Hi, honey. D'you fancy a cherry boy?' Mike indicated Sparks, who in the glare of the electric lights was flushing violently. The whore rubbed her hip against his bare arm.

'Hey, cherry-boy? Really? You real cherry-boy?'

Her voice was husky, but the face, though heavily made up, had an odd, youthful innocence, the dark almond eyes and a wide, well formed mouth smiled intimately. Her pink tongue flickered over the gloss of lipstick.

'What's your name, honey?' Mike asked.

'Lola, sailor boy ... Lola!' She flourished the last syllable and turned back to Sparks. 'You want a good time, Cherry-boy? Lola show you *the best* . . .'

'Oh, you'll get the best, Sparky, the very best number one dose of clap.'

'No' Lola swung round. 'Lola clean girl . . .' She had never ceased to undulate her body sinuously against Sparks, whose senses were reeling irresistibly. Mike's joke had gone far enough.

'Okay, Mike, let it go at that.' I had expected some sort of argument, but Mike acquiesced with a shrug. 'Go on Lola, no business tonight ... hey, Four-Eyes, tell Lola to go away . . .'

Four-Eyes rushed up solicitously and shooed Lola away. She protested, screaming imprecations at us. Sparks's face displayed a chain of conflicting emotions: regret, relief, embarrassment; but no one at the other tables took any notice and Mike had sunk into a sudden introspective mood.

'You had a lucky escape there,' I said lighting a cigarette.

'She was *very* . . .' he searched for a word.

'Erotic.'

'Yes, erotic.'

'You're right about that, but it would have made you feel a bloody fool if you'd gone off with her.'

'Why?'

'She was a "he", not a "she"; a *kitai,* a sexual ambivert, a transvestite, a hermaphrodite. At best a woman locked in a man's body, at worst a raging queer ... sorry.'

The colour that had so quickly mounted up to Spark's face, as swiftly drained away.

'It's all right,' I went on, 'we all make the same mistake, you'll find a lot of that sort of thing. Unfortunately they don't prepare you for it at school.'

'Jesus Christ, I think I'm going to be sick . .

'Oh, for God's sake, no!' Mike stirred into life. 'Don't spew. Come on, let's go.'

We arrived at the foot of the gangway at the same time as Embleton. The seaman wore working clothes and carried a pot of black paint which he tried to conceal from us, but we were not interested in him, only anxious to get Sparks aboard and into his bunk.

I was on deck again at dawn. Shaking the fumes of debauch from my head I recalled Embleton and his paint-pot. Its purpose slowly dawned on me as I stared ahead at the stern of the American ship. There I saw he had completed the work left unfinished by her own negro seamen. The Isbrantsen freighter now bore the name *Flying Arsehole*.

'Oh, shit...'

I took myself aft, as though some guilt attached to my person, leaning on the rail and trying to gather my fuddled wits. From across the narrow waters of the harbour which had been named after Sir Henry Keppel, the naval officer most responsible for clearing these waters of pirates a century earlier, came the scent of vegetation. Oleander? Flame-of-the-forest, hibiscus or frangipani? The green island beyond the narrow strip of water kept its secret, but I was reminded of the note Columbus made when he first smelt the forests of the Indies: 'Oh, the smell of the mornings.'

Voyage East

The City of Angels

There were other nights ashore, for we remained four days at Singapore. They were mere candle-burning forays into the darker side of life, purchased at the expense of sleep, antidotes to our peculiar existence. Most of us remained faithful to whatever we believed in.

'Listen,' I overheard the Purser say to Sparks on the morning after his brush with the *kitai*, 'forget it, you're suffering from alcoholic remorse ... look, if you were at University you'd be *expected* to be shacked up with a sociology student.' To the sober, self-contained and discursive Purser, sex and students of sociology were one and the same thing. 'Just forget it.'

But *Antigone* had not brought us here for such philandering, however amateur. We were here to work, and work we did, from 0700 to 2300 daily, the mates relinquishing the deck at midnight to the Senior Midshipman. The other apprentices assisted with the cargo work, sitting for hours in the 'tween decks, ensuring the cargo was not broached. 'Cargo-watching' was the ultimate in boredom, a thankless task in the dreariest of surroundings; this was not what Conrad or Stevenson had promised, sitting glaze-eyed, guarding a stow of pilferable goodies. For us of more senior rank it was an endless patrol of the deck, a climbing down and climbing up of hatch ladders, of wrangles and disputes over damage and dunnage with gang-leaders and foremen, of searches for lost bits and pieces, the location of over-stowed items buried thanks to Liverpool's slovenliness. All these varied chores made up our work, a sweaty, exhausting contrast to our lordly hours on the bridge. For those four days we took bites out of the 'general' with which our 'tween-decks and holds were filled, landing cartons and boxes, cases and crates, drums of cables and drums of chemicals, bags and bales, cars, lorries, personal effects, spirits, beers, foodstuffs and odd pieces of machinery. We loaded little. A small consignment of silvery tin ingots for Kobe, assiduously tallied in and stowed no more than five tiers high lest their weight prove too much for even *Antigone's* massive scantlings. There were a few more odds and ends of coasting cargo for Bangkok and Hong Kong.

On the second afternoon of our discharge I was accosted by a short, bristling *roinek* in the khaki of the British Army. On his bare, thick-set and tattooed arm he wore the heavy leather wrist-band and Royal arms of a warrant officer. He regarded my stinking, sweatstained K.D.'s with professional disapproval.

'Duty *officer?*' he asked, his nose wrinkling.

'Yes. You've come for the trucks?'

'Three-tonners' he corrected punctiliously. 'Yes.'

'They're in Number Two. This way...' I led him forward, along the centre-castle.

The Mate, in whites, was already there, leaning on the rail and talking quietly to the senior tally-clerk, an elderly Chinese with a sunken chest beneath his cotton shirt and a distinguished, professorial air. He had a habit of ubiquity, the Mate; one rarely found he was not at the point where, at any given moment, the most exacting critic would have said he should be.

'Ah, the Army's here.' He held out his hand.

We had 'married' the wire runners from all four well-guyed derricks at Number Two hatch in a double-union purchase known as 'Frisco-rig. There was much shouting and hand-waving from the foreman. Above us the winch controller jerked his levers and the winch-drums revolved and stopped, revolved again and took up the strain. In the contactor house, against which we leaned and which controlled the circuitry to the derrick winches, the breakers tripped in and out with a furious clicking. The wires drew tight and the derrick heads quivered as the guys took up the load. The first olive-drab monster rose slowly, then up and over the side where a corporal and a pair of squaddies awaited it.

'There's still plenty going on, then?' asked the Mate as the empty slings came back aboard for the second three-ton truck.

'Oh yes,' replied the soldier. 'The Navy have most of the fun, but our boys are at it in Borneo. On the Kalimantan borders there's plenty going on ...' He deliberately echoed the Mate's euphemism and fished in a breast pocket that strained above his barrel chest. He drew out a wallet and extracted a black and white photograph. It showed two decapitated heads,

Voyage East

their mouths filled with their own genitalia.

'Jesus Christ!' The Mate turned away.

'Don't you believe it when they say the Dyaks have given up headhunting,' he said, amused at our lily-livered disgust.

'See this gentleman gets his trucks,' said the Mate, turning away.

'Oh, there's plenty going on, all right,' said the *rooinek*, tucking the picture away as if it showed his family, quite unabashed by the Mate's contempt. He leaned over the hatch, one glossy boot on the rail. 'Plenty.'

The Mate returned to his interminable paper-work. Chief Officers of cargo-liners rarely went ashore and, while the junior officers and seamen were on the tiles, while the Old Man played golf and the Chief Engineer went shopping for his apparently rapacious wife, the Mate sat worrying at his desk. *Antigone's* Mate was a dedicated man and upon his shoulders fell much of the burden of the ship. For himself it was the heavy price he paid for his impossibly romantic love of the sea-life, the satisfaction of a job well done. But it was a price that might bankrupt the soul.

In the engine-room things were no better than on deck. The Chief had kept his threat: the engineers were 'doing a unit.' This meant a complete overhaul of one cylinder of our main engine. It was hot and heavy work, carried out under the active direction of Willie Buchan, our Second Engineer. A Glaswegian Scot of apparently flabbily obese proportions, Willie Buchan possessed a strength that reminded one of a Japanese *sumo* wrestler. Beneath the pale acres of rolling fat lurked a muscular power of awesome proportions that came into its own when such a job was in hand. Sweat poured from Willie and his team as they toiled in 'the pit', their own name for the engine-room, and he would brook no interruption to his task once it was under way. Intermittently the Chief would pace the upper gratings and stare down as the chain blocks rattled and the head was lifted from Number 5 piston. Piston rings were replaced and the cylinder liner calibrated for wear, the bottom end of the connecting rod was opened up and the shell-bearings checked and renewed if necessary. Given the size of such a 'unit', great skill was required and the work was arduous, all the engineering staff taking part, with the exception of a junior reserved for over-night watch-keeping and responsible for running our auxiliary generators. Whilst engaged upon such a task the engineers ate in a messroom, not the saloon, still in their sweat-soaked boiler suits and ready to turn-to when the indefatigable Willie commanded. After dinner in the evening, however, their day's labour at an end, their thirsts were prodigious and they resumed work next morning with the aching heads of the damned.

It was at this point that the Mate decided to give our hitherto reluctant motor lifeboat a chance to prove itself. He announced his desire to lower it into the water of Keppel harbour at breakfast one morning, sparking off a row that first ignited Willie Buchan, eager and ready for another day's toil amid his machinery.

'But we've had the thing running in the davits ...' he protested, an I've more important work tae do down below.'

'There's nothing more important than the boats, Willie,' said the mate reasonably, his elbow across the back of his chair, his body turned to address his colleague at the next table. The rest of us waited, all conversation suspended in anticipation of collision between deck and engine-room, oil and water. 'You can only run the thing for a wee minute in the devits . . .'

'Aye,' countered Willie sharply, 'but it's the starting that was wrong. It's okay now ...'

'No, we'll put the boat down this morning, give it a good run.'

'But I've plenty o' work for my lads to do . . .'

'We only need one of them, Willie, away now...'

'I'll see the Chief then .. .'

At that moment China Dick waddled into the saloon. His Tiger stood by his chair and tucked him in to the table. He cracked open his linen napkin and stared round the saloon, sensing something ominous in the unusual silence and the exaggerated attentiveness of the stewards as they padded round, apparently oblivious to the disagreement between *Antigone's* great men, but in fact eager not to disturb the progress of the burgeoning row.

'Well Mister,' China Dick said as the Mate turned and bid him good morning, 'little problem, is it?'

'No problem, sir,' said the Mate smoothly, 'I've just asked Willie to lend us an engineer for an hour this morning. Want to lower the motor-boat and give her a good test.'

'Good idea, Mister,' approved China Dick, looking up from the papaya the steward set before him. 'I'm certain the Second'll have no objection to that, eh, Mr Buchan?'

'None whatsoever, surr,' replied Willie venomously as he bent his head over his wheat-cakes. His staff mumbled an unenthusiastic greeting to the Chief Engineer who, too late to rescue his beleaguered department, wanted the Old Man to accompany him on a shopping expedition. Mike volunteered to take the boat away. Again, there seemed in his eagerness that febrile quality that stemmed from his parting from Mrs Saddler.

The muted disagreement at the breakfast-table was a prelude to the main action of the morning. As the motor-boat splashed into the harbour Billy, the Fourth Engineer, bent over the starting handle. The lowering party and others, with nothing better to do, leant over the rail high above. Billy had one hand on the handle, the other on the decompression lever. Suddenly he flicked the handle over. The engine kicked inertly back. Wrapping a rag round the handle, Billy repeated the procedure; again the engine refused to fire.

Unwisely Mike, sitting aft with his hand expectantly on the tiller, made some comment. Flushed and sweating in the heat Billy turned.

'It worked all right in the davits,' we heard him gasp angrily.

'It's supposed to work in the water,' goaded Mike. 'You're *supposed* to have fixed it.'

'I *have* fixed it,' snarled the exasperated Billy, trying again with venomous energy. This no more prompted the engine to oblige than did the stream of advice now descending on his head from the Chief Engineer at the promenade-deck rail. Manfully Billy bent to his task again, fuelled by a sense of injustice and a blinding hangover, working himself into an apoplexy as a huge blister rose on his palm.

'Oh fuck it!'

He collapsed, staring at the engine; the whole boat's crew sat as though stupefied. From above, we all stared down too and even the Chief Engineer was reduced to silence. The boat's skids ground gently at *Antigone's* plating; it was a moment of intense anti-climax.

'You'd better take out the injectors and ...' Mike began.

Billy spun on Mike who still sat coolly on the after gunwale.'What the fucking hell d'you know about bloody diesel engines? Eh?'

'About as much as you do, by the look of it.'

Billy rose, the starting handle in his fist, his face suffused with anger and exhaustion. He took half a step aft as we all watched, fascinated. With resourceful insolence Mike drew the heavy wooden tiller from the rudder stock, beating it lightly into the palm of his left hand. Billy seemed to hesitate, though afterwards he said he lost his footing on the bottom boards and was going 'to beat shit' out of Mike. The hiatus was only momentary, and was ended by a bellow from the boat-deck where, at the forward end, China Dick stared grandly down at the little drama.

'Hook that boat on, Mister, and hoist it up at once!'

The boat was returned to its chocks and the Chief himself joined Billy for an hour. During the afternoon it was lowered again and started first time. Mike adopted an air of triumph when it was learned that a change of injectors had cured the problem.

Later I bore the brunt of Billy's hatred for the deck department. He was understandably upset, almost weeping with rage in the intensity of his emotion. 'Look,' he said, with a pleading desperation, 'I told the Chief the boat needed new injectors the last time it played us up.'

'Don't worry about it Billy,' I consoled; it was not my problem and I could be detached.

'You don't believe me, do you? You bastards are all the same.' By which I knew he referred to deck officers.

'Yes, of course I believe you. Why shouldn't I'

'No you fucking don't...'

And we left it there, for there was no point in pursuing it. We had split into the ancient, antipathetic factions of oil and water which, as every seaman knew, never mixed. The thing would fade away in time, meanwhile it rumbled on over cans of beer drunk in our separate ghettos.

As the period of our stay at Singapore drew to its end the Mate's anxiety began to get through to us, for it was essential that we did not over-carry

Voyage East

cargo, that every item consigned for Singapore was discharged there. Each compartment, from strongroom to holds the size of a parish church, had to be thoroughly searched before departure, neglect might lose us customers and bring the opprobrium of Head-Office upon our heads. The indifferent quality of the Liverpool stow made thoroughness very difficult, though Bob and I, in the company of the Midshipmen, clambered about the nooks and crannies of holds and 'tween-decks, our torches focusing on the marks of discharge and, where these could not be seen, turning over heavy boxes, or dragging cases aside to check. We discovered the hidey-holes of British dockers, little gambling and drinking dens set up behind false stows of cartons where broached whisky from 'accidentally' dropped cases ended up. Usually such jerry-built dens collapsed soon after our departure from the Mersey. As we left each successive discharging port the mass of debris, of broken cases and shredded cartons, of spillages from torn sacks, of broken dunnage, cargo mats, shattered lavatory pans or broken bottles increased, a scene of wasteful chaos that was given the occasional delightful spicing of a turd, or the dark dried stain of urine.

Rain deluged our departure. Banks of cloud rolled across the Singapore Strait from the Rhio Archipelago on the far side. As the clouds covered the sky the world darkened. The high, equatorial sun was eclipsed and water fell in large drops, not the sleeting, wind-driven, stinging rain of temperate latitudes, but the overwhelming, vertically-falling downpour of the tropics. The boat-deck awnings sagged under it, the water-ways ran like streams and the gurgling scuppers could not carry it over the side fast enough, so that shallow ponds rushed across the deck as we began an easy roll. Lightning flashed and rumbles of thunder came from high above. Occasionally there was a sizzling crack and the retina received a fleeting impression of jagged brilliance arcing from sky to sea.

On the bridge we peered into the deluge, looking vainly for the stream of ships dotting the radar screen. Out of the sodden air a large fruit bat flapped across our bow, nearly a yard from wing-tip to wing-tip. And then we ran out from under the cloud and the ship was suddenly steaming in the heat as the sun blazed down upon us again. A dark pall rose astern, a great cumulo-nimbus boiling upwards into an anvil-head high above. Abruptly the heavy traffic of the Strait revealed itself and China Dick handed the ship over to the Second Mate. I lingered to watch another elderly Battle-class destroyer cut suavely across our bow, H M S *Barrosa* heading for the Johore Strait and the Royal Navy's base at Sembawang.

We swung north from the lonely rock lighthouse on the Horsburgh Reef, turning up the Malay coast and into the South China Sea, passing over the wrecks of the *Prince of Wales* and the *Repulse*. The rain clouds remained over Malaya and we ran into a north-easterly gale which brought with it misty conditions and a sudden chill. For two hours one morning I watched a beautiful falcon, blown offshore and confused, flailing about the ship. The gale affected us too, for we missed the tide over the Bangkok bar and after a passage of three days anchored at Ko Sichang.

The following morning we embarked the pilot, weighed and passed the bar, entering the Maenam Chao Phraya and threading our way between dense mangrove trees and lush and variegated jungle. Creeks winding into the interior lined with *atap* huts roofed with the nipah palm leaf, left fleeting impressions of the amphibious people who fish and trade on the Maenam. For them the river was highway and food-source. Curious narrow launches, propelled by outboard motors consisting of long impellor shafts, zipped beneath the overhanging fronds of the trees along the margins of the river. Passengers sat in sedate tandem, so narrow were these craft, beautiful young women in sarongs and blouses on their way to the markets and shops of Bangkok. Heavier lighters churning the muddy water astern of chugging tugs brought teak and minerals to the deep-water merchantmen loading further upriver, and fishing *sampans* bobbed indifferently as our wake tossed them, their occupants busy with the ceaseless business of the hunt, casting their nets for the ugly inhabitants of this thick, eutrophic stream.

At Samut Prakan we passed the Thai Navy at its moorings, diminutive antique-looking warships shaped for river and coastal work with the appearance of shrunken iron-clads of a pre-Dreadnought era. Four hours after passing the bar we dropped anchor and swung alongside, veering our cable to check our otherwise headlong progress against the wharf at Klongtoi, a few miles below the city centre. Within minutes we were

Voyage East

swarming with Thai coolies, small, handsome men whose muscular backs bore the intricate blue tattoos of Buddhist prayers. Barges and junks crowded alongside us and our derricks were winged out, butterfly-fashion, to discharge overside onto quay or lighter. Klongtoi was a small wharf, compared to the long frontage of Singapore; village life went on around us and just beyond the godowns of the wharf the omnipresent jungle crowded in on us as it did beyond the anchorage in the river. We shared the place with two of A. P. Møller's blue-hulled Maersk ships and a Norwegian of the Hoegh Line.

'Don't go near the Mosquito Bar,' I heard the Mate order one of the Midshipmen, 'not with those bloody Scandahooligans in port.'

'No sir,' I heard the Midshipman reply with patent insincerity.

'Well, don't say I didn't warn you …' I heard the Mate sigh despairingly, the moral welfare of his charges beyond his control.

We discharged throughout the night. Hot, windless and oppressive, one felt the teeming jungle was almost palpable in its influence, stirring the darker passions of men. Sleep was in vain, for the night was alive, not merely with the clicking and clatter of winches and the blue fires sparking in the contactor houses, the shadowed slings of cargo jerking over the side to the accompaniment of shouts and commands, the electric glare of the lights and the violent shadows they threw, nor the stinging bites of mosquitoes; all these would have been bad enough without the fact that at Klongoi there was another distraction.

Swarming up mooring ropes hung over the quarters, nimble as monkeys they rose out of their boats to gather on the poop, incongruously dressed in party frocks or sarongs, their high-heeled shoes between their teeth, in a parody of piracy. They were young, pretty and compliant, and they vanished into the Chinese quarters amid excited chatter as the grinning greasers and firemen bore them off after a brief haggling.

'Jesus Christ!'

The Junior Midshipman stood open-mouthed at the sight.

'Get yourself down Number Two hatch, son, if you don't want a dose to take home to your mother.'

The Mate prowled, chivvying the Third Mate and his watch, shaking his head at the irresponsible folly of mankind while screeches and giggles came out of the seamen's accommodation as the tide of harlotry rolled forward. I met him coming up the ladder from the centre-castle.

'Not you too?'

'No sir, I can't sleep. Besides, there's not much point.' I looked at my watch. 'I'm on deck at midnight.'

He grunted. 'We should start loading during the night.'

We discussed the cargo already alongside, an excuse for lingering with prurient curiosity, looking aft from the shadows of the boat-deck and affecting to ignore the calls from the boats that were still approaching the ship from the darkness of the river.

'How the hell do they do it?' He stared at a boat-load of women who made suggestive gestures, rubbing their breasts and jerking their fingers in explicit motions. 'Needs must when the devil drives,' he answered his own question. 'You know, I recall hearing of a ship where the Old Man refused to let 'em aboard. The coolies walked off and wouldna work the cargo ... some sort of a Mafia I suppose.'

'Life's pretty cheap .. .'

'Aye, but what about *them.*' He nodded indignantly at the seamen's house below us, immediately abaft Number Four hatch. 'Half of them are married.'

'They'll take the usual precautions.'

The Mate snorted. 'A condom and the application of an anti-V.D. kit? Don't be bloody daft, Laddie. Most of them won't know which way is up in a couple of hours.'

We were riveted in fascinated disgust. Both of us stood looking down on the ship, stirred by similar compulsions to our shipmates', restrained by fear and our sobriety. Our self-righteousness brought little comfort. Indeed, I felt the Mate to be disturbed with real pain.

'Don't forget you've a girl . . .' he left the sentence unfinished.

It was a long night. The heat, my own desire and tiredness combined to produce a savage mood.

'What's the Mosquito Bar, sir?' asked the young Midshipman as I inspected the floor of dunnage being prepared in Number Two

Voyage East

'tween-deck for the reception of our first parcel of homeward cargo.

'You'll find out,' I snapped unkindly.

I caught Mike creeping along the boat-deck, his fist holding the brown arm of a girl with almond eyes which seemed to my fevered brain to glow in the night.

'Oh, for God's sake Mike, you're a glutton for punishment aren't you?'

He winked mischievously and jerked his head for me to follow. Inside the alleyway he lifted the latch on Sparks's cabin and gently pushed the girl inside, closing the door behind her.

'Sailor's dream,' he whispered.

'That's a bloody awful thing to do.'

'You are a fucking prude. Have a beer.' He put an iced can of lager in my hand and I sucked gratefully at the thing. I lit a cigarette and Mike consulted his watch. 'Five minutes and he hasn't chucked her out.'

'Perhaps he's still asleep.'

'That wee lassie would wake a corpse.'

'How old was she?'

'About sixteen.'

'Good God!'

'Terrible isn't it?' But it was only amusement that danced in Mike's eyes.

Towards dawn the ship slept, satiated; except, that is, for the watch and the working of cargo. We began to load; heavy billets of teak into Number Two, bound for London and Rotterdam. The scent of the wood's oil permeated the 'tween-deck, slowly overcoming the less savoury smells accumulated there. Dawn found us hot-eyed, stinking of sweat, watching the blowzy exodus from the accommodation that revealed the extent of the night's dissipation. The exhausted Midshipman stared again, his tired eyes forced open by the spectacle.

'*Post coitus omnes triste est.*'

He stared at me stupidly. 'What?'

'What *sir*,' I said. 'My Latin may be poor, but that's no excuse to forget these formalities. Would you like to turf all those ladies out of the sailors' cabins?'

He stared again, uncertain whether I was joking. The Bosun saved him the trouble. We could hear his voice haranging the crowd.

'Come on you buggers, turn-to, now ... Roberts you dirty bastard, what would your missus say if she could see you doing that? Get out!' He shoo-ed the last of the girls onto the deck where they stood scratching in the dawn.

'Come on,' I said to the Midshipman, 'let's find our reliefs.'

I was in the bathroom naked before I realised the occupant of the other shower was female. We blinked at each other. She was covered in soap, white whorls rubbed around her lithe golden body and under her arm-pits and breasts in a primitive and erotic decoration. Black hair was coiled above her head and she was luxuriating under the cascade of water. I recognised her as the girl foisted upon Sparks. I stepped into the adjacent shower and ignored Sparks's indignation when he came to see if his bedfellow was all right. It occurred to me, as I lay on my bunk, that I might visit the Mosquito Bar when night fell again.

Less than a hundred yards from the Klongtoi wharf, the Mosquito Bar was set above a row of shops, reached by a low verandah from the dusty street, a long hall of a place, dimly lit and raucous with the pop music that united a generation across most of the world. In and out of the pools of light flitted the slinky forms of the whores, slender figures with extravagant breasts sheathed in the shimmering cheap imitation silk of cheongsams, drenched in perfume, erotic, pervasive and shamelessly salacious. They minced on preposterously high heels which lecherously distorted their legs, setting their hips wiggling lasciviously as they moved to and fro in an irregular arousing promenade.

We sat at tables, laagered for defence, ship by ship, abandoning our restraint as the rounds of iced beer slithered down our eager throats. Sparks had come with us and was very quiet. No one mentioned the events of the previous night; even Mike held his peace. The brave among us danced, the watchers taking bets as to the true sex of our partners, for here too the sexual ambiverts gathered to prey upon the frustrated, and we fought off the combined assault of two 'girls' who showed an interest in the Junior

Voyage East

Midshipman. The continuous accosting, the shameless eroticism, the repetitious spectacle of sinuous and writhing bodies eventually dulled the nerve-ends with its fatuity. A rising tide of noise and aggravation further down the hall signalled trouble and Mike ordered our departure. We stumbled out into the cool of the night.

'That,' I remarked to the Junior Midshipman, 'was the Mosquito Bar. Not somewhere you would wish to find your sister.'

'Save yourself for Japan,' said Mike, negotiating a tamarind tree with some difficulty. From behind us came the sound of breaking glass and a cheer which seemed to slide into a glissando of shouts and screams.

'What's that?' asked the Midshipman.

'The Vikings,' said Mike, 'intent on rape and pillage.'

'Rape and pox, more likely.'

Both the Midshipman and I were exhausted at dawn, for we had returned to the deck at midnight. It proved an unpleasant watch with trouble among the seamen, Embleton getting roaring drunk and picking a fight with Wakelin which had to be broken up in a storm of abuse before a wide-eyed and half-naked audience of whores. As the sun rose, setting fire to the mangroves across the river, the cicadas started their chirruping, a noise that subsided into the back of consciousness so that in recollection it seemed made by the sunlight itself.

The boy was stupefied with yawning. 'Go on, buzz off to bed.' He nodded, yawning still, his mouth in a rictus of exhaustion. 'By the way, the Purser has organised a trip round the temples this afternoon. You'd better go; you'll have nothing to tell your parents if you don't. I doubt you'll be writing home about the Mossie Bar.'

'No ... yes, I'll go.'

We went, a party of us in two taxis, awkward as tourists, ashamed of our lack of culture and largely ignorant of Buddhist rites. At Wat Traimit, the temple of the Golden Buddha, we stared in awe at the five and a half tons of solid gold fashioned into the lotus image of the Buddha. Souvenir stalls marred the sanctity of the holy place, though devout Thai monks moved about the impassive face of the benign image among the whorls of joss-smoke that rose lazily fragrant in the still air. At Wat Pho a massive bronze image reclined, covered in gold-leaf and threatening to burst from the confines of its pavilion, like some Oriental Gulliver. The Buddha was surrounded by other statues and images; one wearing a top-hat was pointed out to us, without provenance, as that of Marco Polo. Coming out of the gloom of the Wat Pho into brilliant sunshine, we passed the tall phallus of a stone lingam.

'Bloody appropriate,' muttered the Purser drily.

Most impressive was the shrine of the Emerald Buddha, set within the precincts of the Royal Palace. Under a sky of oppressive cobalt, the air stirred by a slight breeze, we approached the temple to the faint, insistent tinkling of tiny wind bells set beneath the steeply angled green-painted eaves. Red tiled roofs sloped down in the direction of the four winds of heaven from a central spire of white and gold, their peaks terminating in scimitar finials. The gable-ends were studded with coloured glass and mother-of-pearl, aflame in the fierce sunshine. Huge tusked and glaring devils guarded the approach with sabres, their armour and face-masks white and blue and gold.

After this dazzlement the interior was suddenly dark, the air heavy with the scent of joss-smoke. As our eyes adjusted we became aware of the barefoot padding of silent monks in the saffron robes of the novice; devout Thai youths serving a brief monastic apprenticeship with the begging bowl. The thick coils of incense led one's eyes upwards to the glowing murals depicting scenes from the Buddha's life until, with the burst of revelation, one saw the Emerald Buddha, a serene jade figure at the summit of a great dais. From this cascaded a torrent of silk upon which lay the golden bowls and flowers and smoking joss sticks of the devout. The Buddha was dressed ritually by King Bhuimpol and sat smiling impassively over our infidel heads.

We returned to the ship through the teeming suburb of Dhonburi, shopping at the stalls that crammed the crowded streets, buying mangoes and a stinking durian which tasted of nectar to slake our thirsts. After the subduing influence of the temples, the strident tumult of the streets was almost welcome.

Our ignorance of Buddhism came up in conversation when we returned to the ship. 'Have you read *Sidharttha*, by Herman Hesse?' asked the Mate. I shook my head. 'You should.'

'You've seen the temples, then?'

'Not since I was your age.'

I asked the Junior Midshipman whether he had enjoyed his afternoon. 'Yes, very much. It's certainly something to write home about.'

'Yes.' We watched the first whore of the night swarm over the poop rail.

Captain Richards distanced himself from the crew's lechery. He had little concern, disorderly though it was, provided it did not interfere with the ship's routine. Indeed he had been dissuaded from any form of moral guardianship by the agent, who had confirmed the Mate's story of a British ship-master who had turned his firehoses on the *sampans* as they gathered under his ship's stern. As a consequence the labourers had walked off his ship, refusing to work cargo. The story made some sense of the indifference of the gangs to the presence of their women amongst us. A system run on *'cumshaw'* and kick-backs was probable, though unproven. All manner of oriental business was conducted on such lines, condoned by usage and common practice.

'Oh, the Old Man gets his *baksheesh*,' affirmed the Purser cynically when we were discussing the matter, 'don't you worry about that.'

I never did discover the truth, but had long ago learned that only the naive gave anyone the benefit of the doubt where money was concerned.

We left the wharf at Klongtoi the next afternoon. Along the mudflats small patches of earth and mould adhered to the rotting stumps of nipa palms. Small *sampans* retreated up the creeks that receded into the green-brown lushness of the interior - fronded tunnels which turned purple in the fading light. Women could be seen cooking on the verandahs of huts, children playing among small dogs and here and there the saffron robes of an indigent monk begging amongst them.

The sun set as we reached Samut Prakan, touching the great white *dagoba* with gold. The reliquary stood like a huge, inverted pudding basin from which a tall, tapering series of spirals towered into the sky, rising to a golden needle-point. It caught the departing daylight after the jungle had fallen dark. A few kites wheeled against the sky then, giving up the hunt, glided down to roost, while the clicking chirrup of the cicadas died away.

'Farewell to the city of angels,' said the Mate, staring astern as if in search of some lost illusion.

The river held its jade glow for a little longer as our trembling hull cut through its stillness, then turned the colour of steel and, at last, fell back to the open sea beyond the bar.

Voyage East

Diomed

Perseus

BLUE FUNNEL

Ulysses

Troilus

Voyage East

Rhesus

Keemun

BLUE FUNNEL

Bellerophon

Patroclus

Voyage East

Achilles

Glacous

BLUE FUNNEL

Pyrrhus

Automedon

Voyage East

Neleus

Hector

BLUE FUNNEL

Phemius

A view from forward of a typical 'Bluey'.. do you know which one it was?

Voyage East

The Isle of Fragrant Waters

We steamed south-east out of the Gulf of Thailand, slipping into the familiar, comforting round of the ship's routine, passing 'bits of strange coasts under stars, shadows of hills in the sunshine, men's passions in the dark, gossip half-forgotten, faces grown dim.' Thus reminisced Conrad in the introduction to *Nostromo*, and I recalled '*The Secret Sharer*', a story of his set in the Gulf. He had cause to know those waters, having taken three weeks to work the barque *Otago* down to Singapore with a sickly crew and a jinx to hinder him. Delay was to dog us, too, though not on such a scale, for round Cape Cambodia we began to lift to a low swell, rolling down from the north-east as we followed the curve of the coast of Indo-China across the mouth of the Mekong Delta.

As we edged away from the Vietnamese coast the swell steepened and the wind slowly increased to a strong breeze, bringing to mind the old weather couplet:

Long foretold, long last,
Short notice, soon past.
We were in for a blow.

The Mate began to worry about the cargo, for the stows had been broken down in our discharging, and although the Carpenter had 'tommed-off' what he could, heavy weather could dislodge the wooden planks and beams jammed skillfully and wedged with care to stop the cargo taking charge.

'Where's the bloody lookout?' asked the Mate suddenly.

'On the fo'c's'le,' I replied, whipping up my glasses, to find the catwalk across the bow empty. We had not yet shipped any seas but a sudden sensation of panic uncoiled in my belly that we had lost him over-board.

'Who is it?'

'Embleton, sir.'

'Bloody hell! That bugger skated on thin ice in Bangkok ... get up there and have a look. If he's asleep, leave him and let me know.'

I went forward as a spy, but with expectations less cynical than the Mate's. I descended to the centre-castle, went past Number Three hatch, and paused by the contactor house at the head of the well-deck ladder. I half expected to see a limp body, pallid in the dark swirl of water that had accumulated at the after end of the welldeck. The sibilant hiss of the sea took precedence over the muted rumble of *Antigone's* racing engines as she drove her bow into the swell. The sea rose to her sheer strakes, black and suddenly very close. I chose my moment and made for the forecastle, legs leaden with compression as the ship heaved upwards beneath me, light as a feather as the deck subsided, falling through twenty feet before theatening to crush me again with the massive upsurge of her buoyancy. I reached the forecastle ladder, hoisted myself up and dodged round the windlass. Fearing what I might find, I scrambled over the low breakwater as the cables chinked in the pipes and *Antigone* climbed upwards into the sky. My guts surged into my throat as she fell back. Two geysers of water roared up the hawse pipes and collapsed in dark rushing streams, foaming aft, deflected over the side by the breakwater. I was soaked to the knees, half off-balance, and my torch beam wavered around the triangle of deck beyond the pipes.

Embleton lay asleep, half-tucked under the grating upon which he should have stood his watch, his face as innocent as his mother supposed him to be. Feeling the guilt of the informer, I worked my way back to the bridge.

'He ought not to be up there, sir,' I said, 'she's shipping...'

'He's asleep then?'

'Yes.'

'If he was awake he'd have rung and asked to be shifted.'

The Mate picked up the forecastle telephone, pressing the bell insistently. Lifting the glasses I saw Embleton wake with a feral shrug. His arm went out to the phone.

'You're asleep on lookout, Embleton,' I heard the Mate say. 'Get yourself up here.'

I watched Embleton's progress down the deck, half thinking he would be washed overboard, but he arrived safely. He gasped his denial with an

Voyage East

affronted dignity that made me wonder if I had been deceived.

'You were asleep on lookout,' the Mate repeated, cutting short the torrent of defiance, innocence and outrage that Embleton began. 'You'll see the Master tomorrow morning. Now go below and call your relief.'

Embleton passed me swearing under his breath. I could smell the beer on him. At the after end of the boat-deck he stopped and rounded on the distant bridge.

'Scotch bastard!' I heard him bellow into the rising wind.

The full force of the gale struck us at dawn. Grey and tumbling seas foamed down-wind towards us, their streaming sides streaked with spume, so that the violence of *Antigone's* pitching increased. The regular motion of the swell was now compounded by the wind-driven seas and the ship staggered occasionally, thumping into the walls of water. Her rivets screeched, she panted with a strange clicking noise and flung white sheets of water a hundred feet from her thrusting bow. Later, Embleton was arraigned for punishment. This formal process was held in the Master's cabin and known colloquially as a 'logging', for the entire transaction had to be recorded, verbatim, in the ship's Official Log-Book, a document supplied by the Board of Trade into which all such events, plus dates of boat and fire drills, the list of the crew, their conduct, notes of protest and sundry matters involving the discipline, business and regulation of the ship were recorded. It was distinct from the Mate's, or Deck, Log, which contained the record of weather and navigational details. The Official Log-Book was filled in by the Purser acting as clerk and I wondered, as I joined the Mate, cap under my arm, whether successive occasions such as this had given him his dry outlook.

China Dick sat at his desk looking at the Mate's written report. There was a knock at the cabin door and the Bosun ushered Embleton in, then waited behind him, representative of Embleton's interest.

Embleton looked round at us, scowling at me ferociously. After a moment Captain Richards turned and regarded Embleton.

'Well, Embleton...'

'*Mister* Embleton, Cap'n.'

China Dick ignored the interruption '... Here you are again. You went absent without leave in Penang and were docked a day's pay and your train fare to Port Swettenham. You misbehaved in Bangkok...' His crime in Singapore had gone undiscovered.

'What the fuck did I do wrong in Bangkok?'

China Dick turned to the Purser, allowing the frantic pen to catch up. I could just see the expletive recorded for posterity.

'You know very well there was trouble in the seaman's alleyway. Count yourself fortunate that you didn't end up on the carpet for that . . .'

'There was others involved ... dis is fucking victimisation. Yeah, victimisation. You got a note of that, eh?' Embleton stepped forward, wagging his finger at the Purser. The Purser nodded, his face a mask of neutrality. I saw the Bosun's hand on Embleton's arm, restraining him.

'And now,' went on China Dick smoothly,' you have been found asleep on lookout during the four-to-eight last night.'

'Who says?' Embleton swivelled to me.

'I say, Laddie,' put in the hitherto silent Mate, his voice low and menacing. 'You were asleep on lookout.'

'How d'you know I was *asleep*. I might have ducked down behind the windlass for a quick drag . . .'

'The Fourth Mate came forward and checked,' said Captain Richards with an air of exasperation.

'And you didn't wake me, you bastard.' Embleton turned his fury on me, snarling with bared teeth so that I felt the full force of his malice.

'I told him not to wake you, Embleton,' snapped the Mate. Embleton's eyes remained on my face. He knew he was powerless against the Master or the Mate, but a mere junior officer was a different matter.

'D'you have anything to say?' Captain Richards asked, almost wearily.

'Yeah. I wasn't asleep.' He was on the defensive now, gauging our reaction to his protest of innocence. Our eyes watched, opaque with disbelief and he was compelled to ridiculous justification: 'I was just resting.'

China Dick turned to the Purser. 'D'you have that? Embleton says he was "just resting".'

'I have it, sir, nodded the Purser, his pen continuing to fly over the lined

Voyage East

pages.

'This is a serious offence, Embleton. While I gave you the benefit of the doubt in Bangkok, your conduct does nothing to persuade me that I should do so again.' China Dick's mellifluous English picked his words with barbed precision and we waited for sentence. 'You will be fined two days' pay, your bar account will be stopped and you will not be allowed ashore in Hong Kong.'

'Bloody hell, Cap'n, you can't do that!' Embleton exploded. 'This ain't the fucking *Bounty,* this is the nineteen sixties ... you can't stop my shore-leave. I know my rights!'

'And I know my duty, Embleton! You were fast asleep on lookout and that endangers the ship!'

'You're a right bloody shower, you bastards...' Embleton scowled round at us.

'Come along boyo,' said the Bosun, 'don't get yourself into more trouble.'

We could hear Embleton protesting in the alleyway as the Bosun took him aft. At the boat-deck door he flung one final imprecation at us. 'Bastards!'

'Cythral,' growled China Dick looking up and dismissing us. 'Thank you gentlemen.'

'Always one fly in the ointment,' remarked the Mate in the less tense atmosphere of the alleyway as we trooped out of the Master's cabin.

'The trouble is the buggers don't really want to come to sea,' said the Purser, as if men like Embleton besmirched his own calling. 'They only come to make a few bob.'

'And trouble,' added the Mate.

'Aye, and trouble.'

'Don't know why we bother with buggers like that.'

'Keep the Unions happy and uphold the rule of Law,' said the Mate sarcastically.

'Strike a defensive blow in the class war,' I put in sententiously, knowing the Purser's penchant for such references. He rounded on me with astonishing ferocity.

'Our class has no champions,' he snapped, turning into his cabin.

The Mate raised one prominent eyebrow and pulled his pipe from his pocket.

'Just responsibility, laddie. No power, just responsibility.' And sighing, he too entered his cabin, leaving me in the alleyway feeling stupidly inexperienced.

The ship shuddered as she butted a heavy sea. Outside the wind was increasing and though we assembled on the bridge at noon, the grey scud that overcast the sky prevented our finding our latitude. We were alone in a heaving desolation of water, the sky thick with it and the horizon furred and indistinct. We sank into the gloom of bad weather, retreating to our bunks when our duties were over, breathing the stale, uncirculated air that was also thick with the taint of bad conscience. As I dozed in my cabin in half-hearted pretence at reading, I was disturbed by a faint scrabbling at the door. Sparks, pale with what I presumed was sea-sickness, asked if he could speak to me.

'Yeah, sure. Come in.' Reluctantly I stirred myself, sticky with sleep in the enclosed and humid atmosphere of the accommodation.

'I, er...'

'What's the matter?'

'Well ... it's ... it's bloody embarrassing,' he managed in a rush and I could see the pallor was fear, not sea-sickness. It was more than embarrassment that had driven him to his confession, for I knew what was coming.

'I think I've got a dose.'

'Oh, shit ...'

It was out now and he could let it flow in a torrent of relief. 'I went with one of those Bangkok girls, you know ... she got into my cabin one night and, well, one thing led to another, and ... well, you see, there's my girl-friend ... she's my fiancée really, we're engaged . . .'

'Have you told the Doc?' He shook his head unhappily and I sensed he was close to break-down. 'What are your symptoms?'

'Well ...' he seemed to consider the question.

'Have you got a discharge? I mean does it hurt when you pass water. I'm told it's like pissing through broken glass ... eh?'

'No, nothing like that.'

There was a greater fear than the clap. 'Any hard red spots?' I was doing some sums in my head and cursing Mike at the same time. Sparks shook his head.

'No ... no spots.' He swallowed. 'That'd be syphilis, would it?' he asked, his voice barely audible above the rumble of the engines and the howl of the gale.

'Well it would, yes. But if you've got nothing to show, why are you worried?'

He shrugged. 'It's a feeling ... a sort of pain ... I don't know He was plunged in an abyss of misery.

'Look, see the Doc. As far as I know nothing shows for nine days.'

'But the Old Man'll have to know, and then . . .' Sweat was pouring off him.

'I suppose you didn't use a johnnie, or an Anti-VD kit?'

He shook his head. 'No.'

'Well, don't worry. It *can* be cured.' I forbore to tell him all the horror stories one had heard, or about the symptoms sometimes taking three months to emerge, feeling sorry that Mike's foolish practical joke had had such a devastating effect. 'Look, have a beer and try and forget it.'

'Okay. Thanks.'

'Look forward to Hong Kong.'

'What's it like?'

'In a nutshell, the most fantastic place on earth.'

As we brought *Antigone's* head onto a more northerly course, a mood of cheerful expectancy filled the faces of our Chinese. Despite the gale, the poop showed signs of spring-cleaning. Normally scrupulously tidy, the Chinese nevertheless cleaned everything. Rows of washing danced in the wind alongside the drying bodies of fish and extemporised dust-pans made out of Teepol cans cut in half (the thrifty Chinese fashioned such artefacts out of the ship's refuse). Gaily painted and drying in the gale, these turned

BLUE FUNNEL

alongside the fish and the washing under the wings of the docking bridge.

The Chinese quarters under the poop were a distinct contrast to those of the Europeans. Whereas our cabins were temporary abodes from which we decamped the instant we were given leave, the Chinese regarded the ship as their home. Where we reckoned our service aboard in months - though our senior officers sometimes stayed for years - the tenure of the Chinese was for much, much longer. Their chieftain was Chao Ven Ching, the Number One Greaser, a tall, cadaverous man with a pigeon chest, whose neck was as thin as a chicken's and whose hoarse voice was attributed to the opium he took. Whatever the truth of this claim (and the penalties for possession of the drug were Draconian), he was all-powerful, a man to be reckoned with, who condescended to take orders from the Second and Chief Engineers, holding them in higher esteem than the Mate or China Dick himself.

The Chinese were a self-contained and self-regulating community. They had their own cook and galley, their own customs and hierarchy. They maintained a spotless ship and were rarely any trouble.

The bunk-space of every Chinese crew-member was his tiny home, a neat, personalised cubicle filled with photographs of an extended family, a small vase of plastic flowers, perhaps a shrine or book of Maoist philosophy, a shelf of books, a porcelain bowl and box of *mahjong*. At night, particularly in the still of the tropics, they played *mahjong* avidly, the click of the bricks loud on the messroom table, the excitement high in their conversation, for Chinese seamen were great gamblers and would bet on two flies crawling across a porthole. At Christmas China Dick had sent them all a couple of drinks and at Chinese New Year they would invite us down to their great feast. Occasionally the Mate, gratifying a minor vice, would send aft to the Greaser's cook for a Chinese supper. He and the Purser, the men among us British most wedded to the ship, would relish their surreptitious indulgence with evident enjoyment. But for the main part we did not impinge upon their privacy beyond the Master's daily rounds at sea.

As we bore up for Hong Kong the China Sea showed us its most treacherous face. Though deep it is littered with vast areas of shallows ready

Voyage East

to trap even a modern ship, out in her reckoning. On our passage from Bangkok to Hong Kong we had to pass between the Paracels, an archipelago of reefs, islets and shoals over one hundred square miles in extent, and the Macclesfield Bank, a slightly smaller area resembling a sunken island. In the absence of observations we navigated on dead-reckoning, a process that diminished in accuracy the longer one relied upon it and the slower one travelled. At our normal speed it was surprisingly precise; but at sunset, such was the violence of our motion that Captain Richards ordered a reduction in our speed to 95 rpm, to ease the working of the hull and preserve the cargo from damage. This introduced an element of wind-drift, known as leeway, into our calculations.

Next morning the Mate decided to open up Number Five hatch and inspect one of the stows of cargo. For this purpose small access hatches were provided, but that by the main-mast, giving entrance into the 'tween-deck, led directly onto a stow of cartons.

'You're a wee, skinny fellow,' he said to me, 'away down and check the tomming.'

I did as I was bid, wriggling over the top of the uneven cargo just beneath the beams of the upper deck, my boiler suit catching on every crate, and hampering my progress. I found the edge of the stow when my torch, being pushed ahead, dropped over it and, in a stygian gloom which creaked and groaned as the ship laboured and the cargo bent to the influence of gravity, I squirmed out into the comparative freedom of the hatch to the lower 'tween-decks. Recovering my torch I played its beam on the tomming. Vertical billets of timber were jammed between the deck and deckhead, secured by wedges and with cross-members nailed to them, holding the wall of boxes remarkably secure, except in one place where a kind of 'cliff-fall' had taken place. A few cartons had split open and their contents, some knitted fashion goods, had been strewn across the hatch. I gathered up what I could get out, secured the stow as well as possible and returned to the Mate.

He took the woollen cardigans and turned them over curiously with a grunt. I could sense his irritation at the mishap, trivial though it was.

'Aye. I'll advise the Old Man to note protest when we get to Hong

Kong.'

I met Sparks in the alleyway as I went for a shower. He had the haunted face of the possessed. 'Cheer up,' I said, 'you'll be at it again in Hong Kong...'

He disappeared with a groan.

'You really are a bastard,' I said to Mike as we each drank a beer before noon. He smiled that superior smile of his. 'He's worried sick...'

'Syphillophobia, the Doc calls it. Well-known medical condition among incautious mariners.' He looked at me sideways. 'Besides, you didn't try and stop me,'

'No.' The thought nagged my conscience.

'Hong Kong'll sort him out.'

'I've just told him that and he went wailing down the alleyway.'

'If you can't take the heat of the fire, keep out of the bloody kitchen,' said Mike standing and tossing his empty beer can into the rosy. I felt irritated by his cavalier attitude to Sparks, born as it was out of his own problems.

'Have you heard from your wife?' I heard myself asking.

He turned and looked at me and I saw for a second his own anguish, a compound of guilt and uncertainty.

'Yes,' he replied with a catch in his voice. We stared at each other for a second and then his confidence returned. 'Come on, drink up. Let's go and find Hong Kong.'

Hong Kong found us in the nacreous mists of the following dawn. It peppered our radar screens with the outposts of its teeming population, mixed indiscriminately with those of its giant neighbour, the People's Republic of China. The clusters of glowing dots spread out across our track so that it seemed impossible that we could find a way through to the harder echoes of the Lima Islands beyond.

As the daylight grew the Mate and I anxiously flitted between radar screen and bridge-wing, our eyes straining to adjust between the lambent echoes on the screen and the vacant image lenses of our binoculars.

Voyage East

'Fine to starboard!'

'Aye, I see her . . .'

Antigone leaned to her rudder and we began a slalom among the dense mass of junks patiently fishing the coastal waters off Kwangtung. High-sterned, with their triple, pterodactyl-wings of sail, these craft had an exotic, impossible look to western eyes; yet their technical simplicity, the culmination of almost a thousand years of empirical design, had produced one of the most seaworthy and durable sailing craft in the world. Their windward performance astonished early western observers and their rig has, more recently, been adopted in yacht design. As we swept past the first of these wonderful little ships, some sixty feet in length, we could see her crew hauling nets, a cascade of silver pouring over her rail and into the wooden fish pounds on her deck. At her stern a single old man, his creased face visible in my binoculars, looked up at us, his hand raised. Greeting, or clench-fisted gesture of annoyance? We had no means of knowing, for he and his boat had slipped astern and a frantic three rings from the forecastle bell told where a wide-awake lookout had spotted the next. The Mate had anticipated this and *Antigone* was already listing to port as her helm forced her bow round to starboard.

'Got your arse in a tangle with the Aberdeen fleet, eh Mister?' China Dick puffed up onto the bridge, pyjama bottoms flapping beneath a brocaded silk dressing gown of mandarin splendour. Brought from his bunk by the sudden tilt of the deck, he referred to the home-port of many of the fishing junks, Aberdeen Harbour on the west side of Hong Kong Island.

'Aye sir, and the Whampoa Commune out o' of the Pearl River . . .'

China Dick bent over the radar set. The coiled dragon that wound its way over the blue hillock of his broad back glared balefully at the Mate who stood impatiently aside.

'Another junk right ahead, sir!' I called from the starboard bridge-wing, but the Mate had anticipated again and *Antigone* was swinging to starboard, her deck tilting to the sudden thrust of her rudder.

The mist was lifting now, drawing back its veil as the sun rose, red and watery, revealing the sea studded with literally hundreds of junks. And there were ships too, a white P & O liner ethereal in the morning light but recognisable as the *Chusan,* bound south towards Singapore. Astern of us a tanker was making up towards Hong Kong like ourselves, while a black-funnelled cargo-liner, the *Hanyang* of Butterfield and Swire's, was coming in from the eastwards. Still swimming in wraiths of mist, the islands of the Li-Ma Ch'un-Tao, the Lima Islands, were already abeam, their spiny crests hard-edged against the sky. Ahead, the lighthouse of Wang Lan winked its double flash at us before surrendering to the daylight.

Wang Lan's wink was a reminder that Hong Kong was an anomaly, a place of extremes, its very existence of such moral dubiety that one suspended all judgements and accepted it for what it was: a market place created by the colliding of political dogmas. Such was the violence of the collision that sharp edges were blunted, reduced to impotence, in the face of human necessity and human resilience. The Crown Colony, wrested from Imperial China during the shameful wrangling of the Opium Wars, existed by courtesy of Communist China, and its harbour made possible a pragmatic truce between the Marxist and the Capitalist world.

Now immaculate in his doeskin reefers China Dick took over the con as we swung into the Tathong Channel. To the west of us the high peaks of the Dragon's Back formed the eastern rampart of Hong Kong Island, to the east Joss House Bay and Junk Bay were backed by the rising land of the New Territories. We followed in *Hangyang's* wake as she slowed to pick up her pilot from the launch bucking alongside. Ten minutes later we had done the same and Mr Wong arrived to the bridge, to shake hands affably with Captain Richards and give him his orders.

'We discharge dangerous cargo at Quarantine anchorage, then go 'longside Holt's Wharf.' He bobbed a nod that was almost a bow at the bluff figure of the Mate and added, 'Okay, we go half the speed and come to port now.'

China Dick nodded his assent, the telegraphs jangled and *Antigone* picked up speed again, slowly opening a cleft in the high green hills that formed the harbour's eastern entrance, the Lei Yue Mun Pass. At the start of this narrow gutway, on the headland of Pak Sha Wan, a cargo ship of comparable size to the *Antigone* lay cast ashore, lifted completely out of the water, a victim of the last typhoon.

Voyage East

'Let the wrecks of others be your seamarks, Laddie,' muttered the Mate.

Along the ship's rails heads had appeared, eager to see the bowl of the harbour and the concourse of ships and boats that churned its waters into a froth and all but obscured it with their movements and activity, for no ship was ever wholly idle in Hong Kong, even the warships were besieged by *sampans* and *wallah-wallahs* eager to trade, barter or pimp to their crews.

We anchored long enough for a gang of coolies and a lighter to remove seventy drums of hydrogen peroxide from our fore-deck and then weighed, sliding alongside Holt's Wharf at the toe of the Kowloon peninsula, that salient of mainland China that neatly divided Hong Kong harbour in two. As we swung alongside we passed the men-of-war: the aircraft carrier *Eagle*, the British destroyer *Caesar* and the frigate *Loch Killisport*, in company with the Australians, *Vampire* and *Quiberon*, and the Kiwi, *Taranaki*. The usual units of the United States Seventh Fleet were also lying at anchor: the Guided Missile cruiser *Providence* and two destroyers.

'Look at that,' said the Mate, wearing his tight smile of ironic delight as he contemplated any example of the folly of mankind. I raised my glasses. Passing quite close to the *Providence* a large motorised junk chugged its way across the harbour. At its grubby stern a huge red flag bearing the gold stars of the People's Republic snapped in the breeze and the cargo, of live beef steers going for slaughter, could be clearly seen standing jammed in the junk's waist.

'Those'll be steaks in an hour or two,' remarked the Mate, tamping his pipe and picking up his cap, 'being eaten by the dough-boys.'

It made nonsense of the United States' refusal to recognise the existence of Communist China.

Hong Kong, the Isle of Fragrant Waters, was full of such contrasts. At the wharves deep-water merchantmen discharged their cargoes. At the fifty-odd mooring buoys others loaded, surrounded by junks and lighters whose progress to and from the waiting vessels was ceaseless. From time to time a merchant ship would slip her mooring and depart, to be replaced immediately with another in a seething, endless sequence of movement and activity. Backwards and forwards ran the ferries from Kowloon and Hong

Kong. In the lee of the former the typhoon shelter was black with junks waiting for cargoes or being repaired and overhauled. The roofs of Kowloon's shops and tenements disappeared into the greener country of the north under a blue haze of vehicle smoke rising from its teeming streets. On the other side of the harbour the waterfront of Victoria presented a similar spectacle, the high towers of the taipan's offices, the banks and luxury hotels patronised by American tourists rose up the sides of the Peak. Wealth climbed with altitude, the higher one lived the more space one could purchase, so that towards the top the houses stood in isolated splendour, with groves of trees and lush green undergrowth between them. Even at this wintry season of the year, with the very summit of the Peak wreathed in cloud, the cool isolation of the hillside seemed highly desirable above the almost hysterical movement below. From Holt's Wharf we could see other hillsides, the shanty towns and mean dwellings beyond Wan Chai and Aldrich Bay.

Police patrol launches gave the impression of a watchful bureaucracy, but the sheer scale of this great battle for survival by the Chinese defied true regulation. Under tattered sails junks ghosted through the anchorage bringing cargoes that were, without much doubt, from Canton. Even the millions of industrious hands in Hong Kong could not have produced all the curios, the silk paintings, the lacquer work, the intricately carved ivory, the cruder rosewood, the camphor-wood chests, the bamboo-ware, the ebony figures, the jade and the silks that tourists carried home as booty from a visit to this incredible place. Much came from the 'non-existent' country beyond the border but if provided with a certificate of origin from Hong Kong could be taken into the United States. It was a baffling example of, in the Purser's dry phrase, 'man's hypocrisy to man.'

At water-level subsisted the most indigent of Hong Kong's population. In tiny sampans not much bigger than an average yacht tender, and beneath whose flush-decks people slept, women and girls paddled around the harbour begging from the ships. Propelled by a *yuloh*, a single stern-sweep kept in constant motion by the wrist of a prematurely aged female whose cheap cotton smock and trousers flapped in the breeze, these pathetic craft hung around for hours in the hope of anything they could turn to advantage.

Voyage East

Known as 'dunnage girls', their main-stay in the fight for survival was discarded dunnage, old planks and pieces of wood, torn down tomming and redundant packing that was used in the merchant-men for the protection of cargoes, for keeping vulnerable stows away from the condensation on steel decks and bulkheads. Coconut matting provided for the same purpose was also sought after, as was money, the odd coins every seaman had sculling around in a cabin drawer. To see these scavengers living off the prodigal waste cast off from the ships was a sight to stir compassion in even the most hardened breast, and we had hardly secured alongside Holt's Wharf before the harassed Mate was bellowing at me: 'For Christ's sake get down aft and stop those bloody Middies chucking all my dunnage over the side ...'

If we had been a hive of activity in the Malay ports, the next few days defy description. The ship was like a dying animal beset by legions of flies. She was a Babel of noise, a vast confusion of disparate activity, a conflict of intent and rabid disorganisation from which some odd miracle of sense began to emerge. Holt's commercial empire was seen at its best in Hong Kong where 'things got done', as the Bosun said, in a manner 'that would make a Scouse shop steward fucking weep.'

Within minutes of our arrival the Mate was closeted with Hang Lee, the hatchet-faced sub-contractor who provided labour for the many jobs to be attended to about the ship. News of our homeward cargo was arriving via the agent and the appropriate arrangements were put in hand. The officers' alleyway became a thorough-fare for the Chinese tally-clerks, the foreman, the security guards who were usually Indians, the agent's runners, the powerful Chinese wharfinger and a sweating white cargo-surveyor come to make arrangements for a joint survey of damaged cargo.

Pushing and shoving through this clamorous throng besieging the Mate's door came the barbers and tailors, the laundry-boy and the curio-hawkers, the shoe-maker and the taxi-tout. It was impossible to read one's mail without frequent interruptions and the Purser, driven to almost as much distraction as the Mate by the mass of paperwork that all this entailed, was importuned by the individual members of the ship's company who wanted their 'sub', the advance of wages that formed their spending money in this paradise of bargains.

On deck it was little better. *Antigone* swarmed with Chinese coolies, labourers of both sexes undertaking twenty tasks simultaneously. There were gangs of men trimming derricks to discharge our Hong Kong-consigned cargo; gangs of women, armed with brooms, sacks and scoops, swept our emptying 'tween decks. More men chipped and painted areas of the ship it was impossible to undertake at sea. A gang of carpenters was ripping sections of caulking out of the promenade deck and forcing new oakum and pitch into the gaping seams and a host of black-clad and ancient women, their alopecia hidden under sheets of cardboard covered by black cotton so that they seemed a sect of satanic nuns, hovered over the yawning pit of the deep-tanks as the last of the cargo was ripped out.

These unfortunate creatures, known unkindly as 'Hang's Virgins', worked with a small group of men who erected bamboo scaffolding inside the big cargo tanks. As soon as this framework was assembled they would take their tiny steel scrapers and their brushes below and remove every particle of last trip's residual latex and every scrap of scale, so that the inside of the tank almost gleamed with bright metal, for in Shanghai we were to load wood oil, an almost fabulously valuable substance.

Escape from this bombardment by humanity was essential. Only the stoic Mate endured it without relief. China Dick, exercising the privilege of rank, had disappeared soon after our arrival, carted off by the agent to visit friends ashore. Later, we too went roistering in his wake, our pockets loaded with a month's pay in Hong Kong dollars, to slake our thirst and titillate our cheated senses in any one of the numerous bars that lined Kowloon's main thoroughfare, Nathan Road. Among the tables of these caravanserais glided the almond-eyed whores in the gleaming brocaded sheaths of their cheongsams. This most erotic of dresses covered a girl from calf to neck, yet revealed flashes of leg from ankle to upper thigh as she walked or danced under the dim lighting.

Our group split up, according to inclination, avoiding the exorbitant charges for drinks for the girls who slid next to us on the bench seats, teasing a tumescence out of us. Between bars we were importuned by gangs of Chinese boys offering to conduct us to a good bar, to meet nice girls, to black our boots. Our refusal turned these offers into bald beggary. To give money meant a limpet-like devotion from a posse of conductors, their black hair spiky on their crowns, their eyes bright despite the hour, their hands outstretched. To rid ourselves, we would hurl handfuls of cents down the road and leg it in the opposite direction. Sometimes it worked. A sleeting rain began to fall around midnight. Those of us recalled by duty hailed rickshaws and went lolling back to the ship. Others went their own way.

My own cargo-watch was dominated by the discharge of a sixty-five-ton transformer out of Number Two lower hold. For this we used the ship's heavy-lift, or 'jumbo' derrick, capable of handling seventy tons, and the ticklish business occupied the forenoon. It took an hour to rig the guys (the wires that slewed the heavy steel boom) through a series of lead-blocks onto adjacent winches, effectively paralysing discharge from Number One hatch. The Mate appeared at the critical moment and the ship's crew, under the vociferous direction of the Bosun, who obviously enjoyed the occasion, played to an audience of temporarily idle Chinese labourers. My own role was tutelary, to be called on only if something went wrong. As the heavy transformer emerged from the hold and traversed the deck, *Antigone* heeled to its shifting weight, listing at an appreciable angle until the waiting lighter received its load and *Antigone* rolled back towards the wharf like a live thing.

As the jumbo-derrick swung inboard again to be resecured, the suspended work resumed and the Bosun's audience melted away. Walking aft I bumped into Embleton.

'Oh, aye, it's you, eh?' I could smell stale alcohol on his breath.

'Excuse me...'

'Don't fuck me around, Mister ... I know your fucking sort. You just let me catch you shore-side, you bastard, and I'll fucking fix you ...'

'Get on with your bloody work, Wacker!' The Bosun's grunting bulk rescued me from the embarrassment of public confrontation. I was clearly not to be forgiven for discovering Embleton asleep on look-out.

'Thank's Bose.'

'I should keep you head down, Fourth,' he advised with

uncompromising toughness.

'Good advice.'

'He'll come to a sticky end ...' he waddled off and I made my way aft.

'You should have knocked him down with a belaying pin,' remarked Mike with his usual cynicism when I told him of the incident.

'Say one word out of line and you're in the shit,' remarked Bob, taking over the deck from me. 'What a bloody life.'

'White trash,' said Mike dismissively, all his old self-possession back in place.

'Class warfare,' said the Purser, handing me a bundle of boatnotes for small parcels of coasting cargo to be loaded before our departure.

'Here, Bob, you can have these' I handed them to the Third Mate. 'I'm off ashore.'

'Keep your eye open for Embleton, then.'

'You tell Embleton I'm going to Ah Seng's ... but don't tell him I'm having chow with a Police Inspector...'

I visited and was entertained by friends during our remaining duty-free nights in Hong Kong. After the chaos of ship-board life and the banal pursuit of pleasure along the fringes of Nathan Road, these glimpses of regular colonial life were oases of rest.

Four days after taking it up we relinquished our berth at Holt's Wharf to the *Menelaus,* reloaded our hydrogen peroxide at the Quarantine anchorage and headed for the Lei Yue Mun Pass. About the decks hoses blasted rubbish out of the corners and the derricks were swung inboard and secured. Odd sticks of dunnage were hurled over the side, to the delight of a few sampans bobbing in our wake. Discharging our pilot, we headed for the Tathong Channel and the Taiwan Strait beyond.

Voyage East

Lotus Eating

We left Hong Kong prepared to enter the troubled waters of the Taiwan Strait on our way to Japan. The long civil war between the Nationalist Chinese and the Communists still smouldered across this stretch of water, where the Nationalists retained a lodgement on the islands of Quemoy and Amoy, though the seat of their government had long been transferred to Taipei. Occasional sorties were flown by the warplanes of both sides and one Blue Funnel ship, the *Anchises*, had been caught in this cross-fire. To mark our neutrality we had stretched additional tarpaulins painted with large Union flags upon two of our hatches. Further painted canvas flags were stretched on wooden frames and displayed conspicuously along our promenade decks. Thus provided we headed east, past Pedro Blanco, a small island whose name reminded us of the first western penetration into these seas, that of the Portuguese early in the sixteenth century. Next came Mirs Bay, then Bias Bay, haunt of pirate fleets whose junks marauded all passing trade until well into the twentieth century. Beyond the deep and island-dotted indentations of the coast the neat hachures of long-dead British cartographers on the Admiralty charts showed ranges of hills, plotted from the running surveys carried out by the officers of the Royal Navy in the 1800s. Here and there a neat polygon bore the legend *walled town,* and all along the coast there was a compromise mixture of Chinese and imposed names. It all attested to the view that the Royal Navy's greatest achievement was the charting of the world's seas and coastlines. It was a pity, therefore, that politics intruded: blocked out, in jet-black ink, was any reference to the strait into which we were heading, or the island from which it took its name, ever having been known as Formosa. The name was unacceptable to both factions of the Chinese, imposed during the brief ascendancy of Imperial Japan from which the Chinese had suffered so dreadfully. Refusal to black-out this imperial relic would result in our charts being confiscated by the Chinese authorities.

Off Swatow we swung into the strait and the weather became

increasingly cold with every mile of northing we made. Despite the wintry weather the hardy Chinese fishermen were at sea in their junks, enlivening our watches as we dodged laboriously through them. It was bad enough in daylight, with sheets of driving rain through which they loomed like ghostly apparitions, but at night, with a rough sea throwing back echoes and 'clutter' on the radar screen, they were difficult to locate as they rose and fell in the troughs. Few carried lights, relying on their luck and our good judgement, though a few raised hastily lit hurricane lanterns that flickered on a seamed old face sixty feet below our bridge-wing as we plunged past.

As we cleared the northern end of the Taiwan Strait the fresh, bitingly cold northerly wind met the warm current of the Kuro Siwo, sweeping us north and eastwards across the Tung Hai, or Eastern Sea, to the north of Okinawa. Such a meeting of the elements produced coiling tendrils of mist that thickened, from time to time, to damp rolling banks of fog so that few of us, wrenched so recently from the tropics, now escaped the misery of running noses.

During the forenoon of our fourth morning out of Hong Kong the weather cleared. What we saw looming above the horizon on the port bow brought almost the entire ship's company on deck. The holy volcano of Fuji-yama rose pink and glistening in the sunshine long before the coast of Honshu lifted above the horizon. The sense of excitement that ran through the ship was almost tangible. This was a curious reaction, for both the Chinese and British on board, if they had not actually experienced the evils of war at the hands of the Japanese, had inherited historical images of terrifying intensity. Perhaps the Chinese had better reason to hate the Japanese than ourselves, for the Sino-Japanese war of the 1930s had done immense damage to China's Nationalist republic. Yet seamen are an easygoing race. The sharp contrasts to which they are subject, made them a tolerant breed. For them the nationalistic distinctions blurred: individually we might not love the Japanese, but there were mitigating factors that made them more than merely tolerable.

There was nowhere in those days quite like Japan on the eve of her economic explosion. She had not yet emerged as the world's leading manufacturer; her industrial machinery still relied upon a degree of

Voyage East

plagiarism; but there was a fierce energy in the activity of her ports, and an acceptance of the sailor ashore, that was wholly enjoyable. There was no stuffy neo-colonial segregation that graded men from the merchant ships as the 'white trash' of Mike's cynicism or Hong Kong's collective perception; nor were we the *fan-kwei*, the red-barbarians, to be shunned by the native Chinese. Here in Japan curiosity about the West was growing, despite the humiliation of American occupation. We could anticipate a welcome that would revive our romantic aspirations. There was a sparkle even in the Mate's eyes as we swung into the Uraga Suido and the entrance to Yedo Bay. A spontaneous, unmercenary air attached to the cool depravity of the bar-girls of the great ports of Japan, a simple, uncomplicated joy in the lusts of the flesh, brought a gleam of anticipation to every eye.

After a brief sojourn in the quarantine anchorage while the formalities of immigration and port health were attended to by the Purser and Captain Richards, we slid alongside to discharge. It was very cold, with snow on the roofs of the godowns turned to a filthy grey slush along the quays. As in every other port we visited, work started almost immediately. The labourers had an organised, military appearance, wearing black, jodhpur-like breeches that wound round the calves like puttees and terminated in cloth-topped and rubber-soled footwear that split between the large toe and the remainder. Many wore head-bands, and they wielded their cargo-handling hooks with short, staccato grunts of effort, hauling the cases and bales of our cargo onto the cargo nets with an energy that put our own countrymen to shame. Ruddy-faced, stocky and impressively robust, the wharfies of Yokohama were an intimidating race.

'The Japanese,' said Mike sententiously, 'breed the ugliest men and the most beautiful women . . .' and from this Olympian view we descended to talk of the overnight discharge of calcium napthanate from a cargo tank; this black, gooey substance would require tending and threatened any ideas of abandoned pleasure in the watering holes off Isezaki Street, whither our fantasies were already straying. In the end Sparks and I went in search of a bath. This almost innocent activity had in it sufficient salacious delight to titillate without leaving an unpleasant sense of bad faith; it was much enjoyed by the married men and, on a cold winter's night, after a long day, had a sensuous pleasure all of its own. A taxi took us to the bathhouse and I calmed Sparks's fears, for he was still agonising over his past behaviour and suspicious of a further trap set by those more experienced than himself. He kept muttering about trusting me, leaving threats half-hanging in the air to the effect that if I let him down.... With Embleton's outstanding promises in mind, I began to feel somewhat embattled.

We sat in the foyer of the bath-house, paid our 1500 Yen and sipped beers while we waited. Sparks looked curiously round at lounging Japanese men, and a couple of Europeans, off ships like ourselves. Then the girls came, nubile young creatures clad in white jackets and high-heeled sandals. They smiled and giggled when they realised it was Europeans they had to deal with.

'Go on, off you go,' I encouraged a suddenly reluctant Sparks, who looked terrified of the dark-haired beauty bending over him. She was tugging his wrist with a gentle persistence, talking to the girl appointed to look after me, and there was more giggling, their free hands going up to their mouths as if to suppress their amusement.

'Come on Joe . . .'

'Go on. She won't eat you. Ask her what her name is.'

'Me Michiko ... you come with Michiko Joe-San.'

I stood up, Sparks followed and we were led away to the mirth of the waiting Japanese men.

My own attendant was tall for a Japanese, with a pleasing figure and waved black hair that rolled down to her shoulders.

'Me call Mitsuko,' she announced matter-of-factly as she showed me into the tiled room and kicked off her sandals. I introduced myself and she made several unsuccessful attempts to cope with my name.

'I call you name Fuji-San,' she said smiling prettily and tapping my long occidental nose with a finger.

'*Arrigatou* ... thank you . . .' I replied as she took off her jacket, emerging in a pair of white briefs and a provocative brassière. She motioned me to undress and handed me a towel, directing me into a steam box from which I looked out ridiculously as she prepared a bath, watching the light catch the vertebrae of her spine and the soft curves of her belly as she bent over. But concupiscent thoughts were boiled out of me, like the life from a lobster. Once she looked up and smiled engagingly then came over and stepped up the steam temperature until I broiled helplessly.

'You like, Fuji-San?' she asked, still smiling, and I recalled Japanese attitudes to the pain of others.

'No ... no like . . .'

She released me before I was entirely wasted, though my body felt as though every pore had been forced open, and I was bathed in sweat. I was plunged into a hot bath, limp, inert as a waterlogged rat, the sweat still pouring from me, sunk in a mindless lassitude of well-being. As I dozed, Mitsuko knelt at my head and gently massaged the muscles of my scalp, then suddenly hauled me out and sat me on a tiny stool so that I squatted at her feet. With a lubricious skill she soaped me all over, avoiding only my dangling genitals, rinsing me with pannikins of bath-water until the deck was swimming. My scalp was scrubbed and then I was dunked back into the bath, where I lay like a wallowing hippo.

Again I was brought out and sat on the stool, this time to be deluged with cold water, Mitsuko laughing at my protests and shudders and the spectacular contraction of my genitalia from this savage assault. Declaring herself satisfied, she laid me face down upon a table and began to walk upon my back.

Her feet slid expertly outwards from my spine, the balls of her heels kneading odd knots of muscle, her toes stimulating unguessed at erogenous zones as, in a slow and meticulous promenade, she made several passes from neck to coccyx while I groaned in luxuriating delight beneath her. But this was nothing to the performance to be endured lying on my back. Her strong fingers probed the tense muscles of my legs, over stood-upon in the long watches of our voyage, or cracked the tendons in my arms and gave my head a sinew-snapping twist that made me fear for my life - except that in its aftermath I felt extraordinarily revitalised. During this clinical operation my physical lassitude was such that desire seemed moribund, despite the strange intimacy. To preserve the decencies Mitsuko, her almond eyes averted in deference to my libidinous sensibilities, draped a small cotton towel across my limp penis.

But looking up at her, her breasts alive within the restraint of her brassière as she kneaded my thighs, sitting astride my lower legs, it was impossible not to respond to her presence. The little cotton towel rose like a diminutive bell-tent and Mitsuko smiled at me.

'Ah-so ... Fuji-San ...' she laughed and moved her hands upwards. I surrendered to her ministrations. 'A standing prick has no conscience,' I heard Mike's voice saying, and wondered if Sparks was enjoying himself.

Heavy rain accompanied our departure. We edged down towards the forts and the Uraga Strait, our whistle blasting every two minutes, the Mate at the radar and Captain Richards and myself on the bridge wings. The rain fell in an icy torrent, driven by a strong and cutting north-easterly wind.

'That bloody Masefield,' said the Mate, peering out at me, 'with his "wind like a whetted-knife" bullshit. Perhaps if he'd done more than one trip he'd have written about women like a decent poet.'

I smiled despite my discomfort. The rain had penetrated my duffle coat then my reefer jacket and, running in chilly trickles down my neck, was already filling my shoes.

'Can you see that echo ahead, Fourth Mate?' asked China Dick, stumping anxiously across the bridge.

'Not yet, sir.'

'Put her on dead slow then, and blow that bloody whistle again...'

'Aye, aye, sir.'

Then quite abruptly the rain ceased. I felt myself getting warmer and thought at first that the prickling of sweat was relief at the sight of a ship looming up on the port bow, a freighter of the Osaka Yusen Kaisha which swept past us at unreduced speed heading for her home port. But it was not relief that brought on the muck-sweat; the wind had chopped around and suddenly began to blow with increasing freshness from the south, a warm wind that caused every piece of glass on the bridge, including our binoculars, to steam up instantly. Within an hour we were rolling in a Force 8 gale and the Mate was anxious for his new stows. In Yokohama we had loaded the first of our homeward cargo - piece goods, cameras and tape

Voyage East

recorders, marked conspicuously for Liverpool.

Light as we were, we spent a most unpleasant night of it. By midnight we were labouring through a Force 10 which veered slowly to the west with the glass dropping. It was little better at 0400, except that we had skirted the coast and were headed up into Suruga Bay with the smoky chimneys and cluster of industrial buildings of Shimizu taking form ahead of us as the daylight grew. The further up the Bay we progressed, the greater the shelter. Pine-clad shores and rocky bluffs reminded one of the prints of Hokusai and Utamaro, but the greatest splendour lay ahead of us, for Shimizu sits at the foot of Mount Fuji. The dark, fir-covered slopes rose above us, changing to volcanic scree and talus above the tree-line, then to snow and ice that gleamed in the sunshine.

We were a mere six hours at Shimizu: six hours of frantic loading, mainly canned goods and heavy bundles of plywood, before the Mate's single whistle-blast sent us to stations again and, derricks secured, we once more butted the swells in Suruga Wan. Another fatiguing night passage followed, with little rest below and a watch of intricate navigation and collision avoidance. Dotted with rocks and islets, assiduously fished and busy with traffic of all sizes, the Japanese coast was a stimulating test of our professionalism.

Kobe nestled under a range of hills dark with pine trees and capped with snow, its quays and industrial heart lining the shore and the gentler, residential quarters rising up the bills beyond. Here our mad rush was terminated by Japanese bureaucracy. The port health authorities kept us swinging idly round our anchor for several hours, drawing forth reminiscences from the older hands of pre-war humiliations, when uniformed doctors calling for 'short-arm' inspections (examinations of the penis for symptoms of VD) could cause embarrassment to individuals and delays to the ship. Happily those days were over, though I noticed a worried pallor replace the defiant heartiness that had followed Sparks' bath in Yokohama.

I spent the forenoon with the Second Engineer as we filled an empty deep-tank with salt-water ballast.

'Aye, wee Richard,' Willie Buchan said, 'if you want tae see the real

Japan, come ashore wi' me tonight . . .' He seemed to have buried the hatchet of inter-departmental war.

We began in Clancy's Bar, an all-male-no-bar-girls establishment run by an expatriate Australian with a penchant for all things Japanese. Over a beer we watched a few bouts of Sumo wrestling on the television blinking in one corner. It was clear that Willie and Clancy were old friends.

'You off to see Akiko tonight, eh, you old bastard?'

'Aye, can I use your phone?'

Willie picked up the phone Clancy shoved across the bar and used it with impressively proficient ease. He spoke a few words of Japanese and I could hear a squeal of delight. Ten minutes later we were in a taxi, heading out across the suburb of Iluta to pay our respects to Willie's lady friend.

'Ah'm a fortunate man, you know,' he said expansively, leaning back, his round white moon-face with its undistinguished puggish features happily complacent. 'Ah've known both kinds o' love. The love o' marriage to ma wife Margaret, back hame in Bearsden, an' the other kind . . .' his voice trailed off wistfully and he stared out of the window, suddenly heaving his bulk forward and tapping the driver on the shoulder. 'Here we are.'

We scrambled out and he bent into the driver's window, then straightened up, beaming. 'Why, bless the lass, she's even paid for the taxi.'

We went up some stairs and into what seemed to be a restaurant with low tables and cushions laid on *tatami* matting in an immaculate symmetry. The walls were hung with heavy drapes and a glowing brazier burned in the centre of the room.

Willie pulled off his coat. 'Akiko . . .' he called.

'Willie-San!' She ran to his arms, her dark hair loose, her kimono flying, pinched into her tiny waist by the huge bow of the *obi*. She clung like a limpet to the vast bulk of him and they kissed with the passionate frenzy of old lovers. I saw she was not young, but a handsome woman in her late thirties, with every appearance of great happiness at the sudden arrival of Willie Buchan. I was introduced to her and she inclined her head with a gracious little bow, then sat upon a cushion and drew Willie's wobbling

Voyage East

body down beside her. They nestled together like the prints one could buy in the Motomachi, showing the thousand positions for love.

I drank *saki* with them for half an hour and left them to their idyll.

I was never precisely sure why Willie Buchan suspended the sporadic warfare of our two departments with this intimacy. Some of his sudden friendliness may have been impulsive; but I think not. Perhaps his motivation was more complex, obscure even to himself. I had sailed with him before, coasting the *Antilochus* from Hamburg north-about to Glasgow, where his wife Margaret had come aboard. I knew both poles of his love - so was my invitation a kind of boasting? Was he simply wanting to share his triumph but reluctant to let one of his own engineers off duty? Or was it merely to show one of 'the enemy' how real men took their pleasure and lived their lives to the full? Certainly he was a marked contrast to the dour Mate; a street-wise Glaswegian with little love for Calvinistic souls, whatever their nationality. I thought at the time the matter lay between him and the Mate, and that he saw me as the Mate's creature.

It was of little moment. The crackling bush-warfare flared again in the morning. As our holds were emptied and cleaned and we had gained access to the bottom of the ship, it was necessary to test the wells, drainage pockets from which any water which penetrated the space could be pumped. For this testing of wells the Midshipmen used firehoses to fill them, then the engine-room was requested to check the bilge line and pump them out. For some strange reason the correct selection of valves was a matter of great mystery to Junior Engineers. It could take an hour or two before they had the thing right, and this proved intolerable to Mike. The wait had been punctuated by the usual sending of messages below and the receipt of helpful advice to the effect that the suction pipe was probably blocked by debris. This was refuted by a soaking Midshipman who was required to duck into three feet of filth and satisfy himself the strum was clear, a duty made harder by the fact that half an hour earlier the bored boy had urinated into the well.

But even this had not made any difference, and Mike had carried the war into the enemy camp, raging up to the Chief who had been enjoying a pre-prandial *chota-peg*. Mr Kennington had summoned Willie Buchan who came grumpily, having been woken from an illicit sleep, exhausted after his night of voluptuous excess. Willie raged into the engine-room; within minutes the bilge lines gurgled in responsive fury and the well drained in seconds.

'That's reassuring,' remarked Mike within ear-shot of the embarrassed junior. 'At least we know who to send for if we get caught in a typhoon.' Billy incautiously opened his mouth to shout Mike down but was silenced by the dejected and urinous Midshipman who at that moment slopped past in quest of a shower.

'Excellent training for shit-stirring,' said Billy, evening the score with inspired repartee.

It was in Kobe that I had the unnerving experience of being accused of paternity. At breakfast next morning, trying to read the Purser's copy of the *Mainichi Daily Times* in which our arrival had been announced to the English-speaking commercial fraternity of the Kobe waterfront, I was brought-to by a flurry at the saloon door. One of the dock security officers was asking for the Fourth Mate. There was a stir of interest at Captain Richard's table and I left as inconspicuously as possible, fearful of some problem with the cargo.

'What is it?'

'You come gangway please.' The hand on my arm was unpleasantly insistent; I jerked free, but the urgency and the tight-lipped face suggested an accident. I hurried out onto the centre-castle deck and the head of the gangway where a curious little crowd had gathered.

'This lady say you make her baby, now big trouble, you make much pay money.' He pushed me onto the platform of the gangway jutting out high above the taxi on the quay. There was a babble of delight among the onlookers as I protested. Looking down at the taxi I saw the window open and a face stare back up at me. The guard had repossessed my arm and his free hand stabbed accusingly at my innocent countenance. He shouted something to the effect that I was *Antigone's* Fourth Officer. For perhaps five seconds the girl and I stared at each other in mutual disbelief, then her head withdrew, the window was wound up, and with a gangsterish squeal of tires the taxi and its gravid burden disappeared round the corner of the adjacent godown.

'Not belong right man,' I said to the nonplussed guard, jerking my arm from custody for the second time. I returned to the saloon and my breakfast.

'What was all that about?' asked Mike.

'Case of mistaken identity,' I said, ruminating over corn-flakes. 'Anyone know where Dai Morrison is now?'

'Yeah, shagging sheilas on the old *Stentor,* Mate,' replied Bob in his best Australian. 'Why?'

'I've just met the mother of his first child, and she wasn't too pleased to find a proxy arrived for the wedding.'

'Bloody Welsh goat,' said Bob, shifting his accent gleefully then flushing scarlet as he felt China Dick's baleful glare on the nape of his neck.

RED BARBARIANS

Our dawn sailing from Kobe was such as we should have had from a home port. For me, shackled as luck would have it to the cargo-watch, it unfolded in a series of vignettes: lonely arrivals of men cast out of hotel bedrooms into a freezing dawn, drugged by drink and love, their emotions still some distance astern of them. They stumbled up the gangway, individual bundles of remorse or repletion according to temperament. Even the bellicose Embleton had forgotten his private war and greeted me with a wan and sheepish smile.

Last came Willie Buchan, only minutes before the Mate stepped out onto the boat-deck to recall us to duty with an imperious blast of his whistle. Akiko brought him, bathed to the last in the extraordinary warmth of her affection; he popped from the taxi and stumbled tearfully up the gangway.

'Christ ... oh, Christ,' he mumbled, disappearing into the accommodation as Akiko called a last *Sayonara* after his departing bulk.

'Like the last act of *Madam Butterfly*,' remarked the Mate sourly, lifting the whistle to his lips.

To prolong the agony of departure, we made no clean break with Japan but trailed its tantalising coastline on either side throughout the day. Our passage lay through the five 'inland seas' of the Naikai, the main island of Honshu to the north and the successive coasts of Shikoku and Kyushu to the south. Thousands of islands dotted our route beneath the craggy mountains of sandy rock upon which pines grew dark and mysterious, jewelled here and there with the scarlet arches of Shinto shrines. These congested waters crowded with ferries, fishing boats, junks and coastal traders demanded a high standard of navigation, and we were aided by the presence of our pilot, Mr Yamaguchi.

He was a small elderly man in a shapeless fawn raincoat, his lugubrious face peering through falling folds of parchment skin. He stood alone on the bridge-wing, giving helm orders from time to time, unwilling to fraternise with us.

Voyage East

'Don't ask him what he did in the war,' Bob whispered at me as we wove through the remnant minefields, along the advertised safe passage. Suddenly Mr Yamaguchi turned from the bridge-wing and sucked in his breath in a queer, strained sound, almost as if he was in pain. He bobbed towards us, then having caught our attention he turned and pointed. Another town lay in the distance at the head of one of the hundreds of gulfs that opened from the Naikai.

'Hiroshima,' he said, and we passed the prime meridian of our epoch while Mr Yamaguchi returned to his sad contemplation of the invisible channel down which we thrashed.

The tide caught us in the narrow gut of the Shimonoseki Strait and we were rushed past the ancient town, seven additional knots added to our propelled speed. We discharged Mr Yamaguchi off Moji and as his launch turned away from us he gave us no parting wave, no sign of luck or bon voyage. Then the tide spewed us forth into the wide Strait of Tsu Shima that lay between Japan and Korea where Admiral Togo destroyed the last Tsar's Baltic Fleet which under Rozhdestvensky, had come half-way round the world to fight him.

For us, hostility came from the wind whipping southwards from the tundra of the not-so-distant Siberian Arctic, a bitterly cold wind that froze the salt sea spray as it lifted from the wave-caps, and drummed it on our bridge dodgers or stung our injudiciously exposed cheeks with an agonising pain. The cold became intense as we left the maritime climate of Japan and were embraced by the polar air of the Asian mainland. The bare steel was cold enough to 'burn', the exposed surfaces of bulkheads and the dogs of watertight doors became thickened by layers of ice, while stays and rails were festooned by a rime of icicles. We made an uncomfortable passage, glad of our ballasted deep-tanks but still light enough to be tossed about by the severe gale that screamed down upon us with primordial ferocity.

Our cheeks were wan as jilted brides' while ears and noses acquired the dangerously rosy hue of exposure. We kept our watches hunched in duffle coats, polo-necked sweaters under our thick doeskin uniforms topped with scarves wrapped around our throats. *Antigone* banged and pitched, her empty hull sounding like timpani, moving relentlessly in the close circle of her visible horizon so that we might have been the last living thing on a watery world reversing into chaos. And then we saw other men as we rounded the great promontory of Korea and stood north into the heaving greyness of the Yellow Sea, the fishermen of the Huang Hai. They were aboard motor-trawlers, rugged craft a quarter our size, their bows lifting bodily from the sea, then wallowing into the troughs and sluicing white water aside. They flew the Yin/Yang ensign of South Korea; their tough crews were out on deck hauling nets, though logic and common-sense told us the thing was impossible.

'Those bastards deserve every penny they get,' said the Mate through the side of his mouth as we peered through our glasses at the incredible sight of such hard-bitten men. I could sense in his admiration a regret that we had lost this capacity for enduring extremes, and his unconsummated kinship with such men.

'It makes you think ...' he mused, lowering his glasses at last.

I knew he was thinking of the past and the long rope of tradition that bound him and men like him to it. But it occurred to me that he had been doing too much musing. As far as I knew he had not yet been ashore, but such was his quality of self-sufficiency, so fenced about was he by his competence and so distanced by the responsibilities of his rank, that I did not take this seriously. I only realised its significance with hindsight.

Passing between the peninsulas of Dairen and Shantung we entered the cul-de-sac of the Gulf of Po Hai. The winds that roared about the fringe of the Siberian anti-cyclone, skimming down the pressure gradient crammed between the two weather systems of this corner of the Pacific, now petered out. We were almost entirely landlocked and a still, fog-filled calm settled upon us and upon the smooth waters of the gulf. Four days out of Kobe we dropped anchor off the Taku Bar, where we were to spend six days of frozen misery. That night the fog cleared and a full moon rose, red as an Edam cheese, an oddly appropriate manifestation to herald our arrival off the coast of Red China.

Our only distraction was the celebration of the Chinese New year. It was an irony that our Chinese crew members were unable to spend it ashore - if a shore existed, for we were too far distant from the low, alluvial

Voyage East

coast to see it. The only eminences in the area were the remains at Taku of the Manchu forts razed by the Combined Expedition which landed in 1900 to raise the seige of the Peking legations during the Boxer rebellion. Within sight of the Taku Bar lightvessel we and half-a-dozen other ships swung-to in a desolation of dirty ice-floes and sea-water fulvous with the rich loess of the interior, brought down by the Hai Ho River. Its dun colour only added to the overwhelming impression of drabness.

But our Chinese swept these disadvantages aside in their desire to celebrate. Their courteous hospitality to us was impressive and their messroom under the poop was full of multi-coloured dishes and bowls containing the diverse ingredients of Chinese cuisine. Crayfish and prawns, squid and chopped meat; a sucking pig roasted whole, its eviscerated belly held open by bamboo splints; bowls of sauces and vegetables, water chestnuts, mushrooms and bamboo shoots; the table positively groaned under this mass of food. Bowls of rice, bowls of fish and bowls of soup punctuated the line of main dishes, as did saucers of delicate prawn crackers, cashew nuts, peanuts and other mouth-watering savouries.

Da-Foo, the Mate, was in his element, airing a hitherto unrevealed working knowledge of basic Cantonese, to the evident delight of the Chinese, whose wide grins exhibited rows of gold-capped teeth and a corporate goodwill that shamed our Christmas hospitality. Intent on enjoying the foods, he made me take up the challenge he received to *yam-sing*. It was a terrible responsibility and as well for us that we were at anchor. On the face of it, it was the innocent playground game of ick-ack-ock, in which one produced from behind one's back a fist either balled for 'stone', flat for 'paper', or with forked fingers to make 'scissors'. 'Paper' defeated 'stone' by wrapping it, but was defeated by 'scissors' which cut it. 'Scissors', however, succumbed to 'stone', by which they were blunted. The game got under way after China Dick had departed. The Chinese almost always had the edge on us and we lost disastrously. What made it nearly as lethal as Russian roulette was that the loser had to *yam-sing* a drink, in this case half-a-glass of Johnny Walker Scotch Whisky. Successive rounds were increasingly difficult to stand up for, never mind win.

'*Ay-yah, Tze-Foo* plenty no ... *yam-sing!*'

Bob went down gallantly while upholding the honour of the deck-department, his legs buckling slowly under him, a muck-sweat beading his pale brow. Derisive laughter came from the engineers who clustered round Billy, two games ahead of Bob with one win to his credit and the engine-room Storekeeper for an opponent. The glass of whisky seemed to have had no effect upon Yuen Kau, or perhaps he had a stomach for it. He lost two further games to Billy before slaughtering the hapless Fourth Engineer who was by now emboldened to play again. But the initiative had passed to Yuen Kau and at last Billy too was beaten, literally to his knees, and was helped outside while the Chief Engineer did the decent thing and looked the other way.

'Gone for a technicolour yawn,' said Mike, wisely declining a game on the excuse that he was on watch at midnight.

Only Willie Buchan put up a fight, out-playing the Number One Greaser with a street-wisdom acquired from a Glasgow childhood more robust than our own. The Mate and I declined to go on, both paying the forfeit of supplying another bottle of Scotch.

'You've no fighting spirit,' complained the Purser, 'no stomach for it.'

'It's a waste of good Scotch,' said the Mate, adding, with the relish of the gourmet 'and wrecks good food.'

We did not overstay our welcome; most of us were incapable of doing so after such a parlour game. Bellies bloated and heads spinning in the frosty night air, we slithered on the icy ladder rungs with shouts of *Kung Hey Fat Choy* to usher in the year of the Tiger or the Monkey, or whatever it was. The ship lay still, brilliant moonlight glancing off a rime of frozen moisture on her decks, spars and rigging. Behind me the Mate belched low and appreciatively.

'Beautiful night .

'Bloody cold ...'

'Bloody China.'

Two of the seamen passed us, turning in from a night of cards with the Bosun. Our tracks crossed at Number Four hatch.

'G'night . . .'

Voyage East

'Night...' and then in a stage whisper meant for our ears, '... officers pissed again...'

Morning anchor watch was an agony of cold. During the four hours I spent alone on the bridge the thermometer rose from -11° to -8° Centigrade. One's ears and nose seemed prominently distant from one's reluctant and sluggishly thin blood. Only a few short weeks before we had been broiling in Singapore and Bangkok; now I was glad of my beard, for the assiduously shaved cheeks of others had the look of raw meat. It was difficult to imagine the same anchorage in the summer, when the continental climate inverted itself. A voyage earlier in a different ship I had lain a week at anchor on the Taku Bar in stifling heat, the ship infested with flies which hung over us in a malevolent black cloud dark enough to threaten sanity in its nightmarish persistence. With the flies came small insectivorous birds who gorged themselves into flightless immobility and only added to our sense of madness. For weeks afterwards the dark corpses of flies were to be found in odd nooks and crannies.

Our idleness ended at three o'clock one morning when the Chinese authorities came aboard from an anciently elegant white steam-cutter. We were turned out of our bunks and made to stand about for three hours, while in the comfort of the passengers' lounge the bureaucracy of the People's Republic of China ground its remorseless way. In their high-collared suits of dark blue cotton the two officials, an immigration officer and a doctor, sat at card-tables with our identity documents piled next to them. Two khaki-jacketed and blue-trousered soldiers armed with Kalashnikov automatics flanked them, their unsmiling faces filled with the importance of their task. Beside them China Dick sat awkwardly, his presence necessary for reasons of protocol, while the Purser, an acolyte to this solemn ceremonial, produced the appropriate discharge-book for the identification of each of us in turn.

'What's it for?' asked the Junior Midshipman.

'See if you're a known enemy of the people,' said his mentor and senior.

'Christ!'

'Something to write home about, eh kid?' whispered Chippie, grinning widely at this potent exhibition of proletarian power.

'They might lock Embleton up,' muttered Mike.

'No such luck.'

'Bloody class warfare,' we mumbled, catching the Purser's eye.

If we British objected to standing idly for hours in the pre-dawn cold, we at least had little to fear. For our Hong Kong Chinese the experience could be less pleasant. The aggression of the interrogating officials was occasionally blatant, causing their victims to blanch and tremble so much that China Dick intervened. The arsis of the immigration officer's voice silenced China Dick; the humiliation was irksome to him. The matter blew over and the chastened greaser was allowed to go, leaving the unfamiliar surroundings sheepishly. Both he and Captain Richards had lost face, and this seemed to be the purpose of the ritual. One had experienced similar mass humiliation elsewhere from the anonymous bureaucracies of other countries.

We went forward in turn and extended our hands, palms downwards, to the doctor.

'What's that for?' hissed Sparks.

'See if you've got syph,' said Mike.

'They can tell the general state of a person's health by the growth of his nails ...'

But Sparks was not listening to Bob. He had gone deathly pale and looked as if he was about to faint.

'Woodman, Extra Third Mate.' The Purser's voice purred in my ear and the immigration officer looked up from my papers. He seemed to be considering something.

'You been Imperialist America? United States?'

I nodded. 'Yes, two years ago . . .'

I had endured a similar scrutiny on board the *Telemachus* in Los Angeles: 'You bin anywhere near Red China, Richard?' Yessir, I had visited both poles of the habitable world and neither official had asked me which I preferred. The immigration officer nodded and I moved on to the doctor. He had dark, intelligent eyes that surveyed me briefly; his nod of dismissal

Voyage East

was curt but not unfriendly. I moved off to join Mike and Bob, who had been detailed to attend the other facet of this long-winded procedure, the inspection of the ship. Alert for drugs, stowaways, or the illegal imports of filthy capitalism, we conducted the guards round the accommodation. It fell to my lot to accompany the party inspecting the engineers' alleyway and our own cabins. The soldiers opened drawers, stared at upside-down letters and personal photographs. There was more of curiosity than malice in it, though our Englishness resented the intrusion. Privacy, like individuality, was not a concept readily appreciated by the Chinese mind.

A pile of magazines was rifled and a triumphantly zealous revolutionary cry came from one of the soldiers. As he held one up the centre-fold dropped open and a cascade of impossibly depilated limbs was exposed, above which the pertly arrogant breasts of the Playmate-of-the-Month jutted provocatively. The three guards collected round and for a long, libidinous moment they stared at the glossy-lipped blonde before rounding on me indignantly.

'American!' the leader shouted. I nodded. They turned further pages; still nude, the same girl sat astride a Harley Davidson and rolled on a satin-sheeted bed. They pointed at her expurgated pudendum and burst into chatter amongst themselves. Suddenly the leader thrust the magazine at me.

'American!' he repeated. 'No good!'

In the Mate's cabin their eyes fell upon his tape-recorder. One of them pressed a button and the fiery chords of Beethoven's '*Appassionata*' sonata struck us, producing incredulous expressions on the soldiers' faces.

'Belong favourite music of Lenin,' I offered in an inspired moment, nodding furiously as they looked at me. I held up a thumb. 'Lenin's number one.'

They recognised the name, nodding back. 'Lenin ... Lenin number one ... Lenin good!' The majestic notes of Beethoven must have fallen as discordantly upon their ears as did Chinese music upon our own.

But it was over at last; none of us was declared utterly undesirable and the officials departed, to be replaced by a pilot. Two of the soldiers remained, tall men from the northern provinces, of a stature that had surprised the Americans in Korea. They were there to keep an eye on us, pickets on the other side in the class war of the Purser's phrase. With total impassivity they watched us go to our stations as we edged into the mouth of the Hai Ho. The Taku coast lay like a brown smudge to port, the northern shore a low drab plain, dusted with snow. Brown ice swirled about our bow, retarding our progress as we approached the port of Hsinkiang, a consummately ugly modern sprawl of low concrete sheds, pine power poles and festoons of overhead wiring. The only spots of colour were the flags and hoardings, huge boards depicting the heroic achievements of the Chinese proletariat. Who were we to ridicule their progress? China had been an unhappy country until it seized its own destiny from the hands of the taipans and the warlords. There was a triumphant flutter to the red flags that lifted like oriflammes to the icy northerly breeze sweeping down from Siberia, and perhaps our sense of remote isolation was compounded by inherited guilt.

One of these gigantic hoardings depicted a smiling girl holding a sheaf of wheat and a youth holding a sickle in front of a background of tractors set against the new dawn. Beneath it, a party of some two hundred labourers plodded to work. They were diminished by the naive and powerful image above them, yet it conferred upon their progress an immense sense of purpose as, with their shovels and picks, they went to extend the wharves of Hsinkiang.

The ice had rafted between the ship and her berth, scrunched into an impenetrable mass; it needed the churning of an old steam tug to reduce the pancakes of grubby ice to a slush, through which we hauled *Antigone* alongside. I was the first person down the gangway, to read our arrival draught from the white numerals cut into stem and stern. Men with padded coats and fur caps with flapping ear-covers were heaving the final ropes ashore as I stood by a bollard and read the after draught. Curious, they peered over my shoulder at the Arabic numerals I jotted down, the smell of garlic strong on their breath. They grinned and chuckled to themselves, exchanging remarks, smiling and nodding through wrinkled, wind-burned complexions. I grinned back and one pulled at his chin, nodding vigorously while they shared a huge joke.

Voyage East

'They think you're an animal,' Mike called down from the poop, 'you hairy bastard.'

The seamen turning the ropes up on *Antigone's* after bitts laughed and I heard Embleton agree. 'He's a bastard all right ...'

We were *fan kwei*, red barbarians, hairy foreigners, little better than the beasts of the field with whom our kinship was made manifest by our beards.

'You know,' said the Purser later, when the amusement value of my beard came up for discussion, 'when Lord Macartney's embassy was received by the Chinese Emperor in 1797, Macartney reported the filthy habit of the Chinese of closing one nostril with a finger and blasting the contents of the other over the deck. At the same time the Chinese commented upon the disgusting habit of the foreigners of blowing warm snot into small pieces of silk and concealing the matter in their clothes!'

'They don't teach history like that at school,' said Bob.

'Too complex in significance for the teaching profession to grasp,' said the Purser.

The wharfinger was a bespectacled and enthusiastic young man with a degree and an excellent command of English. Liaison with the Chinese was a happier matter over cargo than over immigration or port health. In contrast with the static disfavour of the latter bureaucrats, our wharfinger introduced a cheerful note of purpose. He seemed an embodiment of the hoarding that silently exhorted effort from the work-force. Meeting in the Mate's office, it was a matter of minutes to assimilate the details of the coming consignments and their eventual location in the ship: that delicate compromise of weight, capacity occupied and eventual destination. Human hair, hog-bristles, hides and hammers would form the bulk of our lading, together with cases of wire nails and other simple manufactures, mainly hand-tools. By the time the meeting broke up, the hatches were already open and after discharging a hundred drums of acetone we began loading in earnest.

The strictest supervision was essential. Of major importance was the matter of ventilation, achieved by the use of wooden planking, or dunnage, combined with rush cargo mats. The disparate climates through which we had to pass, the differing hygroscopic characteristics of various commodities and their liability to taint, their relative weight and value, all had to be taken into account. Hog-bristles and human hair (for wigs, uncompromisingly black though it was) were of considerable value. Arsenicated cattle hides stank to high heaven and could not be stowed anywhere near tea, which readily took up odour and would be utterly ruined by such a juxtaposition. But *Antigone* had been built for this. For all the cunning of her hull design she remained a great floating box, her stock-in-trade her internal capacity. As we prepared to sail from each successive loading port, the last duty of the cargo-officer was to measure her remaining vacant volume - a matter of inspired guestimates and calculations which became increasingly important (and easier to measure) as she filled. The tonnage, in 'space tons' of forty cubic feet, was telegraphed ahead of the ship and the agents arranged the consigning of parcels of cargo accordingly.

Antigone was divided into six hatches, each with its lower hold and 'tween deck. Numbers Three and Four had an additional centre-castle deck while Number One, to increase the forward strength of the ship, had an extra 'tween deck. Number Three hold was divided into deep-tanks for liquid or dry cargo as required, as was the forward half of Number Four. Its after section ran through into Number Five, making an enormous space in both 'tween deck and hold. Below the holds lay the ship's double-bottom tanks, holding our fresh water and bunkers, with additional water-ballast tanks fore and aft. Only the engine room really intruded into this gigantic and voluminous construction.

As if the Mate's work was not complicated enough by the differing and sometimes conflicting demands of individual consignments, their ports of discharge and their liability to produce or absorb condensation, smell and so forth, he had also the matter of the ship's stability to consider. Transversely this affected her ability to remain upright as the sea sought to capsize her; longitudinally this governed her trim, draught and the consequent efficiency of her hull. In general, heavy loads were placed in the bottom of the ship, though this should not make the ship too 'stiff' or it would result in a violent jerking roll, destructive in itself. However, too

Voyage East

little positive stability would make her 'tender', liable to roll with a heart-stopping sluggishness at the slightest provocation. Ship stability, as so much else at sea, was a matter of sensible compromise.

Finally, there were also the small parcels of really valuable cargo to consider. These might consist of mail, spirits, currency, valuable metals, lizard and snake skins, silk, scientific equipment, personal effects, arms and even commodities like pepper or gum. These were stowed under lock and key in either the strongrooms, the fore-cabins or the other small cargo lockers situated under forecastle and poop.

Resolution of all these multifarious demands, demands which exploited the versatility of *Antigone's* breed as a general cargo-liner, placed a heavy and relentless burden upon the shoulders of the Mate. His labour was heroic - as heroic as that suggested by the Communist hoarding. For the rest of us it was different; even in Hsinkiang, amid the barren plains of North China with its history of foreign rape and the present domination of all activity by the single-minded ethics of Mao Tse Tung, we went rollicking ashore. Not that I recall seeing a single woman in Hsinkiang, for even pleasure followed strict principles. There was a Seaman's Club and a Friendship Store and little else; but the Tsingtao beer and the truly magnificent fried king prawns at the former were excellent, while the goods at the latter reflected the New China's desire to acquire foreign currency. Beautiful carpets from neighbouring Tientsin were offered at staggeringly cheap prices, as well as the other usual curios. There were more practical items too, hampers and vacuum flasks and fur hats. I bought one of these for a pound. Folded it looked like a Cossack *papenka,* but possessed sealskin flaps that pulled snugly down over my frozen ears; it came into its own as we returned to *Antigone* at midnight. The wind keened menacingly in the overhead wires which shared the poles with clusters of loud-speakers, silent now after the strident clamour of the day. For hours we had been subjected to discordant exhortations to the port's workers to graft harder and defeat imperialism. The apparent relative poverty of the Chinese language, employing no more than a handful of sounds, made the experience very wearying to western ears.

The moan of the wind was suddenly pierced by the shriek of a steam-whistle and out of the night a monstrous black steam locomotive puffed and clanked past us with a long train of trucks. Fine coal dust swirled about us.

'Coal for that Chinese ship astern of us,' remarked Bob, flogging his body with his arms 'going down to the Chapei power station at Shanghai.'

The train passed at last and we galvanised our bodies forward. Along the wall of a newly erected shed the dockside lights illuminated a painted slogan, white characters on a scarlet background with a thoughtfully-provided English translation: 'Our thinking is guided by Mao Tse Tung and the principles of Marxist-Leninism.'

'Makes a change from sex,' said Bob as we made the final dash for the gangway.

We found where such intellectual guidance could lead next morning, when the off-duty Midshipmen woke to find their accommodation occupied by Chinese soldiers. In pursuance of the fundamental equality of their creed, the two assigned to guard us had entered the half-deck, made themselves tea and, with every appearance of curiosity at such barbarian misuse of porcelain, pissed in the lavatory. The Midshipmen were indignant, but there was little they could do. The soldiers were stolidly indifferent and the subtle menace of their native-made Kalashnikovs deterred further action.

To some extent the Midshipmen were avenged the following afternoon, from an unusual quarter. I had gone on deck to relieve Mike, and witnessed the whole incident. Impatient to get more dunnage into a stow of canned goods, Mike had sent the Senior Midshipman up into the 'tween deck of Number Five hold where a bundle of dunnage planks lay awaiting use. Resentful at having to undertake a task that the gang of labourers should have done, the Midshipman began hurling plank after plank into the lower hold. I waited at the coaming until Mike should finish and clamber up on deck to be relieved. He shouted up to the Midshipman that he had thrown sufficient planks, but the young man, well into his muscular stride, continued tossing dunnage down. The planks sailed gracefully out of the 'tween deck, imperfect aerofoils, descending at odd, cracking angles.

'That's enough!' Mike bawled.

Voyage East

Still the planks rained down and Mike, angering fast and losing face before the Chinese who had feigned incomprehension when he asked them to get more dunnage, now resorted to his last-ditch tactic.

'For *fuck's* sake stop!'

The crudity had more than the desired effect. Although the descending stream of dunnage ceased, it was replaced by a storm of invective from the Chinese charge-hand, who railed against Mike's verbal imperialism. Amid the torrent of invective the universally understood vulgarism was repeated. It had clearly offended the Chinese who saw in the incident the evils of capital exploiting labour. In the 'tween deck above, the Senior Midshipman smirked his enjoyment of this sudden ally's onslaught. Furious, Mike climbed out of the hatch.

'What the hell are you grinning at?'

'Your non-conformity with the principles of Marxist-Leninism.'

'Bollocks!'

'Precisely.'

'Bloody class warfare ...'

We left Hsinkiang in a snow-storm, the flakes sweeping horizontally, direct from the Arctic. It cleared as we steamed out into the gulf and after dark we spoke by aldis lamp to the signal station at Tengchow. Slowly we left the extreme dry cold of the north astern, steaming southwards towards the damp fogs of the Yangtze Kiang. It was a total change of climate, though only of a mere six degrees of latitude, for the temperature rose above freezing. Yet the penetrating damp seemed colder and the germs, frozen in North China, now infected our throats and noses, so that we went miserably to our stations as we moved up the Yangtze Kiang towards the pilot station off Tsungming Island.

This was where it had all started; the first questing Indiamen, the opium clippers and then the lovely tea clippers. Just here, off the Woosung forts, the *Thermopylae* and *Cutty Sark* had cast off their steam tugs and spread studding-sails for the 14,000 miles race to the Channel. Here too old Alfred's *Agamemnon* had arrived, to give the clippers their death-wound and open the tea trade to steam ships.

We swung out of the swift brown stream of the Yangtze and into its narrower tributary, the Whang-Pu. Passing the embrasured ramparts of Woosung where a sleekly modern Chinese destroyer lay alongside, we made our slow way upstream towards Shanghai. Pilotage regulations prohibiting the use of radar compelled us to anchor in fog, which closed in frequently, prolonging our passage. Moisture dropped from every awning spar and funnel guy, every davit span and aerial, cloaking us in a sodden blanket of abjection.

The main reason for our enforced immobility in fog was the density of river traffic, for the Whang-Pu was crowded with small craft. Tugs towing lighters, sampans and night-soil boats were among this floating mass, but it chiefly consisted of junks. Low northern junks with their almost horizontally battened sails, or the high-pooped, batwinged southern variety, worked the winds and tides up and down the river with a masterly, timeless skill. Many of these junks were ancient, bearing the remnants of opulent decoration, their sails over-patched and tattered, their anchor cables twisted bamboo, yet sailing with the efficiency that had established the craft as an ocean-going success long before the Portuguese had ventured into the eastern seas. Nor was their role thalassic, for a Chinese admiral had ventured to the southern tip of Africa before an imperial decree dismembered his navy and set the boundaries of the middle kingdom at its landward frontiers. They were curiously fascinating craft and many had doubtless served the ancient Chinese calling of coastal piracy which had flourished until the Communist victory of 1949.

As we lay at anchor ringing the bell and gong that International Regulations demanded at anchor, these junks ghosted past us. Out on the bridge-wing the Mate stood watching them, his eternal fascination with the seafaring of others undiminished by the penetrating chill of the fog. Eventually it lifted and we made our way steadily upstream. As we passed a long wharf at Pootung the mate pointed out the poorly obscured lettering on the corrugated iron of the godown roof. *Holt's Wharf* it read, long since sequestrated by the Communist authorities.

'There was quite a colony out here when I was a youngster,' said China

Voyage East

Dick, suddenly conversational now that the anxiety of the fog had gone. 'The wharf-manager had a house just over there,' he pointed, 'and there was always a Blue Funnel or a Glen ship alongside, see ...'

I had not imagined Captain Richards as anything other than the portly master he was now. Even the story of him reboarding his torpedoed ship had somehow taken shape in my mind with him in his present physical state. It occurred to me to wonder why he had been called 'China Dick' in the first place, and later I asked the Mate; he refused to answer.

'Ask the Old Man himself,' he replied dangerously. Instead I consulted the ship's memory.

'I thought everybody knew,' said the Purser, amused. 'Well, when he was a young midshipman he had an unfortunate mishap here in Shanghai. He tore his foreskin and had to be circumcised. He was operated on by a woman, a *chi-chi* doctor who told him his penis was a delicate part of the anatomy, like a piece of porcelain ...'

So the old joke at the Shipping Office had been right after all! Time, age and rank had converted the reference from the anatomical to the geographical.

'He's got good cause to remember the place, then,' I said, laughing.

'It was a wide-open city in the days before the Long March,' went on the Purser, 'when the International Concessions were wrung out of the poor bloody Chinese; run as a western enclave in the twenties and thirties, full of gangsters, hoodlums and whores, white Russians and expatriate British police officers and God knows what besides. I've heard it called the most exciting city on earth . . .'

It almost looked as though time had stood still as we rounded the last bend and steadied our course for the Garden Reach. On the west bank the purple skyline was Chicago-Odeon, petrified tombstones of western commercial interference set among the fatal aspirations of Sun Yat Sen's republic. We swung off the Bund where the cruisers and destroyers of the imperial powers once lay, showing their respective flags in 'Warship Row'. Now a few deep-water merchantmen like ourselves, Chinese coasters and the usual multitude of sampans and rag-sailed junks churned the turgid yellow waters of the Whang Pu in a duller scene. Our berth was just downstream from the Bund, below Soochow Creek where lay the British diplomatic presence. Once a posting of considerable prestige, the place now pandered to Chinese sensibilities as 'The Office of the Official of the British Chargé d'Affaire's Office in Peking looking after the affairs of British nationals in Shanghai', a piece of splendidly Orwellian tautology in which lingering remnants of Lord Macartney's handkerchief might still be detected.

But commerce remained even after the flags had gone, just as it had preceded them. The riches of this vast country were still exported by its stoic, industrious and long-suffering people. From the rapacity of foreign exploiters and the Manchu mandarins; through the dissolution of the Celestial Empire and the foundering of the first republic; the anarchy of warlords and the long uninterrupted conflict that began in a war with Japan, went on with China's participation in the Allied effort of the Second World War and tore itself to pieces in the Nationalist defeat by Mao's Communists; China had survived. The dragon had woken to shake the world in Korea, and more peaceful symbols of her collective will to survive poured now into *Antigone's* holds. Sacks of talcum, bone glue, apricot kernels, cotton goods, hides and furs, frozen eggs and prawns, tobacco, ingots of antimony, precious silks triple-wrapped in matting, all found their way below. In the deep tanks we loaded white tung oil, pressed cold from the roasted and powdered seeds of *Aleurites cordata*, the wood-oil tree, which possessed a high specific gravity, polymerised easily and was much used then in the manufacture of paints. The 340 tons we took on board were said to be worth most of the voyage's expenses. It was not the only mysterious substance.

'What is this stuff used for?' Bob asked me as he took over the deck and we watched a sling of bags containing barium bromide being lowered into Number Five hatch.

'Putting in the tea at Wormwood Scrubs.'

'No, seriously ...'

'Seriously, no idea. Don't recall a thing about chemistry beyond the process of turning yeast into alcohol ...'

'Barium, sir, emits electrons when heated.' We turned and stared at the

Voyage East

Junior Midshipman. 'It's used in cathode ray tubes ... you know, for radar.'

'I know what a bloody cathode ray tube is!' snapped Bob. 'Have you got a knife on you?'

'A knife?'

'Yes, a knife, a bloody seaman's knife, for cutting ropes and getting stones out of horse's hooves.'

The Midshipman looked even more puzzled. 'Well, no, actually . . .'

'And I don't suppose you know how to make a carrick bend?' went on Bob relentlessly.

'A carrick bend?'

'Don't keep repeating what I say ... you can't, can you?'

'I'm not sure, sir . . .'

'Of course you can't. That's the trouble with you modern lads. You know all about electrons and cathode ray tubes, but you haven't a clue about carrying a knife or tying a few knots.' Bob paused, and then added accusingly 'Got a comb?'

'Yes ...' The Midshipman reached into the hip pocket of his shorts.

'See what I mean?' Bob turned to me with an expression of mock-despair.

'I don't understand why...'

But the lad got no further, for just then an irritated Senior Midshipman arrived in search of his subordinate. 'The Mate wants you! And quick! Christ, you're really in the shit!'

The two Midshipmen hurried off. Bob and I exchanged glances. Bob shrugged.

'Haven't a clue, chum. Perhaps we should go and find out what's going on.' He looked satisfied at the completeness of the Middy's discomfiture.

'When did *you* last tie a carrick bend?'

'Sod off,' he grinned amiably.

I watched a sling of barium sway down into the open maw of Number Two hatch and then followed him.

The boy was in trouble; potentially very serious trouble, here in a suspicious, wounded and defensive country. We could hear the Mate roaring at him as soon as we reached the boat-deck.

'You bloody, stupid young fool. D'you not understand what you've done? Eh? You could be shipped off to prison or an internment camp. This is a bloody crime against the People's Republic of China! Christ, laddie, this is no joke, this is the big bad bloody world!'

Bob and I passed a Chinese soldier on the boat-deck. He had his head cocked beneath his small-crowned peaked cap and was listening to the row, aware that something unusual was in progress. He began to walk with a predatory gait towards the noise. We accelerated our stride to beat him to its source. The Mate, standing in his cabin doorway, looked up as we entered the alleyway.

'D'you know what this silly little bastard's done?' he asked us rhetorically. 'He's bloody near stopped the ship and got himself arrested. If I hadn't happened to send for the Middies' journals this morning and the Chinks had got hold of his before we sailed, God only knows what might have happened. They've already had the guards in their accommodation once; you'd think they'd bloody learn.'

The Mate held up the Junior Midshipman's log-book, tore a page from it and held it out to us. It was beautifully written, for the Middy had a flair for such things: and there, halfway down the page, was a detailed impression of the Chinese destroyer we had passed at Woosung. In pencil and watercolour, it showed the sleek grey warship in detail. The Mate was right. With cameras forbidden, British intelligence in Hong Kong would be quite interested in the sketch.

Behind me the loom of the guard was tangible. Fortunately Bob and I effectively blocked the access. I could feel my heart beating and next to me Bob was grimacing and gesturing at his chest, drawing the irate Mate's attention to the presence of approaching Nemesis.

'Fancies himself as James Bond,' said the Mate, venting the last of his furious exasperation on the hapless Midshipman as he realised how close we were to the consummation of his fears. He handed back the mutilated book to the Midshipman, struck a match and set it to the torn-out page. The flame caught and flared, and he dropped the charring sheet into his cabin rosy where it expired in a thick twist of smoke.

'Don't you ever do such a stupid thing again. The Chinese authorities are bloody touchy … go on, bugger off.'

We parted to let the shaken Midshipman through. He was suddenly confronted by the guard and brought this log-book up in front of him like a shield, edging past the small figure with the evilly gleaming black Kalashnikov. The guard's expression was suspicious, his finger curled round the trigger of the weapon. Then he said something angrily and turned away. The Mate let out a long breath.

'Christ! He could have stopped the ship!'

In the Mate's eyes that would have been a greater crime than espionage.

Mike and I stretched our legs on the Bund after dinner. Hordes of Chinese cycled vigorously past us, over-crowded buses surged along and dilapidated and overloaded lorries chugged by, fuelled by the collapsing balloons of gas bags tied to their cab roofs. Once we were surprised to see a smartly-dressed woman, quite unlike the androgynous creatures we had hitherto observed with only white socks and bobbed hair as sexual identification. She lay back in a rickshaw, the only one we saw.

'Class warfare, you see,' said Mike, sardonically, trotting out the catch-phrase of the voyage, 'even here in the worker's paradise. I suppose she's the wife of a party official.'

'Or a party official herself,' I added, vague imaginings of Midshipmen under interrogation stirring in my mind's eye.

And we too moved like aliens, head and shoulders above the Shanghaiese, who lacked the stature of their northern cousins. They stared at us with undisguised curiosity and apparent amusement.

'I suppose we all look alike to them,' observed Mike. 'Red barbarians…'

My beard aroused excited comment from a gaggle of laughing children who followed us in increasing numbers until Mike found them irritating, and we sought the sanctuary of the Seaman's Club.

It had once been the Jockey Club, an establishment of such sanctity that, before 1949, our entry would have been proscribed on the grounds of our social undesirability. Times had changed. Inside the palatial foyer stood a huge white marble statue of Chairman Mao gazing benignly over our heads. Along one wall black and white photographs showed the paunchy white police of Alabama beating up negro protestors, a convincing demonstration of American imperialism.

'Now *that*,' said Mike sardonically nodding at the propaganda pictures, 'is the land of the free.'

Above stretched a huge scarlet banner bearing White Chinese characters, and an English translation: *Seamen of the World Unite!*

'Be the biggest piss-up in history,' remarked Mike as we made our way towards the bar. It had once been the longest in the world, an impressive perspective of dark mahogany trimmed with a brass foot-rail, at which stood a lone pair of Jugoslavs from a Rijeka-registered freighter.

'The Purser told me,' I said as we blew the froth off the Tsingtao beer, 'that in the old days, as Master of a Blue Funnel ship, China Dick would have just been tolerated at the lower end of the bar. Apparently where one stood and drank here depended upon where one ranked in the pecking-order of Shanghai society.'

'Jesus Christ, it must have been intolerable,' said Mike. 'You can't blame the Chinese for wanting it all to end, can you?' He smiled amicably at the Jugoslavs.

We sailed the following afternoon, slipping down the Whang Pu in a thin, watery sunshine. As we pulled off the berth and the screw churned up the debris which the river had swept under our stern, it dislodged something which rolled over with a white flash.

It was the body of a man, thin and rigid beneath black pyjamas, the face ghastly with decay.

'Too much people,' said the Pilot.

Voyage East

a CHANGE OF ORDERS

The Mate had the Crowd turned-to on the forecastle long before we entered the Lei Mun Pass on our homeward approach to the Crown Colony. There had been a lightening of spirits as we approached Hong Kong, a compound of excitement at being homeward bound, of anticipation of mail, and of release from the dreary restrictions of the China coast. This feeling was less than just to the Chinese, for of all the world's ports, one need never lock one's cabin in those of the People's Republic, and if there was something intimidating about the heavy-handed presence of guards, we had at least had no trouble from the less tractable elements in our crew. But now, despite the Bosun's eagle eye, Embleton was in high good spirits on the forecastle as he assisted in the operation known as 'breaking the cable.'

This was done prior to making fast to the mooring buoy at which we would load from junks. It meant that one of the ship's anchors had to be lashed in its hawse-pipe with several turns of heavy wire, then a few fathoms of its cable tugged laboriously on deck and disconnected by 'breaking' it at a shackle, the joining devices that made up each anchor cable from standard fifteen fathom lengths of stud-link chain. Once it had been separated from its anchor, the loose end of cable was hauled forward and passed over the bow.

As we approached the buoy a *wallah-wallah,* the local name for a small motor-boat, detached itself from the crowd of water-craft in the vicinity and made for our bow. It contained a crew of three Chinese, two of whom would leap aboard the big steel buoy and shackle our cable to its mooring ring.

'Half-astern!'

The telegraphs jangled and *Antigone* trembled as her propeller began to stir the water under her counter. The cluster of boats awaiting our announced arrival were pitched about as they moved inexorably towards us. The Mate was signalling from forward, one arm raised as he leaned over the bow. The *wallah-wallah* had disappeared from our view on the bridge, hidden by the flare of the bow.

'Full astern!'

The vibration increased, the seething whorls of water up our side boiled white and green and an incautious sampan was whirled away like a chip of wood in a whirl-pool.

'Stop her!'

There was frantic activity on the forecastle. The windlass ground into gear, then slowed and stopped. After a little the telephone rang and the Mate's distorted voice reported the ship securely moored.

'Finished with engines!'

The triple ring was responded to with obvious enthusiasm by the engineers below.

Almost immediately we were again subjected to invasion. A Hong Kong harbour craft brought a pontoon alongside, close above which we lowered our gangway to give safe access to the ship, then first the agent, then the foreman and the tally clerks, the vendors, tailors, shoemakers, coolies and half the world, it seemed, poured aboard with a gravity-defying energy that swept me from my station on the gangway as I attempted to get down it to hail the company *wallah wallah* and read the *Antigone's* arrival draught.

For purposes of individual transport to and from a ship on the buoys, the agents, Butterfield and Swire, hired one of these boats. They ran a ferry service as-and-when required, for a dollar a trip. Scores of these boats touted for business in the harbour or off the official landing places at Kowloon and Hong Kong, the lucky ones flying the house-flags of the Companies which had chartered their services. If one missed the last of the Company's *wallah-wallahs,* the hire of one of the irregular boats could prove expensive, particularly after midnight.

As my own boat approached the bobbing pontoon, having made a slow circuit of the ship to enable me to read the draught marks on *Antigone's* stem and stern posts, I was aware of a smart white launch delivering a passenger to our gangway. The launch bore an unfamiliar flag and was called, oddly I thought, *Dayspring.* Its passenger had vanished by the time I reached the accommodation but as I inscribed the details of our arrival draught on the Board of Trade's form, I heard laughter from the Mate's cabin and, forcing

Voyage East

my way through a crowd of Chinese, I found a red-faced priest in a black soutane sitting on the Mate's settee with a large glass of whisky in his massive paw.

'And who's this fine fellow?' The other fist was thrust out towards me and I was introduced to Father O'Rourke of the Stella Maris, the Roman Catholic mission to seamen.

'The good father's come to save us,' said the Mate, obviously anxious to have the priest gone so that he could attend to the queue of Chinese blocking the alleyway. Father O'Rourke clearly thought such commercial considerations could wait until he had dealt with our spiritual welfare.

'I hear you've all been sinning up in Japan.'

'Prodigiously, so, Father,' said the mate between impatient puffs of smoke as he sucked his pipe into ignition.

'As I thought, as I thought...'

'The draught, sir . . .' I held out the form and the Mate took it with a look of agony.

'And I suppose a fine fellow like you has been fornicating?' Father O'Rourke made it sound like scoring a try in a Rugby International, and I think my denial disappointed him. Perhaps he simply did not believe me. I tried to change the subject.

'What's the ensign you're flying, Father?'

'Why, 'Tis the flag of the Holy See ... as far as Oi know the *Dayspring* is the only vessel in the world to be registered in Vatican City ... and talking of ensigns, I must be off. We've the first ship to fly the Irish flag in Hong Kong arriving at any moment and I must meet her.' He stood, fixing me with a baleful stare. 'At least she'll be full of *honest* sinners, willing to confess themselves...'

He turned to the Mate and wagged an admonishing finger. 'And you, Mister Mate, you give them poor apprentice boys the afternoon off, and I'll take 'em all up to St Michael's shrine and do 'em some decent good. God bless you both.'

And he was gone, leaving the Mate and me staring across the cabin. The Mate blew a cloud of smoke in relief.

'The Dayspring from on high hath visited us...' he said. 'Go and tell those fornicating little bastards in the half-deck that their guardian angel has just got them an afternoon off ... St Michael's bloody shrine ... does he think I've fallen for that blarney?'

The news was not welcomed in the half-deck. If the Mate was prepared to give free time, there were other things Midshipmen could do in Hong Kong.

'Oh, sir!' The Junior Midshipman protested (and I noted this new and rebellious maturity with wry disappointment), 'St Michael's bloody shrine ... do we *have* to go?'

'Not if you don't want the afternoon off. You can stay and help me round the deck.'

'Fuck that,' said the Senior. 'No, we'll go...' I thought I caught a gleam of mischief in his eye. It looked as if the Vatican City's principal vessel might be suffering its first case of desertion before the afternoon was out.

I kept the afternoon on deck. At each hatch, moored side by side, the lighters and junks assembled in accordance with the instructions pencilled on their boat-notes by the indefatigable Mate. As each inner one emptied, it warped out clear, allowing the remaining stack to heave themselves alongside. The high-sterned junks provided a fascinating insight into the domestic life of the water-folk of Hong Kong. Fifty or sixty feet in length, they bore two or three masts. The many-battened sails were lowered to one side, allowing the derrick runners to whip out their cargoes. The cases, cartons, casks and so forth were netted by the males in the junk's crew, for these were family homes, not merely cargo carrying craft. Father and sons laboured in the waist and sometimes an older man, presumably the grandfather of the youngest generation on board, would also help. They were lean men in scanty cotton trousers and tee shirts, often bare footed despite the danger to their unprotected toes as the cases skidded under the snatching impulse of the derricks while the junks bobbed alongside, rocking dangerously in the wake of passing ships.

The poops of these amazing craft provided the family accommodation. Tiny cabins contained sleeping rolls, while across the stern, overhanging the great rudder, a series of cunningly-made cubicles and lockers provided a variety of facilities. Above the rudder stock, where a hole allowed the

Voyage East

tiller to be shipped, a plank formed the shitting-place. To one side a suspended bamboo basket formed a small chicken coop, with a pair of laying hens; to the other were an inset iron bowl containing the charcoal cooking fire, and lockers for food-stuffs. The daughters of this tiny commune cleaned pannikins and woks, or helped the women of the junk to prepare the next meal, another child played with simple wooden toys on the tiny poop-deck, while the toddler of the family was restrained by a piece of string about the waist. On the wife's back the head of the newest arrival bobbed uncontrollably, while a balding grandmother squatted in a black samfoo, and split fire-wood with a billhook. This domesticity ignored our towering presence, just as it did rain and wind, when the only protection was a mat awning that pulled over a rough frame-work set above the poop.

Loading now proceeded apace, for a great deal of our homeward cargo was taken aboard in Hong Kong, much of it of a general nature: plastic goods, curios, toys and the cheap manufactures we were used to having on display in our high street shops. Tinned food, much of it from China, came aboard for the growing numbers of Chinese restaurants in British cities; cotton clothing, Chinese in origin but often made up in the sweat-shops of Kowloon and Wan-Chai; bamboo rattans and some coffee for Hamburg, bags of chili, noodles and caraway seeds; army stores and personal effects together with odd and valuable cases whose contents were obscure. One came aboard under armed guard, a second lieutenant, a corporal and a pair of squaddies accompanying it. The manifest later proved it to contain government cipher equipment.

I was attending to a stow of casts of ginger being loaded into Number Two upper 'tween deck, a complicated matter of dunnaging the deck and wedging each barrel so that its bung was uppermost and its weight was taken on the hooped area, leaving the fat 'bilge' of its middle free to hang between the dunnage beams. It was already late afternoon and a mist was creeping over the harbour, the sun having sunk behind Victoria Peak. Above the babel of shouting, the squeak and judder of braked winches, the hum and singing of the derrick runners in the sheaves and the squalling of a pair of babies alongside, there came the strident sound of singing.

> 'Show me the way to go home,
> I'm tired and I want to go to bed,
> I had a little drink about an hour ago
> And it's gone right to my head....'

I looked outboard and saw the *Dayspring* approaching. Father O'Rourke sat in the stern, unobtrusively conducting this unholy choir with the foot of his crossed over left leg. He wore a beatific smile; though his sense of dignity prevented him from joining in, I felt sure that he was familiar with the words.

I looked anxiously up at the boat-deck, half expecting China Dick to be standing outside his cabin staring at the returning Midshipmen. His absence spurred me to action: if we got the Midshipmen to the half-deck without attracting attention, trouble might be avoided. I ran towards the gangway, tripping over hatch-beams and dodging wires. A tally-clerk waylaid me and I was delayed sufficiently to find the Midshipmen swaying up the gangway, tramping in unison so that the wire fall vibrated and the whole thing twisted under their determinedly drunken exertions.

'For Christ's sake ...' I hissed. Below, Father O'Rourke raised his hand in a gesture of blessing as the *Dayspring* sped away towards the Irish ship a mile away.

'It's the Fourth Officer ... sir...' The Junior Midshipman swayed dangerously and almost fell.

'Where the *hell* have you buggers been?'

'S'nt Mike's shrine ... sir...'

I looked at the Senior Midshipman for an explanation. He was grinning, though experience had taught him to keep his mouth shut.

'St Michael's shrine?' I had never heard of the place and wanted some form of rational explanation.

'Actually,' the Senior Midshipman enunciated with care, 'it was the San Miguel Brewery...'

They got away with it, and the following afternoon went on a picnic with the opposition, sailing off to Telegraph Bay with the Anglican padre

Voyage East

from the Mission to Seamen. Though alcohol was restricted, the padre had played a trump card by bringing some girls along, daughters of British inhabitants of Hong Kong. Dewy-eyed with love the Midshipmen returned with plans for dating these girls in the evenings remaining to us in Hong Kong. Alas, China Dick, summoned ashore that afternoon, had returned with news that turned their triumph to ashes. The Mate explained it to Mike and Bob and myself

'The *Clytemnestra* has a tail-shaft problem. She's to go into the Taikoo dry-dock as soon as the *Ashcan* comes out. We're cutting short our Hong Kong lading, transhipping her Manila cargo and picking up her run ...'

'Christ, that's bloody Borneo,' Mike broke in. 'That'll add a fortnight onto our schedule...'

'Probably three weeks,' replied the Mate uncompromisingly.

'Shit!' I thought of those small indications of marital reconciliation Mike had let slip. 'That's really fucked it!' His mood was venomous.

Bob sighed philosophically; it made little difference to me.

'Well there it is ... we all signed two-year articles...' The Mate lit his pipe.

'And that gives us one more night here,' said Bob.

'Yes, and either one of you two can look after the ship this evening,' snapped Mike, distressed and frustrated by the untimely news. 'I'm going ashore.'

The Mate blew a long plume of smoke from his pursed lips. 'No, you're not' he said. 'I am.'

The lighters with *Clytemnestra's* Philippine-bound cargo arrived the following morning as we were emptying the last of the junks that remained alongside. I had the forenoon cargo-watch and I remember it as a bedlam of noise and confusion. Small ragged Chinese boys, barefoot and anxious, chased me about the deck waving the boatnotes for the cargo in their father's junks. The boat note was an authorisation to load, an instruction from the agents to the ship. They were annotated by the Mate, who indicated where the consignment was to be stowed, and they were

BLUE FUNNEL

initialled by the officer-on-deck as the cargo came aboard. The news that *Antigone* had closed for cargo had gone smoking round the harbour by some telepathy not wholly dependent upon the agents. It may have had something to do with the Blue Peter that Captain Richards had ordered hoisted. The blue flag with its conspicuous central square of white fluttered at the foremasthead, an old fashioned gesture that harked back to the days before telegraphy.

'Boat note, sir, boat note.' The small urchin waved the paper in front of me and I took it from him: fifty tons of iron pyrites due for stowage in Number One lower hold. The hatch had been awaiting the stuff since our arrival.

'You come just in time,' I said, scribbling my initials on the docket. 'You savee just-in-time?'

'Ya, ya,' the boy nodded vigorously, 'jus' in time, ya, ya.'

'Ship sail soon. You belong late.'

'Ya, ya, b'long late ...'

The pyrites had obviously come down from Mainland China. The junk containing it wallowed with its burden.

'You fetch Canton-side, eh?'

'Ya, ya, Canton-side.'

'Number One hatch.'

'Okay sir.' He ran off, bare feet flying, shouting to the hovering junk, waving it forward and clambering up on the forecastle to take a bow line. I went to see the Chief Tally Clerk. 'One more junk, *Crani*, for Number One hatch.'

'Last one?' he asked smiling tiredly, for he had been up all night. 'Hope so.'

'Where's the Mate?' the Purser's face suddenly appeared amid the mêlée of the deck.

'Haven't seen him this morning.'

'No, neither have I.'

'He went ashore last night.'

'I know, that's what's worrying me.'

'The Old Man wants him, does he?'

Voyage East

'Everybody wants him.'

'You mean he's not on board?' I asked, astonished.

'He's gone bloody walk-about.'

'Does Mike know?'

'Yes, he's topside now.'

Mike stepped into the breach, clewing up the paper-work so that when China Dick bellowed for the documents necessary to our departure, Mike presented them to him with the Mate's compliments and an intimation that the Mate was busy elsewhere. As the appointed hour for sailing approached and the Mate still had not appeared, Mike offered his apologies to China Dick, inventing a delay concerning the verification of the remaining space, which Mike charmingly attributed to my incompetence.

'Thanks very much,' I said.

'When you tell a lie it has to be believable,' replied Mike with his usual warped sense of humour.

But even this charade could not be maintained indefinitely. Bob and a Midshipman prepared the bridge while I saw the last of the pyrites swung down into Number One lower hold. The hatch beams went below, and then the hatch boards, one set for each deck, until the weather-deck was reached and the heavy tarpaulins were hauled across. The empty junks pulled away from our side and the Crowd arrived, Chippie and his mate to batten down, the Bosun and his derrick gang to lower the heavy steel booms into their crutches. With the last space figures I made my way up to the boat deck and the Mate's office.

'I can't spin in out much longer,' Mike was saying. 'The Old Man'll have to be told...'

'He hasn't been ashore since we left Birkenhead,' said the Purser, offering some mitigation for the Mate's extraordinary behaviour.

'Well I . . .' Mike's voice tailed off and we turned round. China Dick stood behind us. The moment for subterfuge had passed.

'*Diawl*,' he growled. 'Bloody Mate's missing, is he? That what you've been scurrying about trying to hide, Second Mate?'

'Well, sir, I, er...'

At that precise instant the air was cut by the piercing blast of the stand-by whistle. Through the alleyway door stepped the Mate, immaculately uniformed, a secretive smile on his face.

'Ship's ready for sea, sir,' he said, addressing China Dick. 'I've just blown stand-by.' And then to us, 'Excuse me, I need my hat ...'

'Where the bloody hell have you been, Mister?' China Dick asked, flushing.

'*Been,* sir?' said the Mate with an air of astonishment. 'Why, about my duties.'

China Dick's gaping mouth snapped shut with the force of a gin trap. I think he sensed he was in danger of being made to look a fool. He turned on his heel and made for the bridge ladder.

'Come on,' the Mate chivvied the rest of us, 'didn't you hear the whistle?'

Voyage East

The Land Below the Wind

'At least we get out of this wintry weather,' the Mate remarked to me as we stood our morning watch waiting for twilight to reveal the horizon 'Yes,' I replied. 'Back into whites today, I suppose?'

It was not the question I wanted to ask, but our diversion to Manila, though a passage of only six hundred miles, took us from the wet, windy misery of a temperate winter back into the perpetual warmth of the tropics.

'Too overcast for stars,' said the Mate, staring up at three or four constellations which appeared through rents in the last clouds of that disappearing winter. I said nothing to this uncharacteristic lack of zeal. If the Mate did not want to take stellar observations, that was his prerogative. It was my duty to corroborate his falsehood and I guessed he had other things on his mind. I was correct.

'You're not married, are you?' but he did not wait for an answer, hurrying on. 'Get yourself fixed up, permanently ... the alternative's bloody senseless...'

'You mean,' I ventured, 'casual relationships?'

'I mean whoring ... och, she's a bonnie girl, no bar lassie, and I've known her a few years. Works in an office in Victoria...'

The enigma of the Mate's disappearance was explained, but he was a strait-laced Scot, an uncompromising judge of his own conduct. He sighed.

'Women, we put them on bloody pedestals. Seamen are worse than most at that nonsense. They're either saints or slatterns, those you marry and those you screw. One lot belong up on marble plinths, the others ... well...'

I wondered what the unknown Chinese girl would have thought of his cynicism, or whether he really meant it. The dawning light caught the jutting brow and the thin line of his mouth and I realised he was experiencing the pain of separation, cocooning his hurt in a harsh self-wounding. He pulled out his pipe and began stuffing it with tobacco.

'They still know how to be wife to a man,' he said, as the match flared, separating the whole female sex along an imaginary meridian somewhere east of Suez. He felt the rebelliousness of Western women as a faintly personal insult.

'I mean,' he went on, 'women are even coming to sea now.'

He found the notion of British girls applying for cadetships profoundly disturbing. No doubt he would have treated such a trainee with his usual good sense, but his tone manifested his unhappiness. Like all seafarers, he was conservative by inclination; he felt the presence of women at sea would be an intrusion, a diminution of himself, not as hero, but as provider. He wanted someone he loved to be immune from the laborious toils of his job, and could not understand why women should insist on joining the rat-race.

'I suppose they want power,' he went on; 'to be the arbiters of their own fates.' The aroma of his black shag was snatched away by the ship's wind. 'And I suppose it says something about the consistency of human folly ... proves they're not superior, after all.' With the pipe drawing he turned forward again, leaning on both arms. Then he pulled the briar from his mouth with a jerk of indignation. 'Not to mention the fact that they're doing some poor bastard out of a job.'

I thought I saw the image fall from its cherished pedestal; then knew that, for the Mate, it would remain in situ. He was an old believer, destined to die uncured of his folly. Or proved right by a small miracle.

He put the pipe back in his mouth and spoke through tightly clenched teeth.

'Screw stars this morning.'

Luzon, largest of the Philippines, lifted its jungle-clad peaks above the horizon and we swept past Corregidor Island into Manila Bay. The Filipino capital lay along the far shoreline, a white shimmer that took shape as we approached. Overhead roared a brace of American jet fighters and two Yankee warships loomed jaggedly among the assorted freighters anchored in the roads. We reduced speed, moved through them, embarked our pilot, then passed the breakwater and edged alongside a vacant pier.

'I can't stand this place,' remarked Bob, as he wrote up the log and we

Voyage East

prepared to work cargo. 'Violent lot, the Filipinos. D'you know, I got shot at in some bag-shanty up the coast and lost two teeth when some slant-eyed shit knocked me down a hatch.' Grimacing, he lifted a dental plate with his tongue and a metallic click.

'What did you do? Call him a slant-eyed shit?'

'Funny. No, I caught him with his fingers in the 'tween-deck cargo. He hit me while I was shopping him. Knocked me clean out of the 'tween-deck and I came to spread-eagled on a load of hemp in the lower hold.'

'All in the line of duty.'

'You're bloody flippant this morning.'

'Got some mail to read.' I waved two aerogrammes miraculously forwarded from Hong Kong.

'You bastard...'

'Mind I don't knock the rest of your teeth out.'

'Sod off.'

Bob had his revenge that evening when the officers were invited to attend a shippers' party. It was my misfortune to be officer of the deck and I left the accommodation after dinner that evening to the hiss of showers and snatches of song. Intended to drum up business, the party carried with it that faint whiff of corruption for which Manila has since become notorious. The shippers, prominent Filipino traders and businessmen, arrived with their wives and mistresses. A temporary air of glamour invested *Antigone's* otherwise empty passenger-lounge, so that even the Mate seemed to be back in the pedestal-building business.

Among the guests was a weather-beaten and elderly Finn. Judging by the slender and lovely creature upon his arm, his vigour was undiminished. I saw her only briefly, when I came up to consult the Mate on some detail of our discharge.

'A handsome piece, eh? The result of Spanish and native miscegenation.' He leered, seeing my inattentive eye wandering.

'She's a cracker...'

'And there's hope for an old dog too, you see.' He jerked his head in the Finn's direction.

'Who the hell is he?' I asked. 'Doesn't look much like a shipper.'

'He's Old Man off the ship ahead of us.' I recalled the nondescript Panamanian-flagged freighter that lay beyond our bow. 'At one time he commanded the barque *Pamir* when she was under Erikson's flag, and prior to that he was Second Mate of the *Moshulu* in the last grain race from Australia.'

I could see the Mate was enjoying himself, talking to a kindred spirit, a man who formed a living link with the great tradition, whose company would reinspire him, banishing the megrims of Hong Kong.

'The last grain race,' I said, recognising the title of Eric Newby's superb account of life on the Finnish four-masted barque. I should have liked to talk to him myself, but under the Mate's forbidding stare I tore myself reluctantly away.

Two days were sufficient to discharge *Clytemnestra's* outward cargo and to load her homeward consignments. Bales of hemp for cordage and matting were taken aboard for Oslo, Copenhagen, Liverpool, Dublin and Glasgow; bags of copra for Bremen and Hamburg, out of which swarmed the tiny black insects we called 'copra bugs'. They would henceforth infest the ship until we reached cooler latitudes.

We turned south from Corregidor, slipping beneath the green slopes of the Loro de Pico, heading for the Mindoro Strait and the passage through the archipelago. Island after island passed astern, each one under its mantle of lush, dense jungle. Deep water ran through the strait and navigation was, in Bob's phrase, 'a doddle'.

We were bound for the enclosed expanse of the Sulu Sea, a great triangle of water which was usually calm, its smooth surface mirroring the blue perfection of the sky, puckered here and there by a moving zephyr, or disturbed by a lifting shoal of flying fish being chased by bonito or albacore. Sometimes the distant spouts of migrating whales might be seen, or a turtle would be left rocking in our wake. At night the cloudless arch of the sky showed again the magnificent constellations of the equinoctial belt.

But there was another mood to the Sulu Sea, for it lay in those crucial latitudes where tropical storms were generated, great meteorological upheavals such as the cyclone we had dodged in the Bay of Bengal. Vast warm masses of air that rose simultaneously and were spun off northwards

Voyage East

by geostrophic force, deepened hereabouts into the mighty winds of the China Sea typhoon. This geostrophic force was a function of latitude; below some seven or eight degrees either side of the equator it was negligible, and regions set within this zone were immune from such terrible visitations. Thus was derived the native name for Borneo, to the south of us: 'the land beneath the wind.'

Newly independent Sabah, formerly British North Borneo, was a Malaysian state which, together with its neighbours Brunei and Sarawak, shared a border with the hostile and sprawling Indonesian province of Kalimantan. It was a country of mountainous jungle, primitive and beautiful, the habitat of exotic birds and butterflies, haunt of the legendary *orang-utang*, the 'man-of-the-forest.' Deep valleys lay under a heavy mist every dawn, until the morning sun burnt off this exhalation of the virgin rain-forest. Such valleys and mountain ranges made communication by road impossible. The sea hereabouts retained an importance lost elsewhere on the world's coasts, and its ports were reminiscent of an earlier century, of Conrad and the characters of *Lord Jim* and *Victory*. Occasionally this sense was heightened by the sight of an ancient, superannuated steamer, still earning her Chinese owner a living.

One such relic occupied the other half of the two-berthed wharf at Sandakan, and might have been the S.S. *Patna* herself. We tied up astern of her, dwarfing her 900 gross registered tons.

'She's been around this coast for years,' Captain Richards remarked as he left the bridge and paused at the top of the ladder to look about him. 'Commanded by a Chinaman … a leper…'

Conrad's dark vision of the loneliness of men occurred to me as I watched the Old Man retire to his cabin.

Antigone and the replicated *Patna* lay on the outer side of the wharf. Its inner face was occupied by native coasting craft, the *praus* and *tongkangs* that crept out from the creeks, braving the Indonesian attacks, to bring the produce of their villages to this little entrepôt. Some was going direct to Singapore in the *Patna*, some further afield in our own gaping holds. Beyond the wharf lay the bustling town centre, the police head-quarters, the market and bus station, pulsing with a life that radiated from the focus of trade and amid which our arrival was 'an event.' One caught, just before it vanished for ever, a glimpse of what it must have been to be a seaman in Conrad's day. The big ports were too grand for us now; there were other, newer, preoccupations to amuse their inhabitants; the age of tourism was about to dawn and that vapid spender, jack-ashore, was becoming as despised in the East as he already was in Europe. In the few remaining neo-colonial enclaves, air travel had reduced the sense of expatriate isolation that had made Conrad's generation of merchant seamen welcome. In general we had suffered a down-grading, become the 'white trash' of Mike's perception.

But in such small and remote places as Sandakan then was, sea-transport maintained a precarious pre-eminence, a vital link with the world beyond the jungle and the mountains and the desultory guerrilla warfare that flared sporadically along the border with Kalimantan.

China Dick was aware of this increase in his standing and soon we learned we were to be hosting the local dignitaries. The news caused mixed feelings.

'Load of bloody empire-building snobs,' Billy spat ungraciously into his beer.

'We are of one mind, for once,' agreed Mike.

'I'm not going.'

'Why not? Few drinks, good time...'

'Good time? Bullshit!' Billy turned disgustedly away.

'You'll be there, Billy,' Willie Buchan ordered, 'and in your best bib and tucker!'

'And what the fuck does that mean, Second?'

'Red Sea rig...'

'Bloody hell!'

We mustered as pressed men, in our Red Sea rig of long trousers, open-necked shirts and epaulettes, but became willing enough when we caught sight of the police inspector's daughter and the agent's young wife. As though in answer to Billy's apprehensions, there were the inevitable older, desiccated women left by the vanished tide of empire, but the air of faint disparagement they brought with their clubby husbands and their

Voyage East

perfume, soon dissipated on a wave of good fellowship. It became a jolly, informal, suburban occasion, unmarred by any incident beyond the giggling tipsiness of the agent's over-flattered wife and the excesses of Sparks, who took it into his head to get stinking drunk. He was spirited away by Billy, who had suddenly burgeoned into the life-and-soul of the party.

'Did you get him to bed all right?' asked the Purser.

Billy nodded.

'Was he okay?'

'Tired out,' replied Billy. 'He gave one great big technicolour yawn.'

Those of us with off-duty time next day to take advantage of it, accepted a reciprocal invitation to use the dinghies of the local sailing club. After an invigorating thrash round Sandakan's blue bay we returned aboard to find that a darker side of Conrad's past had caught us.

'How many of them?' I heard the Mate ask the agent, standing in his cabin doorway as I came into the shade of the alleyway after the blazing sunshine of the deck.

'Only two.'

'*Only* two! D'you know how much trouble *one* D.B.S. can cause? Two idle buggers will make a hell's kitchen of this ship, damn it!'

It was an old-fashioned and well-intentioned system, this compulsion to assist distressed British seamen, a hangover from the days when illness, injury or misfortune could leave a man stranded in any port in the world. On application to the British vice-consul, a berth would be found for him on the next passing ship flying the red duster. But a D.B.S. was not compelled to work; he was given his food, a berth and a free passage, and our two passengers, we learned, were not the victims of any misfortune. They had been cooling their heels in custody after a night of drunken and violent revelry. The Mate was experienced enough to anticipate the effect their idleness would have on certain of our crew. He was not to be mistaken.

They came aboard under police escort just prior to our departure, two grubby and cocky young men, unashamed at the spectacle they made, grinning about them and staring up and down at my whites as I met them at the top of the gangway.

'It's a focking Bluie, Jimmy,' one of them said. 'Anyone 'ere from Tranmere?'

The two smartly turned-out policemen seemed glad to be rid of them. 'Take home, sir,' one of them said, 'you welcome.'

'Right pair of prats,' remarked the Chief Steward, emerging briefly from the accommodation rubbing his hand over his paunch. We stood and watched the two vagrants being led off by the Senior Midshipman towards the hospital where they were to bunk.

'Just our bloody luck!' he said, and I recalled he came from Tranmere.

We left Sandakan to a waving of hands and handkerchiefs. Beneath the green spread of a peepul tree, on a sward of lawn stretching down from a white bungalow, the flutter of frocks showed where we received a fitting farewell.

Arrival at our next destination was timed for dawn, for this was a tiny anchorage, encircled by a horseshoe of islands, unlit and dangerous to approach in the dark. With the sunrise astern, China Dick conned *Antigone* into the shelter of Bohihan Island with the help of a home-made chart. (There was no Admiralty chart of sufficient scale and we carried one made by Blue Funnel officers, adding to it ourselves as we gained more information).

Antigone shuddered as her screw went astern, then stopped. China Dick gave the order to the forecastle: 'Let go!'

There was a splash, a cloud of rusty dust from the spurling pipe as the starboard cable rattled over the windlass gipsy, and the ship lay still, awaiting her next load of cargo. Almost immediately we were surrounded by small naked boys in dugouts, part of the indigenous population of fisherfolk, who dived for the loose change we flung into the water. It was necessary to import several gangs of men to handle the large *seraja* logs we had come to load. They arrived from the mainland in a ramshackle motor craft which formed a temporary residence while they worked *Antigone*. On Bohihan itself lived the Chinese Superintendent and his family, the representative of the Borneo Timber Company, who oversaw the collection of freshly felled logs that arrived periodically from the hardwood reserves in the rain forest surrounding Darvel Bay. These were corralled in 'necklaces' of stapled and chained logs, rafted to facilitate

Voyage East

both the towage from the mainland and their retention at Bohihan until the arrival of the monthly ship.

Free of duty that afternoon, Bob and I took the motor lifeboat away in company with some of the engineers, Sparks, and a handful of seamen and Chinese firemen. The engine burst promptly into life and seemed to have healed the rift between departments. We beached the boat, unloaded a case or two of beer, and began to splash about on a tiny sandy islet inexplicably called Honeymoon Island on our chart. Here we fooled about, skylarking in the shallows and swimming over the reef, heedless of sharks, marvelling at the beautiful coral, among fish so fearless that one could tickle them, and so extravagantly coloured that it seemed necessary to touch them to prove their reality.

There was a single tree on the island, a gnarled and stunted thing whose roots clawed at the sand, desperate to suck up sustenance into dry and rustling leaves. Small pools lay among the tangle of its roots and along these curious walking-fish clambered upon their front fins. This discovery so fascinated us that we forgot the tidal source of the water, and within the few minutes of our irresponsible neglect, the heavy lifeboat had grounded, left high and dry by the ebbing tide.

'Bloody hell!' said Bob, suddenly aware of the burden of seniority.

'Marooned on Honeymoon Island and not a judy in sight,' bemoaned one of the sailors. 'You won't arf cop it from China Dick, Turd,' he added happily, tipping back his head and swallowing a beer.

Bob looked despairingly at me. 'We'll be here for hours …' We walked across to the boat and tried to estimate the speed of the rise and fall.

'I didn't even know there was a rise and fall here,' I offered in commiseration. '… at least, not much.'

'I bet Mike did.'

'Well, he scored an own goal. He'll have to stay on deck until we get back.'

'Whenever that is,' Bob added miserably.

We endured hours of being sunburned to a lobster red despite our assiduously acquired tans. We improvidently drank the beer too quickly, preferring it to the fresh water in the boat. This and the sunburn gave us all throbbing headaches. We had tried to minimise the effect of the sun by staying in the water, but the shallows over the reef were warm and the sun's radiation struck through. No one swam beyond the reef. Sudden insecurity had kindled a fear of sharks, and the precipitous descent of the sea-bed intimidated us. Our only profit was a few coral heads and the majestic sight of two white-headed sea-eagles that circled with languidly spread pinions over the summit of Bohihan.

'Hey Turd, have youse seen dem fuckin' vultures?' asked one of the sailors pointing.

'They're eagles, not vultures,' replied Bob.

'Dey'll still eat youse when yer dead,' the seaman persisted, enjoying the discomfiture of the officers.

'When you're dead, mate,' put in the Fourth Engineer, 'nothing'll touch you.'

We were not popular on our eventual return. Our plight had been observed from the ship, but we had been left to our fate. Mike, almost as exhausted as ourselves, was blasphemously succinct. 'By Christ, a fine pair of bloody mariners you two are. Haven't you ever heard of the *tide?* it goes in and out and up and down just like you stupid pricks.'

And, of course, China Dick sent for us. We were arraigned before him in immaculately starched whites which seared our raw skin. It was late, and he had been cooling his choler with the better part of a bottle of gin.

'Well now,' he said, his voice softly modulated with a menacing Welshness, 'are you proposing to insult me with an explanation?'

He looked from one to the other of us, before settling on Bob. 'Well, Mister?'

'No, sir.' Bob displayed a manly acceptance of full responsibility that was in the finest traditions of the Company, not to mention the *Boy's Own Paper*.

'You were careless ... neglected the elementary precautions of good seamen ... displayed a measure of incompetence that surprises and disappoints me.'

His eyes included me in this general condemnation of our professional abilities. Bob sensibly remained silent.

Voyage East

'I shall expect to see your observations as to the tidal heights here added to the hydrographic data on the chart. Do you understand me?'

'Yes sir.'

He waved us away and we slunk into the alleyway.

'Been bad boys then, have we?' lisped the Mate, in imitation of the Old Man. '*Du*, shouldn't have been caught out, should you?'

He fixed us with a half-smile and retreated behind a screen of tobacco smoke, puffing vigorously in the belief that it deterred mosquitoes.

'Bloody cheek,' muttered Bob, aware that the Mate's comment contained a veiled illusion to his own conduct in Hong Kong.

We did not work cargo at night, for there was only a single shift of workmen in this remote place. Before they settled for the night, the Dyak labourers hunkered down on the after deck, where their cook had set up a field kitchen, an affair of dunnage, cargo mats and brazier fire. The evening air was filled with the smell of fried meat and boiled rice. After eating they smoked, gambled and talked, before drifting off to the primitive floating hotel that lay alongside our gangway.

The following dawn they broke their fast then turned to, hoisting the big logs aboard with wire slings and hauling them out into the sides of the holds with bull-wires led through snatch-blocks. It was slow, dangerous work, for the logs were heavy, weighing up to seven or eight tons, and four or five feet thick. Some had been in the water for weeks and were slimy with weed. Occasionally a snake would drop from one, and there would be much shouting and banging to frighten the thing into the depths of the ship. Sometimes the logs were reluctant to be drawn into the 'wings' by the bull-wires, which parted under the stress. As a result our 'Doctor' was kept busy dressing cuts, for the men worked barefoot and often slipped between the treacherous logs.

The timber Superintendent dined with us, telling of the piratical raids of Filipinos and Indonesians and of how, a year earlier, they had pillaged Lahat Datu and killed seven men before being rounded up by the local Mobile Defence Force and a detachment of the British Army.

'After capture, the pirates were sent to walk through Lahat Datu,' he explained, 'and the people called them bad names and beat them.'

'Good idea,' said Mike.

'Sure,' went on the Superintendent, 'then they get ten year in prison.'

'You must feel pretty exposed here,' remarked the Purser.

The neatly groomed head nodded. 'Sure. Little bit,' he admitted, 'but I have two Dyak soldiers on Bohihan and they have a machine gun. You have seen watch-tower? Soon we have a search-light. If pirates come they get good welcome.'

'What do they come for?' asked the Junior Midshipman, to whom Bohihan seemed a place of extreme indigence.

'Transistor radio, tape-recorder, woman.'

'In that order?' asked Mike, helping himself to the Tournedos Rossini.

The grounding of the motor boat had made Bob and me partners in crime. On the evening of our departure from Bohihan I remained on the bridge after handing over the watch. It was a quiet night, overcast and black, the sea empty to the horizon. Somewhere to starboard Borneo lay silent, the teeming life of its jungle brought to us as the scent of the land breeze.

'It was a bloody silly thing to do,' he said, irritated by his own stupidity.

'Look, I was as much to blame as you...'

'No, you weren't. I'm the senior, it was my fault.'

'You were simply relaxed. Anyway, everybody's entitled to the occasional mistake and there was no harm done.'

'Only to my reputation ... hey, what's that?'

He pointed into the darkness fine on the port bow. Was there the faintest concentration of darkness? I stared uncertainly over the dark water while Bob dived for the radar set. A few seconds later he ran back into the bridge-wing.

'There's a bloody great echo less than a mile away. Can you see anything?' I was already staring through the binoculars.

'No, not a thing ... wait a minute...'

But Bob was not going to be caught for incompetence twice. He dashed back into the wheelhouse and *Antigone* leaned sharply to the impetus of her adjusted auto-pilot. A moment later Bob reappeared with the aldis lamp.

Voyage East

He switched it on and played it out to port like a searchlight.

'Bloody hell!'

The hull was low and ghostly in the aldis beam, the unmistakable shape of a British frigate, the Pennant Number F6I clearly visible beneath her bridge.

'What the hell is she doing there with no lights on? Christ! We could have run her down!'

Bob began sending the *AAAA* of the call-up. There was a pause before an answering wink from the frigate, then a peremptory query: *What ship? Where from? Where bound?*

Bob clicked out the reply: *British ship* Antigone *from Bohihan to Tawau. What ship are you and why no lights?*

Back came the riposte with the dedicated and impressive speed of the naval specialist: *British warship* Llandaff. *Was waiting for pirates. Thanks for blowing my cover.*

'Oh shit,' I said.

'Better than another bawling out from China Dick,' said Bob, clicking the lamp again: *Sorry. Buy you a drink some time.*

Llandaff's navigation lights came on and she turned in our wake, abandoning her now pointless vigil.

'What the devil are you two up to now?' Captain Richards stood four-square in the wheel-house doorway, lit from behind in awful silhouette by the dimmed chart-table lamp.

'Oh shit,' Bob muttered.

Tawau was on the very border with Indonesia, its short wharf occupied by the *Hernod* of the Norwegian Asia Line. Offshore the Royal Fleet Auxiliary *Gold Rover* lay at anchor, joined half an hour after our own arrival by HMS *Llandaff*. The roofs of the small town were a tiny smear of red surrounded by the dark green of jungle. Coils of heavy mist lay in the valleys of the forest that stretched away into the interminable hills of the hinterland. Somewhere behind Tawau there was an airstrip from which RAF Beverley transports periodically lifted off with supplies for the isolated

BLUE FUNNEL

army patrols. That afternoon Jardine Matheson's *Hewsang* arrived from Wallace Bay with tales of Indonesian raids resulting in the deaths of several people.

We began loading immediately: bags of gum damar, cubic bales of rubber, sacks of peppercorns, bales of hemp and more logs for Liverpool, Hamburg and Rotterdam. Across the wharf *tongkangs* were landing copra in bulk. Ironically, these heavy sailing barges came from the *kampongs* on Sebatik Island, enemy territory beyond the border. The business of survival crossed political divisions easily. As the copra came ashore it was bagged, and some made its way aboard *Antigone*. Next to these 'enemy' craft lay a nondescript motor *prau*, a barge of undistinguished appearance. During the afternoon we noticed a platoon of Dyak soldiers go aboard and conceal themselves below. Soon afterwards the *prau* fired up her engines and slipped out of Tawau.

'Who belong this *prau?*' I asked one of the tally-clerks.

The man jerked his chin in its direction. 'Special navy ship. Special to catch pirates.'

I watched the Royal Malaysian Navy's diminutive Q-ship vanish in a cloud of exhaust smoke: a more practical proposition, I thought, than a frigate.

Bob and I were apprehensive of reprisals from the *Llandaff,* keeping an eye on her boats as they came and went from the wharf. We had explained to Captain Richards that she had lain in our track without lights and he had done no more than grunt. Our concern proved unfounded; it was China Dick who seized the initiative, and the sequel ran contrary to our worst fears. We had the story from the Purser who had it from the agent who had picked it up on the gossip circuitry of the port.

'The old devil waylaid one of her officers and tore him up for arse-paper,' the Purser explained gleefully. 'Took him apart, you see,' the Purser went on, imitating China Dick's accent: 'told him his ploody warship had no business sitting in international waters on the shipping routes without lights, that he was damned lucky his own officers had their wits about them, otherwise they'd have been cut clean in half, see ...' The Purser abandoned his attempt to ape the Master. 'Then he launched into his

Voyage East

favourite polemic about the Royal Navy being a social refuge and demonstrably sod-all to do with seamanship, and that if they thought they would frighten the pirates, they hadn't the faintest notion of the realities of life. I expect there was quite a lot more.' The Purser finished his beer, belched gently and tossed the empty can into his cabin rosy with a clatter. 'It all stems from the war, of course. I'm surprised he didn't accuse the poor bugger of not being around in 1942 when some Kraut stuck a torpedo in the *Glencoe*.'

'That's the one he got into port, isn't it?' The Purser nodded.

'He really hates 'em, doesn't he?'

'Like poison.'

From Tawau we turned north, through the Balabac Strait, beneath the snow-clad summit of Mount Kinabalu. The strait lay between Borneo and the Philippine island of Palawan and was littered with dangerous coral reefs and islets. Several lighthouses and beacons had been built to guide ships through, but there was no sign of their reassuring flashes during our transit. Whether this failure was due to piratical sabotage, corruption, inefficiency or plain mischance, we never knew. It was not our lot to know, we were mere birds of passage. This not-knowing was one of the frustrations of the sea life, dulling one's inquisitiveness; the opposite of that voracious appetite for gossip that flourishes elsewhere, about the parish pump. We had no parish pump, no fixed watering hole; nor, for that matter, any *need* to know. But the unsatisfied curiosity natural to human beings could produce a sense of isolation and insignificance strong enough to dominate a sensitive mind. Perhaps some of this underlay China Dick's excessive prejudice against the Royal Navy; it was certainly one of the irritants that made seamen drink, and part of the fascination of the Mate's character (and, to a lesser extent, the Purser's), that he had armed himself against such corrosion. But victory over this and other deprivations was never assured, not even in so strong-willed a man as the *Antigone's* Chief Officer.

It seems so small a thing, this not-knowing, and perhaps at the time we barely noticed it ourselves; yet its onslaught was ineluctable and the extent of its damage would be revealed when we arrived home. The world had functioned without us and, for the married men especially, this was a tiny death. At the time we took its manifestation in our stride, picking our way through the complexities of the strait by radar.

And it was beautiful; the sea placid, the air thick with the scent of foliage, of hibiscus and flame-of-the-forest, of oleanders and bougainvillea vines, borne on the night wind. We could only guess at the species which cloaked the myriad islands beyond the obvious, ubiquitous palms. Casuarinas, perhaps, and peepul; tamarind and percha gums, mangroves and durian, and the red jasmine called frangipani. This too was part of our unknowing, an unwilled, frustrating ignorance that bred a thwarted desire to explore, aroused to an almost passionate intensity by the soft, sea-wafted *terral*.

But these primitive surroundings that so delighted me and the Mate were not everyone's idea of paradise. The long, hot coasting was a test of stamina, and sporadic drunkenness was now endemic, breaking into rowdy excess among the junior seamen and led by our idle and disruptive 'passengers' from Sandakan. Sparks roamed the ship almost totally withdrawn from our world, unable to shake off his obsessively specific hypochondria, the victim of a disastrously irresponsible practical joke that threatened his reason. Silent, morose, nails bitten bloodily to the quick, time hung heavily as he kept his statutory watch in the isolation of the radio-room, listening to the stutter of morse and static in his head-phones. Such was his preoccupation with self that I do not think he any longer harboured any hatred for Mike, the author of his misfortune.

As for Mike, his nerves were already eroded by our Borneo diversion. His affair with Mrs Saddler and some form of reconciliation brought by letters from his wife had for a while recharged his cocksure self-confidence, but the continuous hot slog, the lack of proper sleep and the passage of time only made him raw, irritable, impatient and resentful of any delay, however caused.

We made a brief stop at Jessleton, now Kota Kinabalu, then called at Labuan, a port which seemed to beat to a faster commercial pulse, as though our approach to Singapore brought us within the ambit of more energetic forces. Sawn ramin formed the bulk of the cargo loaded at Labuan, stowed plank by plank, each consignment separated by lines of

Voyage East

coloured gouache. This paint was mixed in buckets and laid on by resentful Midshipmen who thought the job too reminiscent of the kindergarten. Much of this resentment was justifiable, born of the knowledge that in Liverpool the streaks of blue and red and green would be ignored, and the planks would be torn out by damaging wires, a percentage ruined in the profligate haste of Western consumerism.

Because of the alteration to our schedule *Antigone* was filling rapidly. As we prepared to sail from each successive loading port our estimations of the ship's remaining capacity became more acute. So too did her stability, and the Mate toiled over long calculations to determine metacentric height, that factor which governed *Antigone's* inherent ability to resist the capsizing moments of the sea. There were also lesser calculations, chiefly concerned with our draught and trim at predicted times in our homeward voyage, tiresome arithmetic that could be rendered fruitless with a change of orders. There was a problem with the cargo pumps below and they would be wanted in Singapore, so that even the sybaritically inclined Chief Engineer could not avoid toiling alongside the indefatigable Willie Buchan and his cohorts. Only China Dick could therefore avail himself of local hospitality, and I recall one shipper's daughter leaping about him in girlish glee as his portly, genial figure waddled towards her parents' waiting car.

'Tell the Mate to have her ready to sail at 1600, Mister,' he said, as he shouldered his golf-clubs at the head of the gangway.

'He's already told me that,' the Mate snapped back, wrestling with some problem just dumped on his desk by the agent's runner.

'He just told me to tell you,' I said, the heat of the Mate's reply warming me in turn.

As predicted, this fractiousness found more permanent and damaging lodgement with our 'distressed' British seamen. They lounged in chairs at the break of the poop, strumming Embleton's guitar and throwing out gratuitously insolent asides at all but those they numbered as cronies. The conventions under which officers laboured obliged us to ignore them, but the Bosun and Carpenter gave as good as they got, thereby raising the level of abuse. It was a shining example of the devil making work for idle hands. Resentful of authority in any shape or form, two or three of our younger sailors began to mix with these reprobates, supplying them with beer, forming a little coterie which, innocent enough at face value, was already intruding on the privacy of the Chinese.

Embleton was the fall-guy; enticed to excess by our 'passengers', he could not be roused from his bunk one morning.

'Like bloody Lazarus he is,' the Bosun reported, 'dead-drunk and pissed his mattress. . .'

Later that forenoon Embleton was hauled before China Dick and deprived of a further two days' pay. It seemed Captain Richards, provoked beyond tolerance, would 'decline to report' on Embleton's conduct when the time came to pay-off. This was a euphemism for dismissal, but Embleton continued his wayward association while old heads wagged prophetically over his folly.

On the berth ahead of us Mansfield's *Kunak* was embarking deck passengers. The Junior Midshipman and I leaned on the rail and watched the last of them hurrying along the wharf...men in loose cotton shirts carrying innumerable parcels, women running awkwardly in tightly wound *sarongs*, trailing whimpering children and accompanied by a leaping and barking pye-dog infected with the hysterical excitement of last-minute departure.

'Where are they all going?' the Midshipman asked.

I shrugged. 'Singapore mostly, I suppose.'

'But why? What for?'

I should have liked to be able to answer him with certainty, but that too was part of the not-knowing and he would have to come to terms with it.

Good news came aboard with the agent at sunset. Mansfield's in Singapore sent word that the *Clytemnestra* would leave Hong Kong the next day and pick up her own schedule at Tanjong Mani in the Rejang River, after which she would proceed to Singapore and load our homeward cargo in the Straits ports.

'We'll gain a week, then,' said Mike brightening, 'and we won't have to go up that stinking ditch of the Rejang.'

'That'll make them sweat off their good time in Hong Kong,' added Bob. 'They'll be days at Tanjong Mani and days in Swettenham picking up their own consignments as well as ours.'

The contemplation of *Clytemnestra's* coming ordeal made light of our own disruption, modified as it now was by the news.

'I was wondering where we were going to put it all,' mused the Mate, staring at the cargo plan on his desk.

'So what happens at Singapore?' I asked.

'Oh, just a few odds and ends and the cargo tanks already booked.'

'Thank the Lord for small mercies.'

It seemed the gods were suddenly with us, even the primitive deities, for we saw the unusual spectacle of a moon-rainbow on our way down the Sarawak coast. The pale, luminous arc faded as the shower found its way overhead, eventually blotting out the moon and deluging us with a chill rain.

Homeward Bound

It was the sharp, acrid stink of latex that dominated our brief homeward halt at Singapore. *Antigone* moved directly to a waiting berth and a stream of ancient Chinese coolie women, dressed identically to their sisters-in-toil at Hong Kong in black samfoo pyjamas and cardboard-stiffened head-dresses, padded barefoot up the gangway. They moved with an arthritically hip-slewing walk, their careworn faces wrinkled as prunes, their hands, clawed by the work they did, brandishing tiny bamboo brushes and small steel scrapers. With them came a handful of athletic young men who, poking bundles of bamboo poles, planks, ropes and cargo mats down Number Four hatch, erected scaffolding within those cargo tanks designated for latex.

Although scrupulously cleaned in Hong Kong, the bare steel surfaces were covered with the brown dust of oxidation and not yet ready to receive the sticky ammoniacal solution. Perched like black birds on the rickety bamboo framework and lit by the patchy illumination of bulb-clusters, the coolie women brushed loose all the rusty dust and swept it from the steel. Then they painted the entire interior of the two cavernous tanks with hot wax which, when it dried, became pure white, a pristine uncracked coating. Against this background their black flapping cotton pyjamas stood out, throwing surreal shadows, while their cackles echoed round the webs, frames and stringers.

Latex in bulk had adhesive qualities and after discharge its residue could only be removed by the use of the wax as a barrier agent. The preparation of the deep tanks took two days, and before we loaded had to be approved by a surveyor, a rotund Englishman who searched for cracks or forgotten corners. Upon his good opinion depended the wages of these unfortunate old women, who stood anxiously silent while the *tuan* inspected their handiwork. Pronouncing himself satisfied, the *orang puteh* retired to the hospitality of the Mate's cabin. The coolie women collected tokens from the foreman, signifying their completion of the work, and made their clucking way ashore. Within the hour a heavy hose was sloshing the viscid, milk-white latex into the tanks. Over four hundred tons were pumped aboard, half for Liverpool, half for Hamburg.

The preparations for the five hundred tons of palm oil which we expected were different. For several days prior to our arrival at Singapore, as *Antigone's* holds had filled with the deadweight of Borneo timber and the need to keep sea-water ballast in her diminished, the engineers had been below fitting steam coils to the emptied deep-tanks in Number Three. These steel coils were fitted with scores of flanges whose integrity had to be tested for leaks before oil could be loaded. Steam from the ship's hot-water system was generated by the Cochrane 'donkey' boiler in the engine room and pumped through these pipes, to maintain palm or coconut oil in a liquid state as we passed to colder northern climes. Without this heat the stuff went solid, could not be handled, and had to be shovelled out, a virtually worthless mass.

It was the carriage of this variety of commodities that demonstrated the versatility of ships such as *Antigone*. Like the derricks that were hoisting aboard a few tons of tin and rubber, some bags of gum arabic and cases of personal effects, they made her a maid for all tasks. But they took labour, man- and woman-power much disliked by hard-headed ship-owners, and it was this very versatility that, among other things, ultimately condemned her class to obsolescence. As we left Singapore through the Western Roads, a Dutch vessel of the Rotterdam Lloyd Line lay at anchor. On her long foredeck were half-a-dozen grey aluminium boxes at which China Dick stared with unconcealed curiosity.

'What the devil are they?' he asked the Pilot.

'They're containers, Captain,' the Pilot replied, and no-one on the bridge heard the sentence of death pronounced upon us.

After the mad scramble of the Borneo coast and the tedious heat of Singapore, a non-stop passage north-west through the Malacca Strait and across the Bay of Bengal was as good as a holiday. We slipped easily into the old routine and became noddingly acquainted with our passengers. They too were delighted not to be delayed by stops at Port Swettenham and

Penang. We had also shipped on board livestock, in the form of a tapir destined for the London Zoo, with which had come a vast bundle of fig-leaves for provender. The long-snouted beast stood unhappily in a large crate on the centre-castle deck, and was fed daily by the Midshipmen. They also had another creature to feed, a boxer kennelled on the boat-deck, the responsibility of the Junior Midshipman. Just acquiring a beard, he regarded this duty as beneath his dignity until he discovered that the daughter of the Foreign Office official who was travelling with her family, had a great liking for dogs, particularly boxers. Exercising the thing became a regularly-attended routine around the promenade deck, at which China Dick scowled disapprovingly until the young lady smiled at him, and we saw something of that avuncularity he had briefly revealed on the quay at Jesselton.

We had left *Melampus* and *Clytoneus* at Singapore, along with the *Glenfalloch,* just preparing to sail direct to London at the same time as the rival *Benloyal,* in a kind of token, latter-day tea-race. In the Malacca Strait we passed *Aeneas* on her way out to Singapore from Belawan, for our course hugged the Sumatran shore, finally departing from it off Achin Head and Pulo Weh. We made good headway at our loaded draft, and Mike grinned again as he made up his abstract log with its carefully calculated speeds, distances and fuel consumption rates. Only Sparks remained depressed by our homeward track; and perhaps the irresponsible Embleton, awoken after the loss of his allies to a belated realisation of his uncertain future. By a stroke of good fortune the Purser had discovered that our two distressed British seamen were under contract to British Tankers and, seeing two BP tankers at Pulo Bukum, had persuaded the agents to arrange to transfer them where they could be legitimately employed. They left protesting, but their departure undoubtedly helped raise the spirits of the ship's company generally.

About the decks the Bosun chivvied the Crowd into the final homeward painting programme, and *Antigone* began to assume the appearance of an Argosy, stuffed with oriental riches and smart as a sultan's yacht. The mood of her seamen became cheerily irreverent. Snatches of song and whistling were heard, and a more sober diligence than had been evident 'on the

Voyage East

coast' began to appear. To borrow again from Conrad, we had fallen once more under the thrall of 'the enticing, dis-enchanting and enslaving life at sea.'

The North-East Monsoon was weakening and the Bay of Begal lay under skies of almost unclouded perfection. Only a low swell disturbed us, though that is hardly the word, for the gentle motion of the ship had more of a lulling rock than a tiresome roll to it. Bound westward, we were retarding our clocks at midnight, lengthening the ship's day and conferring upon it a mood of lingering festivity.

Four days from Singapore the low coast of Ceylon rose blue over the horizon and we passed the Narrows to anchor in the landlocked splendour of Trincomalee harbour. Here we had come to fill *Antigone's* remaining capacity with chests of tea, Broken Orange Pekoe Fannings as the initials on the chests declared, for London, Bremen, Hamburg ...

'But most for bloody Liverpool,' grumbled the Mate, 'to oil the idle wheels of British industry.'

It was a slow process, or so it seemed, for we were in a hurry to be gone. The port lay under curfew, prompted by racial violence between Tamils and Singalese. These riots were the opening gambits of what has since become a bloody civil war, and had already disrupted the port as much as the Christmas cyclone that had uprooted half its coconut palms. To pass the time Trincomalee offered us a score of picnic spots, numerous bays each fringed with palms and scrubby jungle, some inhabited by little settlements of fisherfolk, warm friendly people willing to shin up a palm and trade fresh coconuts for a few cans of Coca-Cola or a packet of cigarettes. From the beaches we would wander into the jungle amid the giant ant-hills and the uprooted trees. Through this wilderness wove overgrown tarmacadam roads, leading nowhere except to the brick ruins of the wartime barracks, the wrennery and the Kinema, Ozymandian relics of past British glory, when Trincomalee had been the base of the Far East fleet following the fall of Singapore. The place was full of ghosts; rusting guns rotted in concrete emplacements and the roofless barrack blocks, inhabited now by bats and gibbons, still had patches of extempore decoration on their poorly plastered walls.

It was odd to read the graffiti of one's parents' generation, but comforting to find frustrated desire plagued them as much as it did us. Amid the palms and the dense undergrowth, snakes and the occasional elephant wandered, though our own observations were confined to hooded crows, the gibbons and bats, and the ubiquitous chiel kites that reminded one of Kipling's *Jungle Books*, for all that this was not India.

Tea was a clean cargo, well marked and rarely damaged. The occasional stove chest was sealed by carpenters, dark skinned Tamils who wielded saw, hammer and nails upon plywood patches which they brought aboard for the purpose. The Tamils wore shirts and *sarongs*, the latter hitched up and rolled in their groin to form marsupial pouches in which they kept the betel leaves, areca nuts and lime which they chewed incessantly. The nut was rolled in a leaf accompanied by a smear of lime and then tucked into a cheek by a horny finger. Betel chewing resulted in our decks becoming spattered with red expectorant, and any remonstration was met with beams of simulated incomprehension. This constant hawking and gobbing made one long for the open sea.

At last, despite the curfew and the work-to-rule and the short-fall of tea chests arriving alongside in the lighters, we finished cargo, actually stuffing the last chests between the hatch-beams. As the hatch-boards went on and the tarpaulins were spread, our own carpenter hovered ready to drive home the wedges. The Tamils drifted away to their waiting launches and the last tally-clerk left the tiny office provided for him in a swirl of litter. The Mate's whistle blew the signal for departure, the Crowd lowered the derricks for the last time and, driving home the final wedge, Chippy trotted forward to stand-by the windlass. The empty lighters were cast off and drifted away until the fussy little tugs caught hold of them and then only the pilot launch was left bobbing alongside us. From the forecastle now came the steady clunk-clunk of cable links coming home over the windlass gypsy-whelps.

At last the forecastle bell rang, the anchor was aweigh.

'Half ahead!'

'Half ahead, sir!'

'Hard a-port!'

Voyage East

'Hard a-port, sir ... wheel's hard a-port...'

We swung for the entrance, the water churning white and marbled green under *Antigone's* stern, and headed out to sea.

Next morning, off Batticaloa, in a sea as smooth as the proverbial mill pond, we ran amongst a school of whales. All about us their grey backs eased slowly out of the water as they spouted, perhaps twenty of them, occupying an area some two or three miles square. Close to us, about half a mile to starboard one of them fluked, raising his great tail and sliding down into the depths of the ocean. Suddenly they all slid from sight, denizens of another world, and we were left under the blue sky, on the smooth expanse of the limitless sea.

We swung west off Dondra Head and off Minicoy picked up our outward track, covering old ground in our romp home. In our watches below we completed the master cargo-plan, filling in the final details of our most recent lading. It was then photographed several times and half-a-dozen copies were thrust into the half-deck with a packet of cheap coloured pencils.

'Blue for Liverpool, red for London, brown for Glasgow, yellow for Hamburg and the transhipment stuff for Oslo and Copenhagen, orange for Rotterdam and green for Dublin. Don't get it wrong or the Mate'll have your balls for a neck-tie.'

'No *sir*.'

'It's like being back at school.'

'It's worse. Now get on with it because it's to go air-mail from Aden.'

'I wish *I* could...'

'Stop trying to be clever and get cracking.'

'But I was going to take the dog for a walk.'

'Get your lady-friend to do that.'

As I left them I noticed the Senior Midshipman reach out for the green pencil. There were only two stows for Dublin on the ship. The Junior Midshipman was left with the blue and red.

West of the Maldives there was no wind at all, so that only the passage of the ship disturbed the air and the night was filled with the seething wash of the wake and the rumble of Willie Buchan's engines. As I made my night rounds the Chinese were back at their mahjong tables, free of the intrusions of guitars and drunken *fan kwei*. They were not homeward bound, they were back to normal, gambling, laughing, smoking: men resigned to their fate, surviving in an over-crowded world. I wondered how long we could hold on to our ridiculous expectations, before we too had to face such realities.

The thought depressed me. I came off the after well-deck and walked forward past the seamen's accommodation. A line of them were sitting under the stars, sharing a case of beer on Number Four hatch.

'What-ho, Four-O,' sang out a wit, aping my southern accent. I recognised Embleton's voice.

I nodded. 'Evening.'

'D'you wanna beer, Fourth?'

I shook my head at Wakelin's offer. 'No, thanks.'

'He won't drink wid us,' said Embleton contemptuously.

'*I* wouldn't drink wid you'n less I fuckin' had to,' put in someone else.

'You don't fuckin' have to.'

'Yes I do; it's your fuckin' beer.'

Laughter drowned Embleton's snarled reply. It was clear he was far from popular.

'What you gonna do when you get home, Fourth?' asked Wakelin in the gloaming.

'Get fixed up wid some judy?' the Bosun's Mate emerged out of the gloom. 'D'you know what I'm gonna do?'

'What's that?'

'Get fixed up wid a rich nymphomaniac widow wid a pub.'

'Don't you think about anything except sex and booze?'

'Dat's not thinkin' about sex and booze; dat's thinkin' about money!'

'Yeah, dey're all rich nymphomaniac widows in bloody Bootle...'

Two evenings later we observed the most spectacular sunset of the voyage. Just after the disappearance of a blazing red sun, the sky was a brilliant vermilion before which a handful of fleecy cumulus was silhouetted

Voyage East

as black as jet. Against this spectacular field Venus blazed as an evening star while, climbing towards the zenith, the sky turned almost green before shading to the purple of the tropic night astern. Smooth as glass, the sea ahead to the horizon was the colour of pewter. The brilliance of the redness was due to dust rising over Africa ahead of us; the strange, preternatural calm, a brief hiatus between monsoons.

The Mate emerged from the chart-room and leaned on the rail beside me. We stared in profound silence as the tranquil night engulfed us.

'Djibouti!' Mike ran his hand through his hair in a wild gesture of disbelief. 'Djibouti?'

'Yes,' said the Mate quietly, taking the draught forms from me as we completed connecting up the bunkering pipes, under the burning slopes of Aden's volcano.

'What the bloody hell for?'

'Steers.'

'Oh bollocks!'

'No, bullocks ... bullocks for Suez, two hundred head of 'em.'

'Shit!'

'There'll be plenty of that too.' The Mate was laughing at Mike's petulant anger, for the detour was minimal. Mike withdrew in pique while the Mate perused the arrival draught figure and compared it with the theoretical value he had calculated. He nodded his satisfaction, then looked up at me.

'You have a little time left to decide, laddie, but the Second Mate will have to choose soon.'

'Choose, sir?' I frowned by incomprehension.

'Aye, between the sea-life and something else.'

I went out on deck. Below, on the after well-deck, the Chinese, the seamen and the Midshipmen were haggling with the bumboatmen.

'Hey, Johnnie, I make you special price...'

The heat was unbearable. I sagged under its intensity and it seemed the voices floated up to me as in a dream 'How much? No good ... twenty dollar last price...'

There was a lot of mail for us at Aden, some forwarded from the Straits ports we had missed out. Reading mine, I thought of the Mate's caveat.

'You got some mail.' Mike stood in my cabin doorway, his tone accusatory.

'Yes.'

'From Penang?'

'Er, yes, and one from Swettenham.'

'Christ!' Again he swept his hand through his hair, then turned and left me. It was obvious he had received no mail himself. For a second I stared after him; then I resumed reading my own letters.

Nor was Djibouti any better in the matter of heat. On the opposite coast of the Gulf of Aden, its air was African rather than Arabian. The bullocks were driven down onto the white and dusty quay by thin Somali herdsmen wrapped in woven blankets and bearing long wands with which they prodded their lowing charges.

'*Pardon, M'sieur. Je suis le...*'

I stared, forgetting, despite the tricolours flying prominently from several buildings as well as from our own foremasthead, that this was a French colony. Somehow the impeccable French, issuing from the small brown face with its intelligent eyes, threw me. I tried to muster my meagre stock of schoolboy French.

'Oh, er, *Oui, bienvenu...*'

'What Does he want?' I looked up. Above me, leaning over the promenade deck rail, the Junior Midshipman's lady friend stared down at me.

'I'm not sure. He's speaking French.'

She suppressed a look of withering scorn.

'I know *that*,' and ignoring me she launched into a dialogue with the Somali that left me foolishly nonplussed. On the quay, wearing epaulettes and a kepi, a French immigration officer grinned up at me.

'*Bravo, M'mselle,*' he applauded as she explained to me:

'He is coming to Suez with the cattle. He wishes permission to come aboard.'

'Thank you, I suspect you will be useful as an interpreter...'

But she had jumped to that conclusion minutes earlier and I felt utterly stupid as I conducted the tall, thin Somali to the Mate's cabin. As I made my retreat from this confrontation I bumped into Sparks.

'You got good news at Aden, then?'

'How d'you know?' He looked sharp, pinched, suspicious. The experience of attending a clinic in Singapore had not eased his neurotic anxiety; if anything, it had made it more acute.

'Well,' I shrugged, 'I suppose if the news had been bad you'd have ...' I trailed off - as though remaining silent about the awful options would avoid any sense of guilt if he should attempt suicide. I did not want to put ideas into his head, though from the haggard look of him they had occupied his mind for weeks now.

'They advise me to have another blood test in a couple of months,' he whispered'.

'Oh, that's just a precaution ... you're all right. You want to put it behind you; chalk it up to experience. You'll be seeing your girlfriend soon.'

'But what am I going to tell her?'

'Tell her? .... Nothing...'

But he wandered off, shaking his head, and I stared after him as the first of the bullocks was lifted by a belly-band and lowing piteously, with its legs rigid, was swung aboard.

They were stuffed on the steel well decks, fore and aft, fifty on each side of the hatches, so that by mid afternoon we had two hundred of them and already the *Antigone* stank like a farm-yard. Runnels of urine and liquefied dung trickled over the side, staining the black gloss of our newly painted topsides.

'Oh, fucking hell,' moaned the Bosun, shaking his head despairingly, 'it's a bloody conspiracy, Boy-o, a bloody conspiracy.' He waved his hand in front of his face as a wisp of hay, blown out of the huge sling then coming over the rail, caught his nose, borne on a hot wind. 'The sooner we're out of this place the better.'

Beyond the sun-bleached buildings, the land rose to distant hills. Almost brown, their surface was dusted with green, a sparse, vestigial savanna that seemed inadequate to support even the lean steers that stood patiently crammed on our decks.

'Got to rig fucking hoses, fore and aft,' the Bosun grumbled, watching the pile of hay on Number Two hatch grow higher, 'better get on with it…' He turned away, starting at the sudden appearance of the tall Somali in his blanket.

'What d'you want, eh?' he asked.

'He's coming with us to Suez,' I explained, adding, 'he speaks French.'

'I don't know what the Company's coming to,' the Bosun said, as if the world had rocked on its axis, and waddled off to turn out the seamen.

The following morning we were clear of the Straits of Bab-el-Mandeb, heading north in company with several other ships. The sun was climbing into an already brassy sky when the VHF radio squawked into life.

'*Antigone, Antigone,* this is Greek ship *Ellenis* astern of you, Greek ship *Ellenis* to *Antigone,* come in please.' I picked up the handset. We had overtaken the *Ellenis* half an hour earlier.

'*Ellenis,* this is *Antigone,* Channel Six. Over.'

We shifted off the international calling and distress frequency to one dedicated to ship-to-ship traffic.

'*Antigone,* this is *Ellenis.* Hullo, good morning to you, please can you help to me. I have a sick man on board, please have you doctor?'

'Stand by, please…'

I phoned for the Doc. After a few minutes he appeared. 'They want a doctor,' I said, 'but in the absence of anything better I thought you'd do.'

'Piss off. What do I do?'

'Press that to speak and let it go after you've spoken so that you can hear him. He sounds pretty worried.'

'Okay.' The Doc took the handset from me and spoke into it. 'Hullo. Ship wanting doctor go ahead. This is doctor speaking…'

'Over,' I prompted.

'Over,' he added, scowling at me.

'Oh, please, Doctor, good morning we have sick man, he has very high temperature and also what you call bad fever, yes? and we cannot find

Voyage East

out...'

It went on for several moments. Once the Doc stopped, motioning for paper and pencil, and took notes, pausing to reflect, as though ruling out certain conditions on the basis of symptoms he had enquired after. He thought of something else and spoke again into the handset.

'Please can you tell me if there is inflammation anywhere?'

'Inflammation ..'. er...'

'Hullo, yes, inflammation ... redness, is the skin red and swollen? Over.'

There was a pause. 'Surely they can understand 'redness', for Christ's sake!'

'Hullo, can you tell me if the man's skin is red?' He repeated, turning to me. 'D'you know the Greek for "red"?'

'Sorry . . .'

'Hullo. Greek ship, is the man's skin red?' again he repeated the question. At last the answer came back.

'We cannot tell you this. It is a black man!'

Doc diagnosed a malarial fever in the end, though he thought it a benign variant and prescribed Paludrine, which the Greek Master had on board.

The heat in the Red Sea was almost unsupportable. Off Hell's Gates a few extra-ordinarily heavy drops of rain fell in the night, bringing down upon us a fine, sandy dust. Those members of the ship's company who had slept on deck woke with sore throats. And just before noon we saw another of nature's curious manifestations, that which had given this sea its odd name.

I was on my way to the bridge from some errand, passing the promenade deck where I noticed the passengers' attention had been drawn to something in the sea. The man from the Foreign Office saw me.

'Excuse me ... can you tell us what it is?'

His daughter was pointing ahead and then we were passing through it, a brilliant red bloom upon the surface of the sea that curled rustily aside as our hull drove through it.

'It must be dust, Daddy.'

'No, it's not dust,' I explained, 'Its the marine equivalent of the first shoots of spring leaves. They are tiny blooms of marine plants called diatoms. They won't last long, because the plankton will multiply in proportion and they in turn will be eaten up by things higher up the food chain.'

'Big fleas have little fleas upon their backs to bite 'em,
Little fleas have smaller fleas, and so *ad infinitum*,' jested her father.

'It's the other way round, Daddy,' she said sharply, and then turned to me. *'Touché,'* she added, smiling with precocious self-possession.

'Each to his trade…'

It was still dark the next morning when we heard the first bellows of pain. On the bridge I could see nothing disturbing the cattle on deck, though the foetid stench of them blew back over us like an exhalation of the damned. But the noise was overwhelming and the Mate went aft to investigate. He came back a few minutes later, tense and silent, striding across the bridge to Captain Richards's voice pipe. I could not hear what was said and shortly afterwards he went below, leaving me puzzled in the growing dawn. I got the answer in the saloon at breakfast.

'That young bastard Embleton's really shit the nest this time,' said the Purser.

'What's been going on?' I asked. 'I've been on the bridge and the Mate hasn't let me in on the secret.'

'Oh, Jock's absolutely furious.' The Purser ordered his breakfast and went on, 'Embleton's been daubing the cattle with undiluted soojee!'

'Good God!'

I went aft to see. The cattle could hardly move, so tightly packed were they, but the tormented animals had cleared an area round them by their incessant movement. Soojee, a strong solution of caustic soda, was used for washing paintwork and in the lamp-room a drum of concentrate was kept in readiness, made up from a bag of crystals by the Lamptrimmer. Embleton had obtained a bucket of this vicious mixture and splashed it on the faces and hides of three steers. He would probably have tortured more had not the outraged Somali herdsman been alerted by the bucking and bellows of his charges, for he slept on deck, curled in the warm hay on the hatch.

Voyage East

The animals, maddened by the pain, still bucked and shook their heads, hooking their stumpy horns into the flanks of their neighbours as they desperately tried to throw off the searing irritation. The Bosun and a pair of seamen stood hosing them down so that they slithered in the dung and sea-water, shivering with fear and pain.

There was no sign of Embleton, who had been locked in his cabin, but his shipmates' protests were loud in their own disassociation from this stupid cruelty.

'He's a right fuckin' hooligan,' one of them snapped viciously.

'Little bastard ... what'd he want to do a thing like that for?'

'Kicks.'

'Kicks? Kicks? Christ, I'd like to kick him, and stick his fucking head in a bucket of soojee.'

'Was he pissed?'

'Probably. He came off lookout at four, s'pose he went on the piss and got this bright idea. . .'

The Bosun caught my eye. It was clear no-one other than Embleton had had anything to with the outrage.

'There's always one rotten apple in every barrel,' he said, spitting the adjective venomously, his Welsh accent prominent with anger.

'D'you know what the bastard said to the Old Man this morning?' said the Mate during the evening watch, referring to the disciplinary session that had been held earlier in the day in China Dick's cabin.

'No.'

'He said, "what Does it matter, Captain, they're going for slaughter anyway." Now what kind of logic is that? Eh? I'll tell you, it's the kind of logic that Hitler used.' He pounded the rail with his fist and walked away. I had never seen him so angry.

We discharged the cattle into barges at Suez, one by one. The blue water of the bay seemed levelled to a glassy smoothness by the weight of the sun's radiation and the distant escarpment to the west shimmered violently. Around the ship swam a pair of huge sharks, grey-blue, clearly visible in the still water, attended by striped pilot-fish. 'Dem nobbies,' remarked a sailor, 'can smell death.' He nodded emphatically at the water.

The sharks, Nobby Clarks in the vernacular sailor-slang, languidly circled *Antigone* until the last steer left us, lowing with pain. A broken leg, fractured in the shufflingly nervous reaction to Embleton's assault, dangled helplessly from its hind-quarters. Sitting on the stern of the barge, the Somali herdsman sat wrapped in his blanket, his wand over his shoulder, while the ragged Egyptians carried off his stock for their abattoirs.

'I wonder what he thought of his association with the white man?' mused the Mate, his anger ebbed.

'What's happening to Embleton?' I asked.

'We'll see to him when we get home.'

After the crushing heat of Suez Bay the transit of the canal was peculiarly unpleasant. There was a drop in the ambient temperature of some 20° C, a plummeting that set our teeth chattering, despite a hurried change into reefer uniforms. As we approached Port Said behind the beam of our searchlight, the same stars that had twinkled over Suez Bay seemed now to shine from an inhospitably chilly firmament, and the wind that met us in the Mediterranean made us pitch, lifting our bow out of the water for the first time since we had left Hong Kong.

'Nine days left,' said Mike gleefully, rubbing his hands eagerly, 'five to the Rock and four to the dock.'

'Yeah,' said somebody, 'it's all over bar the shouting.'

ANTIGONE

Visitations of Fate

When it struck, tragedy hit below the belt, the victim of its malice unforeseen. Had I learned, that sad morning two days out of Port Said, that after a lonely watch in his stuffy radio-room Sparks had thrown himself over *Antigone's* side, I should not have been surprised. Nor would some extravagant story about Embleton have taken me unawares, for he was said to be suffering some of the milder symptoms of alchoholic withdrawal. Even had the Mate fallen victim to some calenture, I should have felt a certain prescience, for no man could remain immune to the corrosion of the sea-life, no matter how true the steel of his character. But to learn of the death of China Dick seemed somehow monstrously unjust.

He had been within months of retirement and those glimpses of a humanity beneath the tough, uncompromising facade reminded us that he had a wife and daughter at home, that he was a family man like many of the ship's company. Though he maintained a low profile throughout the voyage, we had never doubted who had been Master of the *Antigone* or that, whatever dedication the Mate and the Bosun, the Chief Engineer and the Purser and all the rest of us put into the voyage, its success or failure would be judged an achievement of Richard Richards alone. Had Bob and I brought back the motor boat holed on the coral of Bohihan, it would have been China Dick whose name would have been associated with the incident.

'If you do something brilliant,' the Mate had said to me one night when in the last hour of the watch we were discussing the bubble, reputation, 'people will talk about it for a week. If you make a monumental cock-up, they will talk about it for years.'

It was a good aphorism for a Master's responsibilities.

He had died of a heart-attack shortly after dressing that morning, discovered by Mike as he went to make his daily report that the chronometers had been wound. That day the ship was dreary under a mood of gloom; not grief, that was too personal a thing and no one truly mourned him, but a melancholy reflection upon our own transient nature.

The Mate assumed command and we shifted watches, Mike taking the four-to-eight with the Senior Midshipman. I changed, once again, to the eight-to-twelve. Captain Richards stiffened in his bunk, his corpse dressed by the Doctor as telegrams winged back and forth. The Mate was confirmed in temporary command and China Dick's widow requested that, in accordance with his wishes, he be buried at sea. The Bosun and Lamptrimmer set about sewing him into his shroud while a Midshipman was sent aft to lower the ensign to half-mast.

Shortly after dawn the next morning, irrespective of our watches, the entire ship's company turned out of their bunks and mustered in silence abreast Number Three hatch. Unbidden, we had all dressed in our best rig; the deck and engineer officers in their dark, gold-braided reefers, the seamen in scrubbed dungarees, the Chinese greasers in immaculate boiler suits, the stewards in their black trousers and white patrol jackets, and the two cooks in their tall hats, white jackets, aprons and checked trousers.

Her engines stopped, *Antigone* rolled gently in the swell. Disturbed by the strange silence a few passengers appeared above us at the promenade-deck rail. Two women wept discreetly while the daughter of the Foreign Office official cried unashamedly, for China Dick had made a fuss of her, seeing in her, perhaps, something of his own daughter whose childhood he had mostly missed.

We stood round a wooden platform knocked up by Chippy and waited for the burial party, whose appearance startled the passengers. They brought China Dick down from the boat-deck, rigid in his canvas shroud, splinted with steel bars from the engine room. The Bosun and Lamptrimmer struggled with the awkward weight of him and others helped them as they reached the foot of the promenade-deck ladder. The Doctor and the Mate brought up the rear of the cortège, the Mate carrying the Book of Common Prayer, his finger held between the pages as a book-mark. The cover was embossed with the ship's name and the date 1891, that of the first *Antigone* belonging to Alfred Holt's Blue Funnel Line.

They slid China Dick onto the platform and we removed our hats. A low

Voyage East

murmur from the Chinese died away as the Mate coughed for silence.

'I am the Resurrection and the Life, saith the Lord . . .' We bowed our heads, staring at the red ensign laid over the canvas bundle, its bunting just lifting in the wind that moaned softly in the rigging.

'We brought nothing into this world, and it is certain that we can carry nothing out. . .'

He wasn't a bad old bastard, you could almost hear men thinking, his very aloofness a sign of the confidence he felt in his officers, for all their ineptitude in grounding a boat on Honeymoon Island. I recalled the anger I had felt when he admonished me for taking a lunar sight - and regretted it, for he had worn the pink and silver ribbon of the MBE, awarded him as a young second mate for bringing in the torpedoed *Glencoe* after she had been abandoned in convoy during the dark days of 1942. No, he wasn't a bad old bastard at all.

'We therefore commit his body to the deep...'

Bosun and Lamptrimmer lifted the platform, their fingers retaining the hoist of the ensign. There was a slither and in the brief hiatus preceding the splash, a sudden crackling sputter of exploding firecrackers filled the air. Driving off malignant devils, the Chinese paid China Dick their own respects.

'Amen.'

We chorused our amens and they were echoed from the gallery of the promenade deck. Putting on our hats we turned away from the rail. The Mate looked up at Mike, alone on the port bridge-wing. There was a jingle of telegraphs, answered by the duty engineer. *Antigone's* engines rumbled into life with a hiss of air and we gathered way again. Already the rings marking the splash of the burial were dispersed by the wind.

'Away aft and hoist the ensign close-up,' the Mate ordered the Junior Midshipman.

Somewhere far below and astern of us, China Dick's body bumped on the sea-bed, disturbing the ooze, then came slowly to rest.

There was a brightening of the weather as we ploughed westward. Suddenly, on the forenoon following, within an hour the ship's upper-works were dark with the flutter of roosting migrant birds, tired after their long transit of the Sahara. There were hundreds of them, swallows, martins and warblers; and with them a sleek pair of raptors, lanner falcons from North Africa living on easy pickings. Each of the two falcons took a mast-table for their killing field and stained the deck below with guano and pellets, staking out a section of the ship for their individual territory.

We carried the birds steadily west during the day, then in the late afternoon they took off, lifting in clouds and circling the ship. By sunset they had all gone, even the lanners, true corsairs returning to the Barbary coast.

The rearrangement of the watches and the assumption of command by the Mate introduced a note of unfamiliarity into our routine. It was typical of him that, although he relinquished the formalities of his former rank, he still oversaw the final preparations of the ship for her docking. It was assumed that all Blue Funnel liners berthed in Liverpool in the smartest condition. Open to inspection by the Marine Superintendent or even one of the Company's Managers, it was a point of honour for Master, Mate, Bosun and all of us, that our appearance should be a credit to Blue Funnel and a reflection on ourselves. Similarly, the Chief Engineer and Willie Buchan and his staff strove to raise the condition of the engine room to the same pitch of splendour.

With great effort the cattle-dung had been scoured from *Antigone's* well-decks; the final touches were being put to her paintwork, limned-in tiddley-work with fine brushes. Brass was burnished to a gleaming finish by the Midshipmen, and the sailors barbarised the decks to a whiteness that would have done credit to a hospital ward. New derrick guys were rove off and new canvas boat covers spread over the lifeboats. Below, the last regular maintenance was completed and boxed up, the casings cleaned and the cream and silver paint touched up. Here and there an instruction plate was high-lit in red gloss, and copper pipes were polished; the final black paint was added to ladders and the bare steel hand-rails given a coat of fine

Voyage East

oil so that no trace of rust was visible. Store-rooms were cleaned out, linen prepared for the laundry and the already immaculate galley received a spring-clean in honour of the occasion, so that *Antigone* rushed homeward like a great yacht.

Every four hours now, at the change of each watch, the Midshipmen raised the thermometers chained in the palm oil tanks and logged their readings as the heat in the steam-coils brought the thick liquid slowly up to discharge temperature. Such were the cosmetic properties of this oil that they had the softest, cleanest hands of anyone on the ship.

'Hands like poofters,' remarked the sailors good-naturedly as they walked past the toiling middies.

'Sod off.'

'Oooo, don't talk like officers, do they, Spike?'

'Nope. Must be too much working wid us, Charlie.'

'You could tell dey was sailors by the semen on dere boots.'

'Sod off.'

The mood of crude and brittle levity increased as we approached Gibraltar. Passing the Rock we hoisted the four-flag signal that denominated the *Antigone* of Liverpool, and called up the Lloyd's Signal Station with the aldis lamp. The news of our transit of the Strait would appear in *Lloyd's List* the following morning.

But the fragility of our gaiety was proved next morning, for the Atlantic greeted us with a gale, a west-north-westerly gale that butted us on the nose as we stretched out for Cape St Vincent. Cold, damp weather drove down upon us, sending us to our cabins and interrupting the final flourishes of decoration about the ship. It increased in fury during the grey day so that we laboured, pitching in the sea, our well-decks awash with green water and the tarpaulins shiny under the constant deluge. White specks crept across the burnished brass and a rime of salt encrusted the superstructure.

'Bloody weather,' swore the Bosun, shaking his head in disbelief at his ill-fortune.

Off Cape St Vincent we swung north, and the wind veered to head us, keeping us pitching and working as *Antigone* thrust the great seas aside, seemingly eager to sniff the polluted air of the Mersey. At eight o'clock that

BLUE FUNNEL

night I took over from a morose Mike, for whom every second of delay was a betrayal of fate. Miles to the eastward the lights of Lisbon threw a glow on the scudding clouds and on the radar screen the bearing cursor and range marker intersected over the glowing cluster that marked the Berlings.

'She's all yours...'

Out on the bridge-wing the wind screamed and I lifted the glasses to watch a smaller ship than ourselves pitching madly in the darkness. I swept the horizon, then raked it again with my eyes elevated a few degrees above it, a trick for picking up pin-points of light by avoiding focusing on the retina's over-worked blind-spot. Apart from our bucking neighbour there was nothing else about. Then something caught my eye, something nearer, a flicker of black, like a great bat wing sweeping across the ship. For a second I thought I was imagining things, then I saw an inexplicable movement on the well-deck, a second flutter of something huge, suddenly flung up against the sky and whipped to leeward with an ominous, dull crack. Thoroughly alarmed I dashed into the wheelhouse and lifted the aldis lamp from its cradle. The narrow beam stabbed the darkness and the lookout called down from the monkey island above, 'Looked like a tarp, Fourth...'

'Bloody hell!'

Dropping the lamp beam I caught the edge of the hatch coaming with it at Number Two. Bare steel reflected the lamp-light: the hatch tarpaulins had gone. A sea reared up cascaded over the rail, swirling about the hatch and pouring off the after end of the well-deck as *Antigone* lifted.

I ran back into the wheelhouse and seized the telegraph, rang Stand-by and altered course, slowing the ship and heaving her to, head to sea. Quite suddenly the Mate was beside me, now awesomely transformed to the Old Man.

'What's the matter, Laddie?'

'I'm not sure, sir, but I think the tarps are off Number Two.'

'Are they, by God . . .' he turned as Mike too came back on the bridge. 'It looks as if the tarps might have come off Number Two,' he said. 'Go down and have a look.'

'How the hell ... ?' Mike began, but the Old Man cut him short.

Voyage East

'Never mind how! Get cracking!'

I told him the course I had steadied on. 'Three-one-oh, sir, and half speed.'

'Very well.' He jangled the telegraphs and reduced to slow ahead. 'Go and give him a hand. Take the Middy with you.'

The Midshipman had completed writing up the engine movements in the record book. We grabbed torches and left the bridge.

'Get your seaboots and an oily on as quick as you can. I'll see you by the starboard saloon door in two minutes.'

He ran off and I went and took my own advice. Two minutes later we emerged into the centre-castle. Mike was just in front of us. Round the corner of the superstructure we met the full fury of the wind and bent, crouching forward, loping into the lee of the forward contactor house and edging round it to try and assess the extent of our loss. If the tarpaulin was gone there was nothing to stop the sea from pouring into Number Two hold through the interstices between the hatch boards and the beams. Enough sea could start to flood the ship, even float off the hatchboards. That was an extreme possibility; it would be bad enough if water got down to spoil the cargo.

Forward of the contactor house we were completely exposed, though as the ship rose on the seas we felt the shelter of the distant forecastle. Nevertheless our oil-skin coats tore at us and it was an effort to make forward progress. The after end of the well-deck, at the foot of the ladders, was waist deep in water. Mike hesitated, playing his torch beam on the bare boards of the hatch. Part of the tarpaulin remained, about a third had been lifted and torn off by the strength of the wind, shredded past the locking bars laid over the hatch as an added precautionary measure. Simultaneously, Mike and I sensed there was something wrong, illogically wrong. Between us the Midshipman stared, open-mouthed.

'Look sir!' he played his torch beam along the exposed and gleaming edge of the coaming, where the derrick runners of our cargo gear had polished and scored it. The weather edge of the tarpaulin was still secured tightly by the wedges. The canvas showed no signs of strain, no fraying as of natural rupture. Its edge was sharp.

'It's been cut!'

The thought and its implications struck us instantly. Mike rounded on the Midshipman. 'Go and tell the Old Man some bastard's cut the tarpaulins.' Then he turned to me. 'I'm going to get the Bosun and the Crowd . . .' he paused a minute and I sensed the conflicting thoughts racing in his brain. 'I don't believe this is true,' he said, and blown to leeward by his billowing oilskin he disappeared round the corner of the contactor house. I stood for a moment, alone. *Antigone* rose and fell, her flared bow protecting her suddenly vulnerable hold. We would be all right; we would get another set of tarpaulins over in an hour or so. It would be difficult with the wind blowing; perhaps if the Old Man turned the ship down wind it might make things easier...

But the Old Man had different thoughts, thoughts that proved him wiser than I. Coming round the contactor house I heard him bellowing a summons back to the bridge. I scrambled back up there.

'Is it true?' he shouted at me.

'That it's been cut? Yes, it looks like it.'

He swore, itching to be active and irked by the restrictions of his new rank.

'The Second Mate's turning out the Crowd, sir ... perhaps if we get the ship before the wind...'

'Eh? What's that? Run before it? Not bloody likely. She'll scend ...' he waved his hand to port where the seas ran huge, 'lift her stern and bury her bow so that the well-decks fill . . .' he left the rest to my imagination and I saw the justice of his assertion. It might be open to debate at the Board of Trade, but not here and not now.

'They might have trouble with the wind under the tarps,' he added, 'but at least the risk of their being washed overboard will be minimal. No, she's all right as she is...' And he patted the teak rail, as though *Antigone* was a favourite horse.

It took an interminable time for Mike to rouse out the hands. Perhaps it was only a few minutes before the dark and shining figures appeared, but it seemed longer. The Midshipman and I had hoisted the two red lights that indicated we were 'not under command', warning that other ships could

Voyage East

not expect us to take avoiding action. Our neighbour had vanished, but the radar now perversly showed more vessels in the vicinity.

Torchlight flashed momentarily across the wheelhouse windows: Mike was signalling that he was ready.

'Give 'em some light down there,' shouted the Old Man and I flicked the switches. The forepart of the ship was thrown into vivid relief. Figures, leaning against the wind, moved forward. I could see Chippy's bulk attacking the wedges he had so assiduously driven home, which the unknown saboteur had left *in situ*. His mate came behind him with a sack, collecting them lest they float away.

'Shall I go down and lend a hand, sir?' I too was frustrated by my inaction.

'No. You take one bridge-wing and the Middy the other. Keep an eye on the men. If anyone goes over the side…'

'Aye, aye, sir.'

At either extremity of the ship the Midshipman and I watched the struggle on the forward well-deck. I have no doubt now that the Old Man was right in not turning the ship. The greater buoyancy of the stern, the slow speed of the ship and the period of the waves would probably have inundated the low deck and added the risk of a pooping, but the wind tore at the men below and their exertions were almost proved fruitless. Two new tarpaulins were dragged forward and got down onto the hatch in a bundle. Dragged as far forward as possible they were cautiously unrolled and Chippy, Mike and the Bosun tried to secure the weather edge before exposing the full extent of the canvas rectangles to the grasp of the gale. But the impediment of winch beds, the turbulence created across the irregularities of the deck and the force of the gale which now perversely reached its crescendo, made the task all but impossible. We watched a demonic life of its own seize the heavy canvas, saw it tear itself wilfully from the seamen's grasp, saw it flog under the lights, dark and shiny from spray, then lift and threaten to blow away.

For a second or two we thought it had gone. But *Antigone* lifted her bow, throwing the fore-deck into a brief lee. The power of the wind slackened and the canvas flopped, caught by a single corner where Chippy, swearing with the effort, his finger nails torn and bloody, struggled to retain a hold. Men flung themselves bodily onto the thing, as though subduing a monster, and then it was too sodden to lift, and even the gale failed to rend it from them further. Slowly it was dragged once more across the hatch.

But it was too much for the Old Man. He could no longer stand the inactivity; with a shouted 'The ship's yours!' he slid down the starboard bridge ladder and a moment later appeared on the foredeck. Mike was performing prodigies and the intervention of the Old Man, who had again assumed the persona of *Antigone's* Mate, would be unwelcome. I could hear him shouting. Snatches of instructions reached me on the bridge.

'Get some dunnage planks, quick ... and some nails ... nail the bloody thing down, you'll never hold it in this wind...'

The glow of the deck lights blinded us on the bridge to events beyond the limits of the deck. A quick look at the radar reassured me that no ships were approaching close, but there was no warning of the height of the sea that now bore down upon us. We dipped into its vanward trough and the sudden drop in the wind roused my instinctive suspicions, taking my attention from the scene below me. The lights on the forecastle samson posts were almost directly into my eyes but then I saw the crest, grey in the gloom, stretching out on either bow, a ninth wave of ninth waves, precipitous and hoary in its advancing slope, up which *Antigone* began to climb sharply.

'Hold on!' I screamed, my voice cracking with alarm. I do not know whether they heard me or whether their own instincts alerted them - the sudden cant of the deck, the variation in the howl of the wind - but there was another danger that transmitted itself to my own brain: *Antigone* was falling off the wind. The angle of the wave was brushing her aside, her speed, adjusted to a nicety while the wind and sea ran true, was now inadequate to hold her heading before the buffeting she was receiving.

I ran to the telegraph and jangled it to full ahead. Already the auto-pilot, sensing our deviation, was applying helm. Mercifully the engineer below was alert, mercifully *Antigone* was not sluggish to respond, and she was already turning as the crest burst upon her port bow. But the explosion of

Voyage East

white that suddenly flared under the glow of the lights was followed by the boom and shudder of impact and then of solid water, green water, foaming across the rail with a rush that raised my heart-beat in an agony of anxiety. I saw men, black shapes knocked down to heads bobbing with upflung arms, dragged like dolls along the sluiced deck. *Antigone* rolled, water poured over the side at the break of the centre-castle. I could no longer see anyone, for they were masked by the centrecastle bulwark.

'Has anyone gone over the side there?' I shouted to the Midshipman, who was almost overboard himself in his conscientious attempts to keep the party under observation.

'No ... no I don't think so.'

And then it was over. The passing of the great wave brought us a lull. Men fought their way back onto their feet and then by some corporate effort they were dragging the tarpaulin forward, its mass sagging under the weight of water it contained. A plank or two was swiftly nailed to hold it and then came the regular tonk-tonk of Chippy's maul as the wedges went home.

I remembered to slow down again, making a mental note to communicate my gratitude to Billy who was on watch below. A figure loomed on the bridge beside me. It was palely pyjamaed and for a split second my over-strained imagination thought it the ghost of China Dick.

'Everything all right, Fourth Mate?'

'Oh, hullo Chief. Yes, I think so ... a bit of a close shave though...'

'Is that the Mate down there ... I mean the Old Man?' He nodded through the wheelhouse window to where, in a black huddle, the men were coming up from the well-deck and into the shelter of the centre-castle.

'Yes.'

'You can't teach an old dog new tricks, can you?' remarked the Chief Engineer, and I could hear the grin in his voice.

'Get her back on course, laddie,' said the Old Man coming up the bridge ladder. He was soaked from head to foot.

'You all right?' asked the Chief.

'Of course I am,' replied the Old Man. 'What are you doing up here?'

'Keeping an eye on you,' replied Mr Kennington.

'I can manage.' The Old Man's voice came from clenched teeth.

'You're bleeding...'

'It's nothing...'

The red lights came down and *Antigone* resumed her passage. We were under command again, heading north with the Berlings dropping astern.

We were conscious of having been lucky. Just how lucky we were not to know until we opened Number Two hatch in Liverpool and broke the bulk of our cargo. Water had got below, finding its way through the cracks between the hatch boards, but it had done no more than wet the outside of sixty or so chests of tea, and the ample dunnage floors we had laid prevented any cargo from spoiling. A prompt pumping of the hold-well had rid the ship of the water as it drained below, and our only casualties were a score of cuts and bruises borne without complaint. A further satisfaction was that the passengers never learned of the incident.

The strip of tarpaulin taken from the coaming showed the sharp edge of a knife slash, and the following forenoon the Old Man tried to establish the identity of the culprit. It was a horrendously serious crime, no less than sabotage, though why it had been committed remained as mysterious as its perpetrator, for no one could be proved to have done it.

Embleton was widely suspected, though he bore cuts and bruises to show he had played his part in redeeming the situation. Popular supposition blamed him and blamed his ignorance, that he did not know the extremity of the danger to which he had exposed us. But nothing was ever proved, for there were no witnesses to an act that spoke of malevolent vandalism rather than conspiracy.

Off Cape Villano the gale blew itself out, leaving a residual swell to harry our crossing of the Bay of Biscay. Before the Spanish coast dropped below the horizon astern we were again invaded by birds. Some fifty Hoopoes came aboard to roost on the derricks, brilliant with chestnut, black and white plumage and Iroquois crests. They vanished as abruptly as they had come and we ploughed doggedly north-north-east towards the chops of the Channel.

Voyage East

The Channels

The Bay of Biscay and the fog patches of late spring reminded us that we were already further north than we had been when among the ice-floes of the Gulf of Po Hai. Spirits rose with every passing mile, inducing a kind of euphoric madness, a neurotic condition caused by the high, bubbling excitement of imminent arrival. This wild feeling of pure joy induced by return after long absence has been known to generations of British merchant seamen as 'The Channels'. It was perhaps the clearest manifestation of the axiom that anticipation exceeds realisation. We had for a while thrown off that feeling of unimportance that came with the not knowing; in our own minds our return was appropriately Odyssean. Induced by 'The Channels', a few souls mustered in the radio-room to put through telegrams or link-calls, radio linked telephone calls fed into the British phone system via the Post Office radio station at Portishead. The unprecedented invasion of his lonely post almost brought a smile to the haggard features of Sparks, though they clouded when Mike appeared in the doorway.

It was unfortunate that I was fiddling with my radio in an attempt to pick up one of the pirate radio stations then abounding, at the same time as Mike made his link-call. I could not avoid hearing his side of the transmission. The experience was devastating; whatever the man's weaknesses I liked him, had lived with him for over four months and knew him well. Notwithstanding the dislike Sparks felt for him, I do not think even he would have wished for what happened.

I cannot reproduce the conversation, even if I wanted to, for it was the demolition of a whole person, a fragmented dissolution in which I heard only Mike's responses. Into my mind's eye came the image of his beautiful wife. The nub of the matter was that she did not want him home, that there was someone else and that his approach was a potential embarrassment. I wondered if Sparks, signing off with Portishead at the end of that desperate conversation, was able to resist an exquisite feeling of revenge, for Mike had pleaded with his wife, abased himself in an attempt to persuade her to change her mind. She would not, and I, guilty of eavesdropping, hardly dared to face him over the dinner table.

But betrayed he was a better man than when seeking his own petty revenge in an affair with Mrs Saddler. Pared to the exposed nerve, his self-control was masterful. I knew then that he would not give up the sea. His time for choosing was over; the decision had been made for him.

All trace of the gale had vanished by the time we were abeam of Ushant. The sea rolled glassily past us, curling only where the hurrying bow slashed through it. Sea and air temperature coincided and thick, nacreous fog-banks enveloped us. It could not have occurred at a less convenient moment in our voyage, for traffic bound from the Mediterranean towards Liverpool, Glasgow, Dublin and Belfast crossed the routes in and out of the Channel, the main artery between London and the great European ports and the United States of America. Added to this stream of ships the milling fishermen only complicated the radar picture presenting itself to the Old Man.

But he would not slow down. He had a cargo to deliver and a tide to catch, and while we doubled our watches and posted our lookouts, while the siren blared mournfully into the dripping atmosphere and we used our ears as much as our eyes, he sat hunched over the radar screen, sipping endless cups of hot, sweet tea. Occasionally he would emerge and order an alteration of course. *Antigone* would list to the application of her helm, steady for perhaps ten or twenty minutes, then swing back onto her proper heading. We neither saw nor heard anything, for he confided little, aware that he bore sole responsibility for his flagrant flouting of the International Regulations. Yet no-one wanted to delay our passage, so our faith in him was absolute. He came out on the bridge-wing once during my watch, in the mood for a moment's respite. I think he had been huddled over the radar then for about thirty hours. A mug of tea steamed in his hand and he stretched like an animal.

'Still thick as a bag, sir,' I said conversationally.

'Aye.' He paused and fixed me with a speculative eye. 'D'ed you remember those Korean fishermen?' he asked.

Voyage East

I recalled the tough men in the rocking boats that we had passed on our way to Hsinkiang. 'Those bastards deserve every penny they get,' the Mate had said then, and I knew now that he felt he had earned his own place in the long tradition, and had proved he possessed the toughness he had admired in them.

By noon we were west of the Scillies and the breeze came out of the north-west to disperse the fog in half an hour. Gannets skimmed low over the rising sea, and fulmars quartered it on their motionless wings. Herring gulls swooped in to sit attendant upon the flat mushroom-vents that topped our sampson posts, ruffling their feathers and letting forth the shrill wah-wah cry of their species.

'Sound like bloody naval officers at the bar,' quipped Bob, relieving me.

We picked up the Smalls lighthouse in the sunshine of a late April afternoon. Its red and white tower and the pale blue hills of the Precelly Mountains beyond were the first sight of home, just as they had been the last. By the time I went on the bridge for the evening eight-to-twelve watch we had just rounded the Skerries, carrying the flood tide into Liverpool Bay. The Old Man, refreshed after a sleep and a shower, was already there and we leaned on the bridge rail in our old intimacy, though I was sensitive enough to the greater gulf that now existed between us.

'Enjoyed being Third Mate?' he asked me.

'Yes. I think so. And you?'

'Being Master?'

'Yes.'

He sighed, took his pipe from his pocket and tamped it down. With deliberate slowness he lit it.

'Difficult to say,' he said. 'Difficult doing nothing . . .' He paused, and I sensed a climax to our intimacy, a reflection on the friendship we had formed. The burden of responsibility he bore sat well upon his shoulders; he had come through his first trial successfully, and yet he could talk of being idle. I caught a gleam in his eye. 'Look,' he said, staring to port, and I became aware of a strange luminescence in the sky to the northward. Ahead, just over the horizon, the sodium glow of Liverpool lit the clouds, but this was something different, something different even from the last glow of daylight fast fading astern, a deep crimson infusion radiating upwards from the northern horizon.

'Well, I'm damned,' he said beside me. 'It's an auroral glow ... never seen one so far south before. You wouldn't see that if you were ashore.'

Between his two remarks lay the paradox of our existence.

We berthed at Gladstone Dock, embraced by the locks and then by Liverpool's grey and uninspiring dockland. The squalor of our surroundings mocked the pride of our arrival. Why had we painted and prepared our ship for this indifferent landscape? What was this place called home? Where was the welcome, the fatted calf and red carpet? What were these intrusive blue-uniformed rummagers that rifled our cabins in the name of Her Majesty's Customs and Excise? Even the suspicious Chinese did not subject us to these humiliations.

'Bloody class warfare,' raged the Purser.

'This is where I came in,' said Bob, handing me a last and excess can of beer.

'How's Mike?' I asked.

'All right. Why?'

I explained, glad to confess the crime of spying.

'Jeeesus. Poor bastard.' Bob frowned. 'That's why he was muttering about volunteering to do the coasting.'

'Yes, I expect so...'

Whatever happened to us, the life of the ship went relentlessly on.

'Hey, Dick, I want you to meet Julie.' Sparks invaded my cabin, a pert and pretty blonde in tow. He was smiling happily and holding her hand.

'Hullo, Julie.'

'Hullo.' We shook hands and I looked at Sparks. Our eyes met and it was clear his nightmare had passed. She was already telling him of a 'Fab movie at the Empire,' and I felt him sucked ashore and whirled into the life of Liverpool that had been spinning its merry-go-round way in our absence.

'Perhaps she'll let on who she's been seeing while he's been away,' said

Voyage East

Bob as they left us. 'Do him good.'

'Well youse fellows, Wullie's fur Glasgie toon ...' The Second Engineer came in holding out a pudgy paw. 'Ah'm off fur true love ... ' He winked at me and I recalled his farewell from Akiko.

'Some buggers have all the luck.'

'If it can happen to a fat slob like me it can happen to youse fellas. *Sayonara.*'

'Cheerio.'

'Och, where's the skipper? Is he away hame tonight?'

'Haven't you heard?' Bob said. 'They've confirmed his promotion - for the coasting voyage anyway. He's closeted with the Shipping Master and the Commissars. They're trying to get Embleton off the hook.'

'Bugger Embleton.' Willie Buchan looked askance at a blue boiler-suited rummager who peered suspiciously into the cabin as we tossed the last beer can into Bob's rosy with a defiant clatter. 'Right, then.' He moved his bulk into sudden activity. 'Ah'm bound fur Bearsden.' And elbowing the inquisitive rummager aside, he puffed away.

We paid off on board, in the saloon. The ship had passed to the care of the Company's shore-staff. One by one we began to drift ashore. The Bosun was anxious to get the first train to Holyhead and Chippie to be the first into the nearest pub on the Dock Road. The seamen, strange in their shore-going clothes, picked up their discharge-books stamped with the normal 'V.G.' and left in groups. Some had their homes, with waiting wives and families, the younger men their mothers. One or two would make their way to the Sailors' Home, a fortress in Canning Place with the interior design of a prison. Here in a lonely room they would board until their money was spent, and then ship out again, living lives of singular barren pointlessness, sufficient unto themselves alone. The Chinese ignored this exodus of their European shipmates; for them the round of coming and going went on. It was the end of our Board of Trade acquaintanceship. A similar indifference existed on deck, where the Liverpool dockers peeled back the tarpaulins and opened the hatches to begin their systematic ravaging of our careful stows. To them,

BLUE FUNNEL

Antigone was just another China Boat and we were mere birds-of-passage, drifting our way home to be met by our friends: 'Hullo, how are you? When are you going back?'

We left Mike on deck, his lonely isolation complete. He raised his hand in farewell, his face blankly unhappy.

'Poor bastard,' commiserated Bob.

'Poor Mike...'

On the quay the four Midshipmen were piling into their taxis. Only the first-tripper looked back. His face was leaner than when we had crouched over the bucket of filthy dock water and watched the silver hydrometer spin and bob.

We met the Purser, a bundle of documents under his arm.

'What happened about Embleton?' we asked as we dragged our gear along the deck.

'Bloody class warfare,' he called back, and hurried off.

Bob looked at me and shrugged. 'Come on.' We struggled down the gangway to the waiting cab. Getting in I chanced to look up. Behind us came the shipping Master and the Marine Superintendent together with a representative from the Seamens' Union. Clearly Embleton's fate had been decided one way or another. The Old Man was seeing them off, wearing his usual preoccupied expression. He caught my eye and nodded a farewell, one of those men who, as Conrad put it, 'live on illusions which somehow or other help them to get a firm hold of the substance.'

But was that substance really tangible? Had not Conrad with his gloomy foresight already sensed the core of disillusion: 'the seaman of the future shall be not our descendant, but only our successor ... History repeats itself, but the special call of an art which has passed away is never reproduced.' The Old Man's private tragedy was that he was ideal for a calling that was already passing into history. He could exist only as long as *Antigone* existed; as long as Britain could afford the profligate waste that attended the carriage of general cargo in open stows.

I waved farewell and climbed into our taxi.

Voyage East

'Lime Street Station,' we commanded the taxi-driver, and fell back into our seats as he let the clutch in. A fine rain began to fall as we turned the corner of the shed and lost sight of the *Antigone*.

Eager now to be off, we bent to the prevailing breeze of corruption; two ten-shilling notes slipped beneath our baggage passes and Customs clearances were expertly palmed by the policeman on the dock-gate. Refusal to comply with this 'perk' meant one's personal effects were spilled out and rummaged in the rain.

'I don't know what the hell they think we're going to smuggle in,' remarked Bob as the cab jerked forward, avoided a lorry and accelerated down the Dock Road. 'Got to keep us in our place, I suppose…'

'Class warfare,' I said, thinking of the Purser.

'Fancy a last drink at the station?'

'Why not?'

The end was anti-climax. We slipped home unnoticed. Britain turned no hair at our arrival, just as she has turned no hair at our extinction.

BLUE FUNNEL

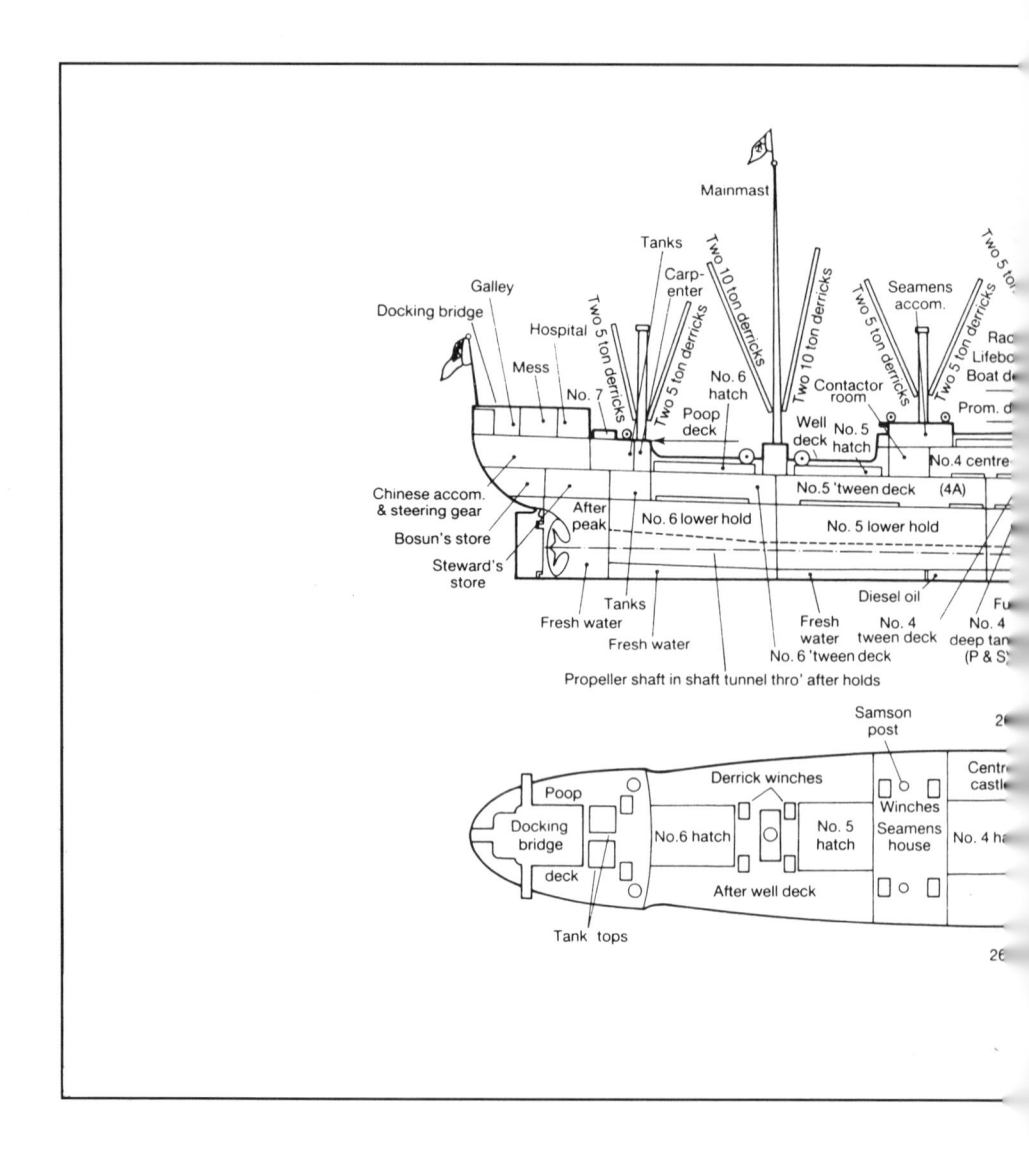

Voyage East

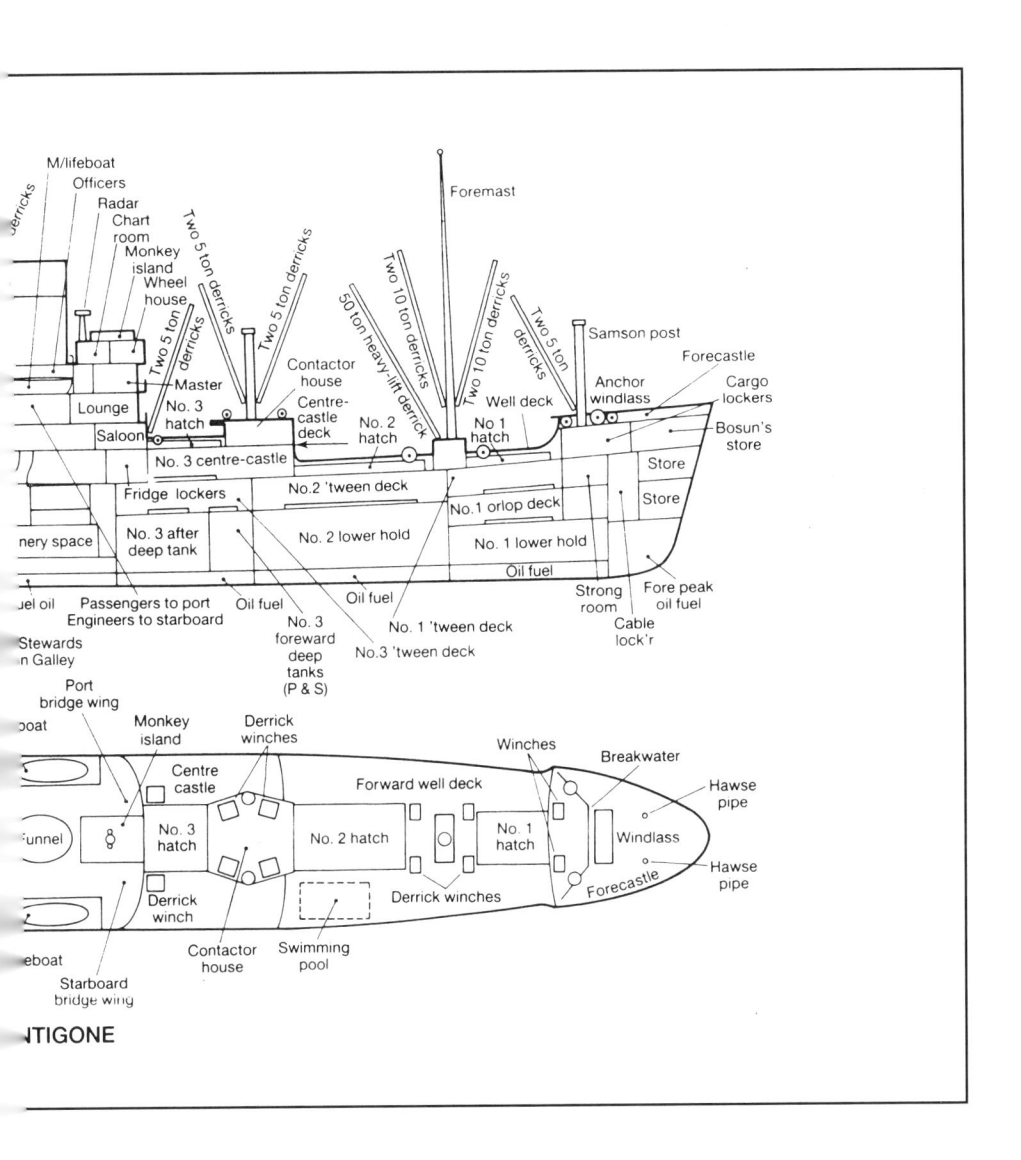

[Ship diagram — side elevation and plan view labels:]

Side elevation labels:
- M/lifeboat
- Officers
- Radar
- Chart room
- Monkey island
- Wheel house
- Derricks
- Two 5 ton derricks
- Two 5 ton derricks
- Two 5 ton derricks
- Two 10 ton derricks
- 50 ton heavy-lift derrick
- Two 10 ton derricks
- Two 5 ton derricks
- Foremast
- Samson post
- Forecastle
- Anchor windlass
- Cargo lockers
- Bosun's store
- Master
- Contactor house
- Centre-castle deck
- No. 3 hatch
- No. 2 hatch
- Well deck
- No 1 hatch
- Lounge
- Saloon
- No. 3 centre-castle
- Store
- Store
- Fridge lockers
- No.2 'tween deck
- No.1 orlop deck
- nery space
- No. 3 after deep tank
- No. 2 lower hold
- No. 1 lower hold
- Oil fuel
- Fore peak oil fuel
- uel oil
- Passengers to port
- Engineers to starboard
- Oil fuel
- Oil fuel
- No. 3 foreward deep tanks (P & S)
- No. 1 'tween deck
- No.3 'tween deck
- Strong room
- Cable lock'r
- Stewards
- n Galley

Plan view labels:
- Port bridge wing
- oat
- Monkey island
- Derrick winches
- Winches
- Breakwater
- Hawse pipe
- Centre castle
- Forward well deck
- unnel
- No. 3 hatch
- No. 2 hatch
- No. 1 hatch
- Windlass
- Hawse pipe
- Derrick winch
- Derrick winches
- Forecastle
- eboat
- Contactor house
- Swimming pool
- Starboard bridge wing

ITIGONE

MORE BOOKS, DVD'S & VIDEOS FROM AVID

Note. All prices here include postage and packaging within UK.
See rear of this book for order details.

THETIS -THE ADMIRALTY REGRETS
-THE DISASTER IN LIVERPOOL BAY

by C.Warren & J.Benson

The definitive minute by minute account of this terrible tragedy in 1939 when 99 men lost their lives as HM Submarine *Thetis* undertook her first and only dive. With new photographs and documents as well as a new foreword by Derek Arnold, a survivors son, and a new postscript by maritime historian David Roberts. Why didn't anyone cut open the submarine? Why was there no urgency in the Admiralty's rescue system?
Did the Admiralty really regret?
ISBN 0 9521020 8 0   £14.50

HMS THETIS - SECRETS AND SCANDAL
by David Roberts

This book uncovers some shocking hitherto unpublished details of the events and aftermath of this terrible Submarine disaster in 1939.
Why did the Official Inquiry blame nobody, explaining it away as *'an unfortunate sequence of events'*? Why did the civil action on behalf of the widows fail? Did the Admiralty cover it up? How much did Churchill know? How were those left behind treated?
' A book that shocks' .... Sea Breezes
ISBN 0 9521020 0 5   £12.50

FORGOTTEN EMPRESS - THE TRAGEDY OF THE EMPRESS OF IRELAND
By David Zeni

A highly detailed account of the loss of Canadian Pacifics' *Empress of Ireland* in the St. Lawrence Seaway in 1914... with a fascinating connection to the Dr.Crippen Murder case.
'...dubbed 'The 'Forgotten Empress'...the second in a shocking trio of tragedies at sea...sandwiched in between the disasters of the Titanic *and the* Lusitania, ...*it was a sudden death... that sent Liverpool into mourning...*' Liverpool Echo

ISBN 1 902964 15 2   £14.50

LUSITANIA
by Colin Simpson

Almost a century on the story of the *Lusitania* continues to be shrouded in mystery and suspicion.

What was her real cargo?
Why wasn't she protected?
Why did she sink so quickly?

Simpson exposes the facts, the fictions,

but most of all...**the truth.**

"The truth at last" - Sunday Times
'*A book that clamours to be read...*' - The Observer

ISBN 0 9521020 6 4   £12.50

CHILDREN OF THE BENARES
- A WAR CRIME AND ITS VICTIMS

by Ralph Barker

Foreword by Beth Williams (née Cummings) - the only Liverpool Survivor

The Ellerman and City passenger liner *City of Benares* left Liverpool on Friday 13th September 1940 carrying a precious cargo - 90 children from the bombed cities of Britain bound for safe haven away from the war - to Canada.

Four days later, without warning, she was torpedoed and sunk by a German U-boat in mid - Atlantic. 256 people were lost including, at first count, 83 of the evacuee children.

An event that shocked the world in its brutality, much use of the atrocity was made by the British authorities in an attempt to persuade the United States into joining the conflict.

However it was not long before the parents of the lost children, who had entrusted their loved ones to the evacuation scheme, began to suspect those same authorities of neglect, when they learned that the promised naval escort for the convoy had abandoned the unarmed ships twenty-one hours before the U-boat struck!

There were allegations of crew rushing the lifeboats, poor equipment and even racial prejudice in the ensuing clamour for an explanation. Yet somehow a formal investigation was avoided and the scandal covered up.

The Children of the Benares is a gripping story of the disaster itself and exposes at last what went on behind the scenes at the Ministry of Shipping and the British Admiralty.

It is a chilling tale of fallibility and human survival.

ISBN 1 902964 07 1   £14.50

JUST NUISANCE AB - HIS FULL STORY by Terence Sisson

The amazing but true story of the only dog that was officially enlisted into the British Royal Navy, a Great Dane whose name was Nuisance, his official name and rank was Just Nuisance AB.
Famed for his preference for the company of navy ratings (he wasn't too keen on Officers) in and around the famous World War II naval base of Simonstown, South Africa, Nuisance helped many a sailor rejoin his ship after a night on the town.

ISBN 0 949989 38 X   £10.75

THE GOLDEN WRECK - THE LOSS OF THE ROYAL CHARTER
By Alexander McKee

The effects of the great hurricane of October 1859 were to shock the nation. 133 ships were sunk, 90 were badly damaged and almost 800 people lost. More than half of those that perished were on one ship - The *Royal Charter*.
Bound from Australia to Liverpool with returning prospectors, she was almost home when the freak storm hit her off Anglesey.
News of the wreck soon spread and the *Royal Charter's* other cargo, gold, became the focus of people's attention.
Was all of it ever recovered?
If not, where did it go?
The worst shipwreck in Welsh history, this is the story of the *Royal Charter*...and her **GOLD**.

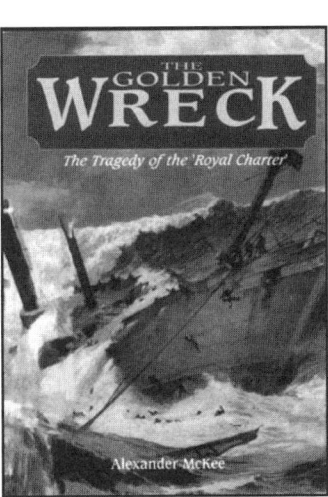

ISBN 1 9029640 2 0 £12.50 inc. p&p

THE ALABAMA AFFAIR
-THE BRITISH SHIPYARDS CONSPIRACY IN THE AMERICAN CIVIL WAR
by David Hollett

Reveals the turmoil and intrigue surrounding a deal involving the British government, the now defunct Merseyside shipyard of Cammell Laird and a country engaged in civil war, America.

The Confederate blockade runner *ALABAMA* did enormous damage to Union shipping during the war.

What was involved?
How was the conspiracy organised?
Who were the shadowy figures at the centre of the controversy? The *Alabama Affair* answers all the questions.

ISBN 1 902964 3 2 2   £12.50

FASTER THAN THE WIND
- A HISTORY GUIDE TO THE LIVERPOOL TO HOLYHEAD TELEGRAPH
by Frank Large

Take a journey along the one of most spectacular coastlines in Britain, the hills and countryside of North Wales and Wirral. The views are quite superb, and on a clear day it is possible to see just how shipping information was signalled along the coast to and from Liverpool.

Contains full details of the intriguing and little known sites of the substantial remains of the Liverpool to Holyhead Telegraph Stations.

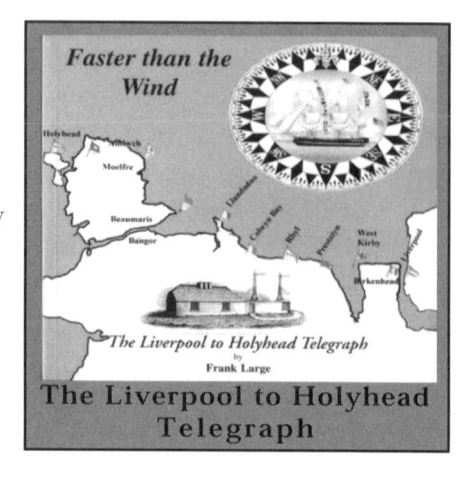

ISBN 0 9521020 9 9   £12.00

IRON CLIPPER *'TAYLEUR'* – THE WHITE STAR LINE'S 'FIRST TITANIC'
by H.F. Starkey

Iron Clipper is subtitled 'The First *Titanic*' for it tells the story of the first White Star liner to be lost on her maiden voyage.

The *'Tayleur'* tragedy of 1854 and the *'Titanic'* catastrophe of 1912 are disasters which have so much in common that the many coincidences make this book appear to be a work which is stranger than fiction.

ISBN 1 902964 00 4   £9.50

SCHOONER PORT – TWO CENTURIES OF UPPER MERSEY SAIL
by H.F. Starkey

Meticulous research of two centuries of shipping and shipbuilding on the Upper Mersey including Runcorn, Widnes & Warrington. 'Schooner Port' contains a wealth of information and makes a very important contribution to our knowledge of the maritime development of the North West of Britain.
Contains rare photographs and illustrations.

Recognised as the only authoritative work on this particular subject '
    - Sea Breezes

ISBN 0 9521020 5 6 £12.50

LIFE AT LAIRDS - MEMORIES OF WORKING SHIPYARD MEN
by David Roberts

"When Cammell Lairds has gone and we are a generation or two down the line who will answer the questions ...
'What did they do there?' '
What was it like?'
This book answers the questions."
– Sea Breezes

'A Piece of Social History' - Liverpool Echo

ISBN 0 9521020 1 3   £ 9.00

CAMMELL LAIRD - THE GOLDEN YEARS
by David Roberts.
Foreword by Frank Field MP

Looks back at the world famous shipyard's history with particular focus upon the 1960s and 70s when Lairds were engaged in the building of Polaris Nuclear submarines. A unique look at the history of this yard that contains many photographs and references.

'Captures life in the prosperous years of the historic Birkenhead shipyard'
Liverpool Echo

'Puts into perspective...the strikes...the Polaris contract...and those who worked at the yard' - Sea Breezes

ISBN 0 9521020 2 1   £9.00

{**Cammell Laird** - Old ships and Hardships: on DVD. £16.95 inc. p&p in UK}

THE LIVERPOOL LIFEBOAT DISASTER OF 1892
by Jim Sullivan
One man's search for a missing piece of history -

The unsung heroes of the seas around Britain are remembered in this real life tale of the early days of the lifeboat service.

'A labour of love that deserves to be told... a story of astonishing courage, brilliantly researched.'

Alan Bleasdale

ISBN 1 902964 10 1 £9.50

CLAN LINE IN PHOTOGRAPHS - THE COMPLETE SERIES
by Tony Blackler

Charles Cayzer founded a shipping company in 1878 which was to become, in 1890, Clan Line Steamers Ltd. More than 100 years on all the ships with the familiar two red bands on a black funnel have disappeared from the oceans along with the company, but they are not forgotten.

Clan Line is still very much spoken about in today's shipping circles. and as far as we know, there has been no definitive history written about the whole company, generally known throughout the last century as Cayzer Irvine & Co. Ltd. These three volumes of old photographs compiled from the collections of Bob Briscoe and the author (both ex-company employees) will certainly go some way to revive old memories.

VOL I: THE FIRST FORTY YEARS: 1878 –1918 £10.00
VOL II: FROM PEACE TO PEACE 1918-1945 £10.00
VOL III: THE FINAL YEARS 1945 - 1986 £11.50

All Three Volumes for £27.00

DVD
BLUE FUNNEL - Voyages and Voices

Vittoria dock in Birkenhead was the home of what was once the biggest, and probably the best, General Cargo shipping company in Britain; Alfred Holt's... perhaps better known as *'The Blue Funnel Line'* or ' the *'China Boats'*. Many thousands of people, both passengers and crews sailed on famous ships like *'Hector' 'Patroclus', 'Laomedon'* and many more. This film has been compiled with the help of never before published film taken all over the world by some of those men who actually sailed with 'Blueys' on many of their well-known vessels.

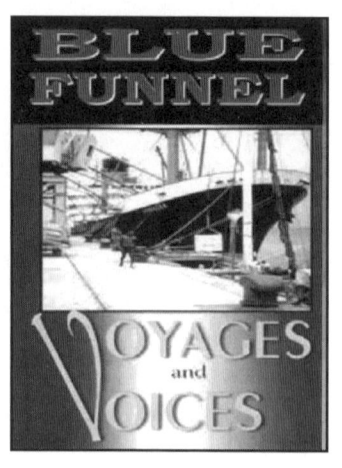

This DVD contains some of the sights and sounds of typical Blue Funnel voyages; leaving the home shores of the UK, sailing through both the Suez and Panama canals, the legendary gilly gilly man, Hong Kong, Singapore, Kobe, Tokyo, and other 'exotic' ports.
We also see and hear the thoughts and memories of some of those who actually sailed with 'Blueys' over their working lives, from Able Seaman to Captain, Steward to Engineer.

'reviewing it was an absolute pleasure.....a treasure trove of life at sea over some five decades....for anyone who has been to sea or who just enjoys being in the company of seafarers'……….. Sea Breezes
'The film is a must for anyone who sailed with 'Blueys' or who sailed in the merchant navy of old.'
……….Shipping Today and Yesterday
£16.95

DVD

CAMMELL LAIRD - Old ships and Hardships

The story of the world famous shipyard at Birkenhead.

After an extensive search for moving footage of this world famous shipyard at work a film of the history of this enterprise has at last been compiled.

Shows how the company came into being and how Cammell Laird served the nation through two World Wars, building world famous vessels like the *Rodney, Hood, Mauritania, Ark Royal, Windsor Castle* and many more, up to the tragic day in 1993 when Cammell Laird was shut down.

The story of the yard is also told through the voices of the men who worked at Lairds;
Welders, cranedrivers, electricians and plumbers, they tell of the hardships of building ships in all weathers and the lighter moments that came from some of the 'characters' of the yard.

£16.95

VIDEOS

'ALL IN A DAYS WORK' VOLUMES I & II
- A LOOK AT WORKING LIVES ON THE RIVER MERSEY.

The River Mersey is still an active and thriving river and filmed here are some of the ordinary people and vessels that work on the river. Not for them the 9 to 5 daily grind, they work with ships, on ships and around ships; they enjoy life on and around the sea and they are using the wealth of experience that they possess. Here then are stories of a living, working river, and the ordinary people that work upon it.

£14.99 each

Overseas formats are available prices on request.

ALL PRICES INCLUDE P&P IN UK.
FOR OVERSEAS ORDERS PLEASE CONTACT AVID PUBLICATIONS (SEE BELOW)
TO ORDER BOOKS , DVDS OR VIDEOS DIRECT CONTACT:-
Avid Publications, Garth Boulevard, Hr. Bebington, Wirral, Merseyside UK.
CH63 5LS. Tel / Fax (44) 0151 645 2047

for more information see our website at:
http://www.avidpublications.co.uk or e-mail info@AvidPublications.co.uk

Avid Welcomes new authors.